Contents

From the Directors of HEUNI and KICJP

Mr Kauko Aromaa and Prof. Dr Sang-Ki Park

In 2004, the United Nations Secretary-General in his report to the Security Council wrote that in articulating "a common language of justice…, [c]oncepts such as justice, the rule of law, and transitional justice are essential to understanding the international community's efforts to enhance human rights, protect persons from fear and want, address property disputes, encourage economic development, promote accountable governance and peacefully resolve conflict…To work together effectively in this field, a common understanding of key concepts is essential"[1].

We both the directors of European Institute for Crime Prevention and Control, affiliated with the United Nations (HEUNI, Helsinki, Finland), and Korean Institute of Criminal Justice Policy (KICJP, Seoul, Republic of Korea), two members of the United Nations Crime Prevention and Criminal Justice Programme Network of the Institutes (PNI) are pleased to contribute to the development of a common language of justice with this anthology.

Although the precepts of democratic governance such as fair and speedy justice, transparency, accountability and citizens' engagement are universal, there is no single recipe for contributing to the development of a common language of justice. Rather a comprehensive approach needs to be adopted.

Therefore this anthology, which comprises 21 contributions written altogether by 26 authors, has been probably one of the few, if not the only one worldwide, that takes up the challenge of developing effectively a comprehensive and common language of justice from an international criminal justice perspective, and seeks to offer very intercultural context to advance its precepts further.

We are looking forward to readers' criticism, inspiration and their own work in this promising field of international criminal justice education and training. We hope that this pioneering book will contribute useful insights for the international crime prevention and criminal justice community. Ahead of it there are two important international conferences: World Civic Forum – Building Just Societies. From Vision to Action (Republic of Korea, 2009) and The Twelfth United Nations Congress on Crime Prevention and Criminal Justice (Brazil, 2010), both of which, in their own ways, may further contribute to the rule of law in the world.

---

1 S/2004/616, The rule of law and transitional justice in conflict and post-conflict societies, *Report of the Secretary-General*, para. 5.

Foreword

Eduardo Vetere[1]

Almost at the conclusion of his "*Adventures in Criminology*", written at the end of his long, distinguished and varied career Sir Leon Radzinowicz commented the following:

"I cannot claim to have been in all parts and corners of the world, or to have studied them all in depth. But I have travelled enough, observed enough, recorded enough, and read enough, to be able to characterize their predominant philosophies and practices. In very many parts of the world, including parts of Europe, the system of criminal justice is amorphous, disjointed and stagnant. In many countries it is torn by chronic turmoil and punctuated by savage convulsions, the inevitable consequences of recurring political and social upheavals. Often there are pious proclamations of goals to be pursued, which are flagrantly contradicted by ugly realities; or else brutality is openly paraded in the hope of maximizing deterrence and fear. Often the system of criminal justice is perceived and enforced as a self-perpetuating bureaucracy, a self-contained machine deliberately cut off from wider influences and reliable reassessments. I am aware that these are harsh statements, but they simply reflect harsh realities. The exceptions to such strictures are very few, accounting for a very small proportion of the countries of the world. At least four-fifths of the world's population of over 5 billion people are as hungry for elementary criminal justice as they are for essential commodities. The annual reports of Amnesty International and of Human Rights Watch – terrifying but authentic accounts of violations of human rights across the world – are as important, if not more so, as the accounts which reveal the working of criminal justice as a whole. Indeed, one of the most disturbing interconnections brought out since the early 1970s is the one between human rights and penal standards. They condition and influence each other and neither can achieve satisfactory achievement without the other".

If I quoted extensively from a Great Teacher and Scholar, one of the Fathers of Comparative Research in Criminal Law and Criminology, it was not only because I wanted to pay a tribute to Sir Leon as one of my predecessors in the United Nations Secretariat

---

1 Former Director of the Division for Treaty Affairs, United Nations Office on Drugs and Crime (Vienna, Austria); Director of the Centre for International Crime Prevention (United Nations Office on Drug Control and Crime Prevention, Vienna, Austria); Executive Secretary of the eighth (1990), ninth (1995) and eleventh United Nations congresses on crime prevention and criminal justice (2005).

who contributed in the early days of the Organization to the establishment of what later became the Crime Prevention and Criminal Justice Programme, but because I firmly believe that what he so authoritatively stated almost ten years ago is equally valid, relevant and crucially true also today. This is why I consider this book as an 'essential commodity' for its future readers, not to be limited to the academic and scientific community, or to graduate and post-graduate university students in Law, Sociology and Political Science or to criminal justice practitioners – from police officers to judges, prosecutors, lawyers, prison officials and other correctional personnel - but to reach a much wider audience, from policy-makers and diplomats to educators, social workers, instructors and activists, particularly in view of the growingly evident inextricable nexus between 'human rights and penal standards', as well as of the increased awareness of the need for their universal protection and application, without double standards, at home and abroad, nationally and internationally.

There are, however, other reasons for which I felt honoured to have been invited to write this foreword: firstly, before becoming an 'international bureaucrat', I started my career at the University and - with respect to a widespread campaign of public education for the internalisation of values which emphasize the importance of international standards and norms towards a culture of lawfulness - I am convinced that the role of academic institutions is fundamental; secondly, I have a profound esteem for the editors of this book, with whom I have been working together for so many years, and who should be congratulated not only for their initiative in conceiving the idea, but also for their stamina and perseverance in bringing it up to its end with successful results; thirdly, many of the contributors are very good and old friends, with whom I truly enjoyed being associated in different ventures and challenging projects and who have always been extremely generous and enthusiastic in providing their advice and support to the United Nations; fourthly, the book is a rare example of the comparative and cross-cultural multidisciplinary approach in the criminal justice field, with the various contributions covering very topical subjects, whose technical and theoretical aspects are admirably blended with their practical implications and pragmatic outcomes; and, last but not least, in reading through its six sections about the various experiences across the world related to teaching and training, very important memories started to emerge related to the context in which most of the United Nations standards and norms were formulated, all the excitement and hopes when they were developed, all the anxiety and fears till the moment of their final approval, the challenges to be faced to promote their implementation, the problems and difficulties still to overcome to ensure their application, the gradual but ineluctable shift from the so called soft law consensus-building towards the long gestation process and the relatively short but painstaking negotiations of more comprehensive and mandatory international instruments, such as the United Nations Convention against Transnational Organized Crime with its three Protocols[2] and the United Nations Convention against Corruption[3].

There is no doubt that first the United Nations Committee of Experts on Crime Prevention and Control and after the Commission on Crime Prevention and Criminal Justice, together with the quinquennial United Nations Congresses, played a very important role in preparing the ground and in crafting most of those instruments for their final more formal approval or endorsement by the General Assembly or the Economic and Social Council[4].

I was fortunate enough to service most of the meetings of those bodies, witnessing therefore every moment of this fascinating and complex process, starting as an incredulous and almost lost young professional officer at the Fifth Congress at Geneva in 1975, which approved the United Nations Declaration against Torture and Inhuman or Degrading Treatment or Punishment, through all the successive ones, including as their Executive Secretary, up to the last Eleventh Congress in Bangkok (2005).

While it has been a long, unbelievable and unforgettable experience, with all the related satisfactions, trepidations and frustrations - especially during the few parentheses of peace-keeping missions in Cambodia, Iraq and Western Sahara - it is also undoubted that I was lucky enough to find inspiration,

---

2 General Assembly resolution 55/25 of 8 January 2001 (United Nations Convention against Transnational Organized Crime; Protocol to Prevent, Suppress and Punish Trafficking in Persons, Especially Women and Children, supplementing the United Nations Convention against Transnational Organized Crime; Protocol against the Smuggling of Migrants by Land, Air and Sea, supplementing the United Nations Convention against Transnational Organized Crime); General Assembly resolution 55/255 of 8 June 2001(Protocol against the Illicit Manufacturing of and Trafficking in Firearms, Their Parts and Components and Ammunition, supplementing the United Nations Convention against Transnational Organized Crime). See further: http://www.unodc.org/unodc/en/crime_cicp_convention.html#final.
3 General Assembly resolution 58/4 of 31 October 2003 (United Nations Convention against Corruption). See further: http://www.unodc.org/unodc/en/crime_convention_ corruption.html.
4 For the history of the United Nations Crime Prevention and Criminal Justice Programme, see: Benedict S. Alper with a Foreword by William Clifford, Crime: International Agenda. Concern and Action in the Prevention of Crime and Treatment of Offenders, 1846-1972, Lexington, Mass., Toronto, London, Lexington Books, D. C. Heath and Company, 1972; Manuel Lopéz-Rey, A Guide to United Nations Criminal Policy, Brookfield, Vt., Gower Publishing Company, 1985; Roger S. Clark, The United Nations Crime Prevention and Criminal Justice Program. Formulation of Standards and Efforts at Their Implementation, Philadelphia, University of Pennsylvania Press, 1994; Reece Walters, Social defence and international reconstruction: Illustrating the governance of the post-war criminological discourse, Theoretical Criminology, vol. 5 (2)/2001, 203-221.

encouragement and support from two exceptional persons, who have always and consistently been available to provide advice and help: the late Professor Gerhard Mueller and Professor Cherif Bassiouni. Both of them deserve a particular mention here, for the powerful mark they have left in the United Nations work in the field of crime prevention and criminal justice, for their most impressive and innovative academic publications and scholarly articles, which have been breaking new grounds - influencing entire new generations of lawyers and criminologists around the world - and for their engagement in the international scientific community, as well as for their acclaimed and widely recognized standing as Teachers and Educators.

In his textbooks "*Criminology*" and "*Criminal Justice*", published in 1994 and co-authored with his dear spouse Freda Adler and William Laufer, in addition to several 'windows of the world' covering specific United Nations activities, Gerhard includes an entire chapter devoted to 'Comparative Criminology' and to 'International and Comparative Criminal Justice', respectively, of which I would like to highlight the following passages:

> "In view of the globalization of the world - brought about by recent technological advances and the enormous increase in international commerce, both legal and illegal - comparative studies in criminology have become a necessity...There are a number of requirements for successful comparative research: studying foreign law, understanding foreign criminal justice systems, learning about a foreign culture, collecting reliable data, engaging in comparative research, and, when needed, doing cross-cultural empirical research. The accomplishments of criminologists who have engaged in comparative studies form the foundation for further research. The tools of comparative criminology should prove useful in helping both individual nations and the United Nations solve some of their common crime problems. The United Nations and its agencies continue to do very practical work to help nations to deal with crime on a worldwide basis"..."U.N. activities in crime prevention and criminal justice are broad-ranging. Many aim at assisting individual countries in their own crime prevention and criminal justice efforts. Some are designed to provide technical assistance by improving the capacity of governments to deal with their domestic crime problems in a humane manner; others are directed at dealing with international and transnational crime. Of particular significance are the norms, guidelines, principles, standards and models pertaining to a wide range of criminal justice issues...Considering that only forty years ago there was no agreement among the governments of the world as to what constitutes humane criminal justice

procedures, the world has come a long way in a short period of time. The countries of the world have agreed on a basic set of standards for the humane administration of criminal justice. These standards extend to all areas of criminal justice, from crime prevention to policing to prosecution and adjudication to corrections. Some countries have taken the standards very seriously, by enacting them into law or by adjusting their laws accordingly, and by using them in the training of officials. Some have ignored them. And some are undergoing change."

While Cherif, in his 'Introduction' to the "*Compendium of United Nations Norms and Standards*" entitled "The Protection of Human Rights in the Administration of Criminal Justice", also published in 1994, writes the following:

"This compilation brings together, for the first time, all the procedural norms and standards applicable to criminal processes, whether national, regional or international. The instruments are systematically arranged. The listing is in chronological order by category, irrespective of the legal source of the given instrument and the United Nations organ or body that produced it. Some of these instruments are embodied in multilateral conventions binding on their signatory states. Others are still at the stage of resolutions. But these enunciated human rights may also be binding on states by their reaching the level of customary international law or 'general principles of international law', or both.

The procedural instruments contained in this compilation are exhaustive, and some additional commentary and explanatory material is added on a selective basis, thus providing the reader with a single comprehensive source of all the norms and standards.

As the world community's commonly shared values coalesce around a basic human interest sought to be protected, we witness its inclusion in a more specific instrument, and, as the need and opportunity arises, the right is embodied in a legally binding instrument or it receives the same level of recognition as part of customary international law or 'general principles of international law'. This dynamic evolutionary process has been on the move since the Universal Declaration of Human Rights. It is likely to continue in the years to come, probably with a greater focus on implementation, now that the ideological confrontation between East and West has ended. However, the challenge of enforcement is going to be greater than that of enunciating norms and standards. This decade will therefore witness an unprecedented vitality and growth of enforcement mechanisms and procedures. They, too, like the elaboration of norms and standards, will undergo an evolutionary stage which is likely to culminate in the establishment of an international criminal court which will adjudicate the more serious depredations".

We now we have the International Criminal Court, functioning and in operation. But, how can we dissociate its establishment from all that Cherif Bassiouni did to transform this idea into reality? He managed to prepare the ground for this to happen through a number of international meetings and seminars hosted by his *Istituto Superiore Internazionale di Szience Criminali* (International Institute for Higher Studies in Criminal Sciences) in Siracusa (Italy); continuing to develop and refine the underlying concepts; channelling and expanding the required political support, gradually but steadily; chairing the drafting committee during the Rome Conference; and energizing the coordination work for the follow-up activities necessary to promote the entry into force of the Rome Statute.

In fact, further to the creation of the International Tribunals for the former Yugoslavia and Rwanda in 1994, and as Kofi Annan emphasised in his last report on the Work of the Organization (A/61/1), "the establishment of the International Criminal Court in 2002 was the realization of a long effort to end impunity and undertake through the rule of law that those who commit the crime of genocide, crimes against humanity and war crimes will no longer be beyond the reach of justice. This important step demonstrated the international community's commitment to a permanent and universal mechanism to ensure that, as regards those most serious crimes, impunity will not be tolerated"[5].

And this leads me to a crucial issue, which is touched upon in most of the contributions contained in this volume, and that is so well enunciated and elaborated by Mr. Aromaa and Dr. Redo in the introductory chapter: "the global criminal justice message" which we should transmit is "the importance of the rule of law in teaching and training".

While in the past different interpretations had been given to the concept of the rule of law as originally conceived by A. P. Dicey in his "Introduction to the Study of the Law of the Constitution" (1885) – including: common ethics, supremacy of the law, restraint of arbitrary power, separation of powers, the principle of 'habeas corpus', the principle 'nulla poena sine lege', the principle of proportionality, judicial independence, equality before the law, state protection for all, supremacy of civilian authority, prohibition of summary justice, and this listing could still continue – from a United

---

5 Doc. A/61/1, Report of the Secretary-General on the Work of the Organization, para. 108.

Nations perspective it was Secretary-General Boutros Boutros-Ghali who, for the first time in his "Agenda for Peace" in 1992, recognized that "there is an obvious connection between the rule of law and...the achievement of true peace and security in any new and stable political order"[6].

We owe to his successor Kofi Annan to have 'articulated a common language of justice', using the words of Kauko and Slawomir, in his report submitted to the Security Council in 1994 entitled "The rule of law and transitional justice in conflict and post-conflict societies"(S/2004/616), which elaborated on previous material contained particularly in his Millennium Report "We the people"(A/54/2000), as further refined in a major report submitted five years later to the General Assembly entitled "In larger freedom: Towards development, security and human rights for all" (A/59/2005), which was also drawing on the recommendations made by a High Level Panel on "Threats, Challenges and Change"(A/59/565). In such reports, as well as in other remarkable statements, Kofi Annan has been periodically and regularly reminding us – as the conscience of the world – that "every nation that proclaims the rule of law at home must respect it abroad and that every nation that insists on it abroad must enforce it at home", stressing the need to restore and extend it throughout the world as a "framework in which rather than might making right, right would make might" and as one of the main "legal principles that constitutes our Organization's foundation".

At this point, it is very legitimate to pose the following question: If the rule of law constitutes the 'foundation' of the United Nations - which is concerned with many other priority issues, from international security to development, from disarmament to environmental protection just to mention the first ones that came to my mind – why the rule of law cannot be the main message to transmit at the global level in our teaching and training programmes in crime prevention and criminal justice? In this connection, we would have a short memory if we would forget that the Ministerial Meeting held in Versailles in 1991 in its 'Statement of Principles and Programme of Action of the United Nations Crime Prevention and Criminal Justice Programme' solemnly stated that "We believe that justice based on the rule of law is the pillar on which civilized rests. We seek to improve its quality. A humane and efficient criminal justice system can be an instrument of equity, constructive social change and social justice, protecting basic values and peoples' inalienable rights. Every right of the individual should enjoy the protection of the law against violation, a process in which the criminal justice system plays an essential role" (GA res. 46/156,

---

6 Doc. A/47/277 - S/24111, An Agenda for Peace Preventive Diplomacy, Peacemaking and Peace-Keeping, Report of the Secretary-General, para. 59.

Annex, op. paragraph 2 and Doc.A/46/703). Similarly, how to forget that at the Ninth United Nations Congress, held in Cairo in April 1995, there was a substantive agenda item on "International cooperation and practical technical assistance for strengthening the rule of law"(A/CONF.169/4)? As a matter of fact, the Congress also adopted a resolution on this topic in which the Commission on Crime Prevention and Criminal Justice was invited to encourage the Secretary-General, as a way of strengthening the rule of law, to include the reestablishment and reform of criminal justice systems in peace-keeping operation, as well as to call on all relevant international, intergovernmental and non-governmental organizations to continue cooperating with the United Nations in developing manuals and training curricula and in organizing courses in the various areas of crime prevention and criminal justice (A/CONF.169/16/Rev.1).

Five years later, the Tenth Congress also had a specific agenda item on "Promoting the rule of law and strengthening the criminal justice system (A/CONF./187/3) and the relevant recommendations contained in the "Vienna Declaration on Crime and Justice: Meeting the challenges of the Twenty-first Century", endorsed by the General Assembly in its resolution 55/59, reflect the rich discussions that took place in Vienna in April 2000 on that occasion (A/CONF.187/15/Rev.1). Finally, the last Congress also made specific recommendations in its "Bangkok Declaration" expressing support for a "more integrated approach within the United Nations in relation to the provision of assistance for building capacity in crime prevention and criminal justice, and in cooperation in criminal matters of a transnational character, as a contribution to the establishment and strengthening of the rule of law" (A.CONF.203/18).

To conclude, the rule of law is not only important for education and training, but also fundamentally necessary to reduce the "hunger for elementary criminal justice", thus permitting to conjugate more effectively security with legality, as well as reconciling public safety with respect for individual rights and freedoms.

Towards a Common Language of Criminal Justice across the World: The International and United Nations Experience

Kauko Aromaa[1]
Slawomir Redo[2]

Introduction

The world is one. But delivering one criminal justice message across it has never been an easy task, even now in the era of globalization of education (Palermo 2004; Evans 2005; Tomasevski 2005). That one global criminal justice message is about the importance of the rule of law in teaching and training.

This article reviews international and United Nations experience in this field. It addresses traditional and modern teaching and training approaches and techniques. In conclusion, it seeks to contribute to the emerging need to consolidate the global educational and training agenda on which there seems to be too little common work to deliver more effectively one criminal justice message in the name of the rule of law.

In 2000, in the United Nations Millennium Declaration Member States resolved to strengthen respect for the rule of law in international as in national affairs, and the capacity of all our countries to implement the principles and practices of democracy and respect for human rights (A/RES/55/2, para. 24). In 2004, the Secretary-General of the United Nations in the report to the Security Council noted that in articulating a common language of

---

1 Director of the European Institute for Crime Prevention and Control, affiliated with the United Nations (HEUNI, Helsinki, Finland). The author was a researcher/senior research officer/research, Director of the Finnish National Research Institute of Legal Policy (1970-1999), President of the Scandinavian Research Council for Criminology (2000-2003), Chief Editor of the *Journal of Scandinavian Studies in Criminology and Crime Prevention* (1999-2002); Chairman of the Research and Validation Committee of the European Union Crime Prevention Network (2006); President of the European Society of Criminology (2006-2007); invited Emeritus Professor of the University of the Cataratas (Foz de Iguassu, Brazil, 2005). Edited/co-edited 6 books, authored/co-authored two criminology textbooks, and authored about 60 articles and about 150-200 other reports/publications.
2 Doctor of Law; United Nations Office on Drugs and Crime, Vienna, Austria. Author of three books, co-editor of three books. Authored about 45 articles on various crime prevention and criminal justice issues, mostly covered by the United Nations treaty and customary law. The views contained in this article do not necessarily reflect the views of the United Nations Secretariat.

justice for the United Nations, concepts such as the rule of law, justice and transitional justice are essential to understanding the international community's efforts to enhance human rights, protect persons from fear and want, address property disputes, encourage economic development, promote accountable governance and peacefully resolve conflicts (S/2004/616, para. 3).

For more than half a century the international community has worked to articulate collectively the substantive and procedural requirements for those concepts. There is now massive documentation and literature, numerous global, regional and sub-regional standards and norms, and an unaccountable number of reports, books, articles and other publications.

Within the United Nations alone, as a computer search of its optical disk system[3] shows, there are about 1,000 various United Nations documents on human rights education. Over the past 30 years (1987-2006), the General Assembly adopted every year one resolution on human rights education. In some of those resolutions there were consolidated recommendations for a follow up through the *"United Nations Decade for Human Rights Education, 1995-2004"* [4] and the *"World Programme on Human Rights Education"*. [5]

In response to those resolutions, numerous outputs emerged. While it would be impossible here to list them all, just in the way of example one should mention a series of the human rights training and educational material, covering also the criminal justice field, prepared in cooperation with the United Nations Office on Drugs and Crime (UNODC)[6].

Some of these recommendations have been followed not as "material" (publications), but on a joint programme basis, *i.e., "The Global Human Rights Cities Program"* (2005-2008) by the UNODC, the Office of the United Nations High Commissioner of Human Rights (UNHCHR) and other United Nations agencies.[7] This *Program* is carried out with the involvement of the "Global Compact" - a voluntary corporate citizenship initiative of more than 1,000 largest corporations. The initiative has two objectives: mainstream business activities around the world; and catalyse corporate action in support of the United Nations goals, including fighting human rights abuses and corruption. With over US $

---

3 http://www.ods.un.org.
4 A/RES/58/181, "United Nations Decade for Human Rights Education", 1995-2004.
5 *E.g.,* A/RES/59/113B, "World Programme on Human Rights Education".
6 See: Office of the High Commissioner for Human Rights, Publication list, December 2006, http://www.ohchr.org/english/about/publications/docs/pubEn.pdf
7 The United Nations Environment Programme, the International Labour Organization; the United Nations Development Programme, the United Nations Industrial Development Organization. See further: http://www.citiesprogramme.org/programme_history.php.

5,000,000 budget, including funds for training in a new vocation of "human rights community educators", the *Program* has not only entered the national agendas but also city agendas (UNDP 2003; Jahan 2004).[8]

The above resolutions and follow up action document very advanced, comprehensive, elaborate and practical coverage of educational issues in the field of human rights. They do and should serve as a model on which one can act in pursuing specific actions relevant to the education in the criminal justice field.

This is important, because there are less resolutions on human rights in the administration of justice. In principle, in the past 30 years, they were adopted every second year.[9] In that time, there were even fewer (nine) resolutions directly on anti-drug education[10] (as a follow-up to the two General Assembly resolutions of 1990 and 1998 containing political declarations and global programme of action)[11]. Last but not least, there is only one General Assembly resolution on criminal justice education.[12] In effect, there are very few United Nations educational manuals, books, reports or other publications on either anti-drug or criminal justice education, but there are numerous on "grass roots" training and public awareness for substance abuse prevention.[13]

This article, and, generally, this book, is an attempt to make a targeted contribution to international and United Nations crime prevention and criminal justice education and training at the undergraduate/graduate and post-graduate level. It focuses on education and training throughout the world, in terms of programmes, projects or other initiatives (ideas) that may contribute to a more effective and humane treatment of offenders and victims of crime, and to crime prevention. The articles in this book seek to advance instrumentally the aforementioned common language of justice - in fact, criminal justice - by looking into the modalities of

---

8 The goals of the programme include instilling in communities a sense of ownership over human rights as a way of life; enhancing democracy, peace, security, and social justice; and strengthening the infrastructure that supports human, social, and economic development (Jahaan 2004, 4).
9 In the period 1984-2005, the General Assembly adopted sixteen resolutions on "Human rights in the administration of justice".
10 A/RES/59/163 and A/RES/60/178, "International cooperation against the world drug problem."
11 A/RES/S-17/2 of 23 February 1990 and A/S-20/4 of 10 June 1998.
12 A/RES/45/122, "Criminal justice education". However, in the same year when this General Assembly resolution was adopted, the Economic and Social Council (ECOSOC) also adopted the resolution on "Prison education" (1990/20) and on "Education, training and public awareness in the field of crime prevention" (1990/24).
13 Among various guides, written in a reader-friendly manner, there are a number on youth drug abuse prevention programmes. See further: UNODC publications at: http://www.unodc.org.

delivering the rule of law message in the two settings: academic and training, both in terms of real (physical/personal) and virtual (indirect) contact with the audience; in short, through distance learning. Distance learning is, perhaps, the greatest change in contemporary higher education, aside from the advent of personal computers (Lanier 2006: 244). It led to "several social and economic trends ...that are driving the interest in its development and shaping the political debate about its implementation" (Rubiales *et al.* 1998: 31).

There are six substantive sections in this book. The general section which opens it, is the first one to tackle very challenging policy issues surrounding the topic of the rule of law internationally and in the United Nations, in terms of the relationships between security and justice issues (and *vice versa*), and as far as delivery of the precepts of the rule of law in practice is concerned. The second section deals with an innovative technique for getting across the world the essential part of the rule of law message, that is international precepts of criminal justice and crime prevention through distance learning. The third section deals with the same challenge but in a real classroom setting where more experiences have been gathered to share them with the reader. The fourth section shares the experiences in training in various criminal justice academies in Europe and the United States. The fifth section addresses the substantive international criminal justice training and teaching agenda. The last section deals with training experiences in crime prevention, including cybercrime, thus taking the book back to the point where virtual academy training is a top priority, in view of rapid and dynamic evolution and expansion of this form of computer crime which cannot only be effectively counteracted by traditional teaching and training methods (real academy).

The idea for preparing this book on real and virtual teaching and training emerged in 2005 in Toronto (Canada) at the annual meeting of the American Society of Criminology, a non-governmental organization with consultative status with the United Nations Economic and Social Council. One of the editors of this book, then on a sabbatical leave from the United Nations, through a number of specially focused panels with papers of criminal justice academic researchers and practitioners involved in training and teaching issues, collected their contributions to this volume. Subsequently, throughout 2006-7, additional contributions were made to this anthology which now includes altogether 21 articles.

Particular contributions to this book, while all of them clearly international, in their contents reflect, however, various degrees of the common language of criminal justice.[14] This language is

---

14 For an interdisciplinary analysis of the concept of a common language of justice, see Slawomir Redo, "For a common language of justice: translating

integrated to a various extent in criminal justice education and training across the world. It appears that neither the international criminal justice community at large nor the United Nations community have yet attained a sufficient degree of comprehensiveness in technically dealing with criminal justice education and training in one common language. Europe and North America may be exceptions, for on both continents the integration processes have been so much advanced beyond the economic sphere, that also human rights and criminal justice education have been there more commonly and jointly articulated and pursued than in any other continent (Eskridge 2003; Bufkin 2004).

Human Rights and Criminal Justice

The above suggests that, in principle and practice, there is no difference between the concepts of teaching and training in human rights and criminal justice, in the sense that whatever is in the field of criminal justice, it is, or may be, also addressed in the field of human rights. In this sense, both are interrelated and complimentary.

Whatever the Human Rights Council (earlier the Commission on Human Rights) and the Commission on Crime Prevention and Criminal Justice (earlier the Committee on Crime Prevention and Control), whatever other United Nations policy making fora have separately or jointly contributed to the United Nations standards and norms in crime prevention and criminal justice, has always been a mutually reinforcing and complimentary process.

This is probably best reflected in the General Assembly resolutions on "human rights in the administration of criminal justice". There, all legal substantive and procedural requirements worked out and adopted in the United Nations within its human rights programme, and all such requirements coming from its crime prevention and criminal justice programme are the same. Further, in more than sixty years of development of both programmes in the United Nations, there has been a continuous mutually reinforcing process of elaborating and strengthening the precepts of the rule of law. However, technically (that is not in the sense of the aforementioned legal procedural requirements), the human rights and criminal justice programmes have partly different aims and working modalities.

---

words into deeds, *Aktualne Problemy Prawa Karnego i Kryminologii* Wydawnictwo Temida 2, Białystok, 2008.

They also address partly different aspects of the global crime and justice picture. The eventual aim from the human rights perspective is their full observance in crime prevention, criminal justice and beyond – in the social, economic and cultural sphere. The eventual aim from the crime prevention and criminal justice perspective (in short: criminal justice perspective), is, perhaps, best encapsulated in a strategic mandate of the UNODC, capturing the essence of its programme, which is working *"Towards security and justice for all: Making the world safer from drugs, crime and terrorism"*,[15] in a humane and effective way, and using in that process United Nations legal instruments, its own and other international best practices.

The most recent and best example how both human rights and criminal justice approaches are blended together is the development of a "common justice package", that is *Model Codes for Postconflict Criminal Justice,* as a follow up to the so called "Brahimi Report" on peace keeping operations which reflected upon the practical and legal difficulties that had been faced by the United Nations in delivering justice in postconflict States on the United Nations Peace Operations (Report of the Panel, para. 81).

Based on consultations that took place after the publication of that report, the United States Institute of Peace and the Irish Centre for Human Rights, in cooperation with the Office of the High Commissioner for Human Rights and the United Nations Office on Drugs and Crime, launched that *Model Codes* project, the ultimate aim of which was to create a set of model codes that could be used as tools by both international and national actors engaged in the criminal law reform process in postconflict states around the world. In pursuit of this aim, the model codes were drafted in a way that takes into account their potential cross-cultural application and use, in addition to the inevitable exigencies of a postconflict environment. The substantive provisions of the codes were inspired by a variety of the world's legal systems, which were blended to create a coherent body of criminal laws tailored to these exigencies.

This "common justice package" consists of four codes: the *Model Criminal Code,* the *Model Code of Criminal Procedure,* the *Model Detention Act* and the *Model Police Act.* The *Model Criminal Code* is a "criminal code" or "penal code" similar to those found in many states that focus on substantive criminal law. Substantive criminal law regulates what conduct is deemed to be criminal, the conditions under which a person may be held criminally responsible and the relevant penalties that apply to a person convicted of a

---

15 See further, UN doc. CTOC/COP/2006/ CRP.4, Towards security and justice for all: Making the world safer from drugs, crime and terrorism, Note by the Secretariat, http://www.unodc.org/unodc/organized_crime_untoc_2006.html.

criminal offence. The *Model Code of Criminal Procedure* focuses on procedural criminal law, which is a body of rules and procedures that governs how a criminal case will be investigated and adjudicated. The *Model Detention Act* governs the laws and procedures to be applied by the criminal justice system to persons who are detained prior to and during a criminal trial and also to persons who are convicted of a criminal offence. Finally, the *Model Police Powers Act* sets out relevant powers and duties of the police in the sphere of criminal investigations, in addition to relevant procedures to be followed in investigating criminal offences. Moreover, the *Model Police Powers Act* contains additional provisions on police powers and duties and the relevant procedures to be followed by police in the maintenance of public order.

As of this writing, the model codes are due to be published in a three-volume series in 2007/2008. The already published first volume contains the *Model Criminal Code* and its accompanying commentaries. The second volume consists of the *Model Code of Criminal Procedure* with commentaries. Finally, the third volume comprises of the *Model Detention Act* and the *Model Police Powers Act* and their accompanying commentaries. Each of the three volumes include the "User's Guide to the Model Codes". The model codes will also be available online, once published.[16]

What has already been fully published is the *Criminal Justice Assessment Toolkit*,[17] a standardized and cross-referenced set of tools to enable United Nations agencies, government officials engaged in criminal justice reform, as well as other organizations and individuals to conduct comprehensive assessments of criminal justice systems; to identify areas of technical assistance; to assist agencies in the design of interventions that integrate United Nations standards and norms in crime prevention and criminal justice; and to assist in training on those issues. It should be noted in particular that the assessment of criminal justice systems in postconflict societies may present additional challenges, therefore – in the anticipation of those challenges – the *Toolkit* draws also on the model codes.

Criminal Justice Education and Training or Continuous Criminal Justice Education?

At first sight, the concepts of education and training may imply that "education" is restricted to the academic environment and "training"

---

16 http://www.nuigalway.ie/human_rights/Projects/model_codes.html.
17 Criminal Justice Assessment Toolkit, United Nations Office on Drugs and Crime, Organization for Cooperation and Security in Europe, Vienna – New York, 2006, http://www.unodc.org/pdf/criminal_justice/INTERNATIONAL_COOP.pdf.

to the post-academic environment. This book does not strictly follow this division, at least as far as the first concept is concerned. This is because of a more encompassing concept of continuous criminal justice education – a part of a "life long le@rning society" (Gorard and Selvyn 2005) – which extends to post-graduate trainees, the concept demonstrated in this book.

International Criminal Justice on the Training and Academic Scene

The book starts with the present introductory article, in which the current authors review various training projects of the UNODC (the United Nations Secretariat's administrative and conceptual follower of the United Nations Crime Prevention and Criminal Justice Programme and of the United Nations International Drug Control Programme). In its contents, the article touches on traditional and modern teaching and training techniques, hence the references in the text of the book to "real" and "virtual" academies.

The United Nations Drugs and Crime Programme

The general mandate for the UNODC education and training efforts originates from the United Nations standards and norms in crime prevention and criminal justice. Currently, all these standards and norms amount to 3 drug control conventions, 2 conventions against transnational organized crime, and corruption, 13 universal conventions against terrorism, and over 55 soft law instruments.[18] Through them the UNODC addresses interrelated issues of drug control, crime prevention and international terrorism. This mandate is pursued largely through a set of global programmes and projects generally organized around the thematic areas (drugs, crime and terrorism).

Formally, initial results of the implementation of this general mandate (and the specific, afore mentioned, 1990 General Assembly and ECOSOC resolutions) have only emerged in 1995. In that year, within the United Nations Crime Prevention and Criminal Justice Programme,[19] the manual on "*Basic Education in Prisons*" (1995) was published. The manual has not been used for a specific field project but was and still may be seen as a general reference material. But, in fact, the United Nations Crime

---

18 See further: http://www.unodc.org/unodc/index.html.
19 Established by the United Nations Assembly in its resolution 46/152 (Annex) of 18 December 1991. See further: http://www.un.org/documents/ga/, res/46/a46r152.htm.

Prevention and Criminal Justice Programme, and the UNODC as a component part of it, has been for many more years involved in criminal justice education and training, both at the headquarters and field level.

Numerous training courses for law enforcement officers, prosecutors, judges and prison officials on the topic of United Nations standards and norms in crime prevention and criminal justice were conducted by the UNODC in its Headquarters (Vienna, Austria). Although this entity is not a training establishment *per se*, it clearly is a place where authoritative (if not also original) course syllabi have been developed and implemented on the subjects covered by its mandate.

The multitude and number of the UNODC HQ training activities makes difficult to present them in this article. However, a few observations may be helpful. Namely, that the UNODC responds to a great variety of calls for training. The response addresses professional needs of the entire international and domestic crime prevention and criminal justice sector, including law enforcement officials, defence lawyers and specialists in forensic medicine, the diplomatic community, the public health sector (drug and HIV/AIDS professionals), urban authorities and non-governmental and other civic community members, including media representatives. UNODC has thus a very broad institutional and international expertise enabling it to review and consolidate its diversified and long-developed experience. This may enable new proposals how best to advance the international and United Nations criminal justice teaching and training justice agenda that may be of interest to other agencies and institutions, including universities and training schools around the world.

UNODC's competence is reinforced by the accomplishments of the institutes of the afore mentioned United Nations Crime Prevention and Criminal Justice Programme. They have made their own inroads into the criminal justice education and training field.

The United Nations Interregional Crime and Justice Research Institute (Turin, Italy), one of 15 such institutes of the global Programme Network of Institutes (PNI),[20] has recently announced its Masters of Law Programme on "International Organizations, International Criminal Law and Crime Prevention".[21]

---

20 http://www.icclr.law.ubc.ca/Site%20Map/Related%20Sites/United_Nations_
Network.htm. PNI operates in the framework of the International Scientific and
Professional Advisory Council of the United Nations Crime Prevention and
Criminal Justice Programme (ISPAC, Milan, Italy), established in 1990 by the
General Assembly of the United Nations (resolution 45/107, Annex, para. 28).
21 http://www.llm-guide.com/university/537/unicri-united-nations-
interregional-crime-and-justice-research-institute.

UNICRI's educational Programme intends to provide participants with specific competencies in the field of international criminal law; in-depth knowledge of the international instruments for the prevention and punishment of international and transnational crimes as well as of acts of terrorism; and insights into the United Nations and other international organizations' activities and policies. This 1,500 hour, 6-module programme will cover International Organisations; Institutions and Sources of Law; The United Nations System; International Treaties in the Field of Criminal Law; International Criminal Law; International Criminal Jurisdictions; Interstate Co-operation on Criminal Matters; Relationship between International Criminal Law and National Legislations.

UNICRI, in partnership with the University of Turin, the European Institute for Crime Prevention and Control, affiliated with the United Nations (HEUNI, Helsinki, Finland), and the Dutch Centre for International Police Co-operation (NCIPS) has recently completed a training programme targeting trafficking in human beings, developed for international law enforcement personnel. Three three-day training sessions for personnel deployed or to be deployed in peace-support operations in the Balkan area were conducted at the UNICRI HQ in Turin, Italy, in May-June 2006. These involved a total of 35 participants from 17 European countries. The programme also comprised a Trainers' Guide (UNICRI 2006).[22]

International criminal justice education and training has also been the mandate of another member of the PNI - the International Institute for Higher Studies in Criminal Sciences (IIHSCS, Siracusa, Italy). In its work programme the Institute has annual specialization courses (40 contact hours) in international criminal law for young penalists (up to 35 years of age). These courses include moot courts where participants take part in simulated court proceedings, that include drafting briefs and participating in oral argument. The institute provides also technical assistance regarding rule of law, due process, criminal procedure issues and human rights. Officials from a number of different countries including Iraq, Afghanistan, Egypt, former Yugoslav Republic of Macedonia were involved in the training.[23]

The United Nations Asia and Far East Institute on the Prevention of Crime and the Treatment of Offenders (UNAFEI, Fuchu, Tokyo, Japan), the oldest of all United Nations-related institutes, since its establishment in 1962 until now has staged 135 international training courses on various international crime and justice topics.

---

22 UNICRI: Trafficking in Human Beings and Peace-Support Operations. Pre-deployment/In-service Training Programme for International Law-enforcement Personnel. 1st edition 2004, 2nd edition 2006, available from UNICRI.
23 http://www.isisc.org.

So far, more than 3,200 law enforcement and criminal justice officials from 113 countries (including Japan) have attended these courses.[24]

Limited space prevents from even a cursory review of their contents. However, as in the case of UNODC HQ courses, they addressed United Nations topics which before the emergence of the two United Nations conventions against transnational organized crime (2000) and corruption (2003), covered earlier United Nations standards and norms in crime prevention and criminal justice, starting with the Standard Minimum Rules for the Treatment of Prisoners, adopted by the First United Nations Congress on the Prevention of Crime and the Treatment of Offenders (1955).[25] Topics ranging from offenders and victims of crime through criminal justice management, crime and drug prevention to computer crime have been before and after adopting the conventions by the General Assembly very often at the focus of training, as they are nowadays. Training material (experts' and trainees' papers) is regularly published and distributed, and is also available through UNAFEI's web site.

The United Nations Latin American Institute on the Prevention of Crime and the Treatment of Offenders (ILANUD, San José, Costa Rica), another member of the PNI, has hosted a number of regional and national training seminars on human rights and penitentiary systems in Latin America.[26] Some of such seminars were co-organized by the International Centre for Criminal Reform and Criminal Justice Policy (ICCRCJ, Vancouver, British Columbia, Canada), and the Raoul Wallenberg Institute (University of Lund, Sweden) - other members of the PNI.

Separately, these two institutes have been involved on their own or with other partners in criminal justice training. In addition to the training on human rights and penitentiary systems (for Chinese and Ugandan officials), ICCRCJ conducted regional training seminars on the control of money laundering, and terrorism. Technical cooperation with China has been especially dynamic. The Centre published in Chinese books that were employed as instructional texts in the Legal Aid Centre's National Legal Aid Training Project

---

24 http://www.unafei.or.jp/english/pages/Distributionparticipants.htm.
25 For a review of most of these standards and norms see: The Application of United Nations Standards and Norms in Crime Prevention and Criminal Justice, Peace Centre, Castle Schlaining, Stadtschlaining, Burgenland, Austria, 10-12 February, 2003, UNODC and the Ministry of Justice, Austria, 2003, http://www.unodc.org/pdf/crime/publications/ standards%20&%20norms.pdf. The entire set of United Nations standards and norms in crime prevention and criminal justice (55 instruments) appeared in the "Compendium of United Nations Standards and Norms in Crime Prevention and Criminal Justice" (UNODC, Vienna, 2007).
26 Programme on Penitentiary Systems and Human Rights, http://www.ilanud.or. cr/derechoshumanos/actividades_e.htm.

sponsored by the United Nations Development Program in ten cities in China. The Centre's Legal Aid Project was the foundation for the development of a China-Canada bilateral Legal Aid and Community Legal Service Project that started in 2004.[27]

The Centre's international training workshops, in turn, involved, for example, the International Criminal Court Technical Assistance programme, held in 2000-2002 in the Pacific Islands (Cook Islands/New Zealand), in Central Africa (Cameroon), the Caribbean (Jamaica). The workshops were also organized for the Southern African Development Community (Namibia), and for the Economic Community of West African States (Cote d'Ivoire). Cumulatively through these five workshops, the three pillars (government, civil society and media) have worked together to directly sensitize and provide training and assistance to approximately 400 delegates from 80 countries.

Concerning the Raoul Wallenberg Institute, every year it organises international training programmes on human rights in Lund, with funding from the Swedish International Development Cooperation Agency. About 25 participants from developing countries are admitted to each one of these programmes. The primary profile of participants aimed for is key persons, such as policy makers, decision makers on different levels and trainers, at institutions with a human rights mandate, mainly government institutions involved in the administration of justice.[28]

HEUNI conducted a series of training courses for police and other practitioners on violence against women, starting from Poland (1997), next addressing Lithuania (1999), and, finally, Estonia (2001 and 2002). Furthermore, HEUNI has developed another form of technical assistance, the so-called HEUNI stipendiate programme in the framework of which already more than 170 junior experts and practitioners, mostly from Eastern European countries, have been able make study tours where they have had the opportunity to visit Finnish experts and authorities relevant for their particular interests in criminal justice and crime control issues.

HEUNI's principal profile is targeting officials and academic researchers, producing research-based information and analytical work on topical crime prevention and control issues. Typical representatives of such work are the periodic analytic reports on the United Nations Surveys on Crime and Criminal Justice (comprising Europe and North America), and research reports on, to name some recent examples, a global inventory of what is known about trafficking in human beings, a study of the smuggling of people into the European Union, or a global comparative survey on violence against women.

---

27 http://www.icclr.law.ubc.ca/Site%20Map/Programs/China_Program.htm.
28 http://www.rwi.lu.se/coop/itp/overview.shtml.

These kinds of education and training activities, pursued also by other United Nations institutes, have all been implemented at the sites of those institutes or at the host venues. These, in their own way, "real criminal justice academies", have been until now the core of the education and training activities of the United Nations Crime Prevention and Criminal Justice Programme.

On their face, these activities merely represent a number of topics, hours, participants, outcomes, *etc*. But in reality each and every one is a very different activity which needs to be customized to the needs of its audience. The student audience of the UNICRI Master of Law Programme (graduates and young professionals) differs in composition and age and from the IIHSCS's young penalists and middle ranking criminal justice officials. And so is with the UNAFEI's Asian and other countries' official audience, and HEUNI's audience of officials and academic researchers.

The other part of the United Nations drugs and crime mandate - the United Nations International Drug Control Programme[29] - began its own training in a different area and with a different method. The area is e-learning for drug control and crime prevention, and the method is an interactive computer-based training (CBT).

CBT is a part of a broader training strategy - the "UNODC Global e-Learning for Drug Control and Crime Prevention" initiative. UNODC defines e-learning as "a structured, purposeful use of electronic systems or computers in support of the learning process" (UNODC 2006: 3).[30]

CBT started in 1995 with a regional and thematic focus by a project "Enhancement of Drug Law Enforcement Training in East Asia". It was a part of a larger law enforcement program between UNODC and, at the beginning, six South East Asian countries – Cambodia, China, Laos, Myanmar, Thailand and Vietnam. The project now covers 6 training centres, in: Cambodia, Fiji, Jamaica, Nigeria, Thailand and Turkey where it is highly popular and in great demand (*Ibidem*).

In Turkey, the CBT has been carried out within the international training programme by the Turkish International Academy against Drugs and Organized Crime (TADOC), established in 2000 in partnership with the UNODC. TADOC provides training to law enforcement in Turkey and also to countries of the Economical Cooperation Organization, Black Sea Economical Cooperation, and other countries that have mutual cooperation agreements signed with Turkey. Training in TADOC ends with "Kirkpatrick's Four

29 Established by the General Assembly resolution 45/179 of 21 December 1990, see further: http://www.unodc.org/unodc/en/resolution_1990-12-21_1.html.
30 Courses delivered through Internet, intranets and extranets, presented on interactive CD-ROMs or lessons delivered via television are examples of e-learning.

Levels of Evaluation" (Kirkpatrick 1994).[31] "TADOC has effectively reached its targets with respect to envisaged trainings and international cooperation, and accomplished achievements in a very short period of time" (Turkish Drug Report 2005: 63).

In all UNODC-related training centres, training aimed at enhancing basic skills and knowledge relevant to successful drug interdiction (land controls, airports, seaports), including risk management for senior managers, controlled deliveries, and drug identification. Over time, the project has expanded to include other topical training issues such as money laundering and human trafficking.

More than 50,000 law enforcement officials (1995-2006) have so far been trained. Over an 11-year period, it was delivered through 157 training centres in 26 countries in 13 languages (IEU BRIEF 2006). The training is available on a continuous basis, which allows personnel to be trained relatively quickly. The computer is the trainer, which means training is not dependent on the availability of expert consultants.

The CBT component of e-learning was evaluated (*Ibidem*: 3). Among the major findings, the following ones are particularly relevant for this book:

1. At the pre-training phase, one should conduct a needs assessment to help shape the training milieu;
2. Concerning student selection, it presently appears to be a function of participants' supervisors. While this may be adequate, a more systematic approach may be needed for additional or advanced training;
3. There is a need to provide a sufficient number and variation of training courses in order to provide opportunities for a progressive training plan, including refresher courses;
4. The programme has resulted in a more integrated approach to training, one that recognizes the need to include participants from multiple agencies. It has facilitated inter-agency cooperation;
5. There is consistent evidence that the CBT programme is valuable and has filled a need for basic law enforcement training across regions and countries;
6. The positive impact from the training appears to be significant as reflected in increased knowledge and skills, and in on-the-job behavioural changes;

---

31 In the sequential order: "Reactions", "Learning", "Transfer", "Results". According to this four-level model, evaluation should always begin with level one, and then, as time and budget allows, should move sequentially through levels two, three, and four. Information from each prior level serves as a base for the next level's evaluation. Thus, each successive level represents a more precise measure of the effectiveness of the training program, but at the same time requires a more rigorous and time-consuming analysis.

7. Data from student surveys and other sources show a high level of satisfaction with all aspects of the CBT.

Realistically, it should be noted that the UNODC e-learning initiative to date consists solely of the CBT. Soon, however, the lessons learned from the CBT project may benefit another component of the UNODC's e-learning initiative, a virtual anti-cybercrime forum.

The latter initiative only emerges in a consolidated form from an array of various initiatives separately pursued before and at the Eleventh United Nations Congress on Crime Prevention and Criminal Justice (2005). At that event, the impulse for creating the virtual anti-cyber-crime forum came from the Congress' general workshop on "Measures to combat computer-related crime" (A/CONF. 203/14), and a special training by public and private sector (Asian Development Bank/*Microsoft*) in the framework of the "International workshop on cyber-crime and digital forensics". In effect, in 2006, the first expert meeting on the creation of a virtual anti-cyber-crime research and training forum was organized by the Korean Institute of Criminal Justice Policy, member of the United Nations Crime Prevention and Criminal Justice Programme Network of institutes, in cooperation with the UNODC (Report 2006).

Implementing the mandate given after the Congress by the United Nations Commission on Crime Prevention and Criminal Justice, the expert meeting discussed possible contents of a technical assistance project, the scope of which would be the development of a model training course for law enforcement personnel from developing countries with a rolling curriculum that included cyber-crime control and prevention. The project would include a virtual expert forum under the auspices of UNODC to facilitate the exchange of information on new trends and approaches in the fight against cyber-crime.

The experience of the United Nations University (UNU, Tokyo, Japan) with online learning opportunities (including its Water Virtual Learning Centre, developed by the UNU's International Water, Environment and Health Programme) has been considered by the above expert meeting.

The Way Ahead: Three Objectives

One of the recommendations of the expert meeting on a virtual anti-cyber-crime forum held in 2006 was to encourage the creation of such fora on other criminal justice and crime prevention topics (Report 2006). This book seeks to contribute to this objective. But there is also another one for this book: assistance in enhancing criminal justice teaching and training in real academies. Finally, this book documents that there is a need to move from the level of anthology (as this one) - perhaps the first of its kind in the world - through, hopefully, many and various monographs on international criminal justice teaching and training, to putting on the global decision-making agenda the criminal justice teaching and training issues and proposing action-oriented solutions. They should move the topic ahead, in terms of more coordinated, concrete and incisive promotion and development of the rule of law. And this not only in real and virtual academies, but also in the field of project-based humanitarian operations across the world.

Getting the criminal justice message across the globe implies extending it beyond real and virtual academies into the field of humanitarian operations. In short, into peace keeping and peace building missions that are now so many, involving police personnel from 112 countries. The United Nations and the Organization for Security and Cooperation in Europe are among those which have been working on civil policing issues with their national police counterparts. In these issues the lack of common language of criminal justice and crime prevention among police officers recruited for these missions from so many countries and cultures, is a serious impediment to a more effective delivery of law enforcement services. In dangerous and highly politicized environments characterized by conflicting guidance and limited or non-existent judicial systems, this lack is not only hazardous, but also counter-productive to joint work (Schoenhaus 2002: 5-7).[32]

The answer to the absence of a common criminal justice language does not lie in the uniformization of education or training. Two approaches should be pursued parallelly: content- and experienced-based.

The content for the common language is provided by the United Nations standards and norms in crime prevention and criminal justice. These standards and norms - soft and treaty law - are also a common denominator for all 192 Member States of the United Nations. While sometimes they are regarded as "the lowest common denominator" (hence, as if not applicable in more advanced domestic legal systems), they do also declare or even stipulate the requirements above those existing in those systems, not only domestically, but regionally (Redo 2003). These standards and norms offer content-based information allowing to draw from a common substantive source.

---

32 See also: United States Institute of Peace, Progress in Peacebuilding. The Work of the U.S. Institute of Peace, Washington, D.C., 2006, and Duncan Chappell, John Evans, The Role, Preparation and Performance of Civilian Police in United Nations Peacekeeping Operations, Schlaining Working Papers 1/99.

The second approach is common sharing of experience-based information for education and training of very diversified audiences. Although the United Nations strives for a common language of justice, such audiences need to be taught or trained in that language in their own specific ways. More often than not the audience is very sensitive to their national concerns, sometimes (*i.e.*, especially when high-ranking officials take part in the activity) to the point of reacting to arguments of political nature. Science and politics, especially when it comes to security issues, may create a volatile solution – quite a counterproductive context for teaching and training in the name of a common language of justice. That is why, in order to support the common language of justice, there is a need to go beyond a mere set of internationally developed criminal justice curricula or programmes. Special pedagogical approaches, extra-curricular activities may have to accompany teaching and training in order to facilitate a mutual understanding and successful outcome.

This is quite a dynamic and long process. It has limits. One of the tools for its enhancement is the evaluation of the programmes. There are no publicly available results of their evaluation. It may be worthwhile to make an effort across the Programme's network to develop a common basis for such evaluation, provide it publicly and move together ahead with recommendations on the standardization of the United Nations criminal justice education and training. The recent review of the administration of justice activities of the United Nations Office of the Higher Commissioner for Human Rights (Flintman and Zwamborn 2003), is a good demonstration of evaluation, for which there is also an increasing number of tools (UNODC 2004).

In conclusion, in teaching and training, using a common language of criminal justice requires both content- and experience-based information. This book is a contribution towards this end.

Review of the Contents of the Book

The book goes now into a broader theme of the rule of law and transitional justice. It informs the readership what these concepts mean internationally, taking into account that the United Nations is one of the key providers of the precepts of the rule of law and transitional justice. In the article by Jean-Marc Coicaud (*"The United Nations in the international security and criminal justice politics: making the rule of law work"*), where he explains these concepts, the author emphasizes that "the rule of law", although a self-evident concept at the heart of the United Nations mission, beyond it may still remain a peripheral concept. That is why the title of the book is *"For the Rule of Law"*, since it seeks to advance it rather than taking it for granted. This article documents how difficult it is to deliver the precepts of the rule of law in practice. The same applies to the article on *"Training and effective support of comprehensive justice and security reforms: Outcomes to date and lessons learned"* by Yvon Dandurand, Curt T. Griffiths, and Vivienne Chin. These two articles document how difficult it is to deliver the precepts of the rule of law in practice.

The latter article takes this issue from the difficult realm of politics into the not less difficult realm of technical assistance. Their authors emphasize that "although aid institutions engaged in rule-of-law assistance do attempt some 'lessons learned' exercises, many of the lessons produced are superficial and even those are often not really learned". Moreover, there is "the unwillingness of aid organizations to invest sufficient resources in evaluations, and the tendency of both academics and lawyers not to pursue systematic empirical research on rule-of-law programming." Nonetheless, based not only on their own experience, but also on the experience of many others, including the experience of the UNHCHR and the United Nations Development Programme, the authors share the lessons learned from the rule-of-law programmes, which indeed seem to be useful for successful technical assistance delivery.

To meet this objective, new methods need to be found, and clearly distance learning is one of them.[33] Jacqueline Schneider, the author of the article *"Distance learning: An alternative service delivery for criminal justice training and high education"*, points, however, to the many new problems distance learning brings. Emphasizing that distance learning is a very lucrative university business, she also stresses that its impact on students and faculty staff is very poorly researched and evaluated.[34] Profits must be weighed against the other potential problems that may underline the new system of delivering higher education. She finally argues that only in the United Kingdom the evaluation of distance learning courses has reached a level that other countries do not have.

Rodrigo Paris Steffens *("Distance learning as a tool for the effective dissemination of United Nations criminal justice instruments to future law enforcement officers: The case of ethnic and gender issues")* argues two points. First that, although the new methods enable to modify the distance learning course syllabi easily by including in them information on international legal

---

33 One of the biggest distance learning providers in the world (250,000 students) is the University of South Africa (UNISA). It offers a diverse choice of study fields at levels from certificate to degree, ranging from animal health, agriculture, law, business, education, humanities (http://www.unisa.ac.za).
34 And indeed this may be confirmed by *e.g.*, Lanier (2006), cited also later in this article. See also Snell and Penn 2005: 19-36.

instruments not really known, at least, by a part of the audience, the course instructor in the United States must persuasively explain the relevance of such instruments for the practitioners of criminal justice there. Secondly, that one has also be aware of the fact that the new medium unfortunately facilitates misreading of instructor's comments, which may be taken as abuse of students' human rights. The author speaks in this sense of the "minefield", but there are also on the students' side reasons to be worried about (weak motivation/cheating), as other already published research has shown.

This first point, but generalized (*i.e.*, as the need for developing genuinely international and progressive criminal justice course syllabus), has been taken up further by Jesus Dámasio. He explains in his article how his law school in Brazil teaches alternatives to imprisonment via satellite *("Education via satellite technology applied to promotion of non-custodial measures")*. The promotion of alternatives to imprisonment by the United Nations is an important issue for the United Nations. Since 1990 (adoption of the United Nations Standard Minimum Rules for Non-custodial Measures (The Tokyo Rules)), adopted by General Assembly resolution 45/110 of 14 December 1990), this may be considered equally important, as since 1955 has been the promotion of the implementation of the United Nations Standard Minimum Rules for the Treatment of Prisoners.

The need for developing genuinely international and progressive criminal justice course syllabus, has also been addressed by a number of other authors in this book writing about it in the context of a real academic classroom setting.

Frank Hoepfel, the next contributor to this volume, opens its next section by addressing the topic of *"Teaching criminal law in its international dimension – Where to start?"*. Before reading the answer, one has to explain that development of criminal law in its international dimension is a part of progressive development of international law in general, as stipulated by the Charter of the United Nations (art. 13 (a)).[35] The mandates of the United Nations drugs and crime programme include various international criminal law instruments with which it pursues much of its work against organized crime, including illicit drug trafficking, corruption and terrorism, thus also contributing to the implementation of the Charter. Over recent years, in line with the progressive development of international law, the two new conventions (against transnational organized crime and corruption), have been added to the three already operating United Nations anti-drug conventions (Chawla and Pietschmann 2005; Joutsen 2005). All of them expand the international criminal law field enormously, hence there is a real

---

35 See also Corell (2002).

need to teach the students about its new complexities, in a way that is effective. The author emphasizes therefore, that to get the message through to the students, it needs to be an attractive subject at law schools. That will only work, when it is not too complex. Given the steady movement of the contents of this matter, it actually is less feasible to teach it, and to pre-process it in terms of introducing it into textbooks.

In the article by Philip Reichel on *"Using the topic of torture for interrogation to teach about international standards and the rule of law"*, the author reports that he surprisingly found out that there were really no effective legal arguments that could change students' support for using torture as a means of interrogation, despite an innovative interactive innovative method which he used in the class.[36] Clearly, this finding is as "explosive" as the "minefield" through which another academic had to go while teaching students human rights in the administration of criminal justice – the second point mentioned above.

Next, Michael Platzer in his article *"New ways of teaching students about international criminal justice"* writes about even more moving experience gathered in Austrian and Australian universities, initially developed through a case study method. After enhancing it with the new experiences observed and discussed with his Australian colleagues, Platzer in his article shares a great deal about new teaching techniques. Applying these techniques, reports Professor Rosita Dellios, one of the evaluators of Platzer's criminal justice course at the Bond University in Australia, "is a real bonus for students... The students assessed him as "very knowledgeable about the United Nations. [H]is many personal stories that are relevant and interesting...allowed detailed discussions...encouraged debate and student input".

Subsequently, Mangai Nataranjan, describes in her article *"John Jay's Bachelor's Degree in International Criminal Justice"*, a criminal justice college of The City University of New York (USA), which teaches students from 135 countries in the world. This article is another contribution to the challenging but growing effort of internationalization of the criminal justice academic agenda in the United States. This international educational agenda has now expanded to one-third of the criminal justice colleges there (Cordner *et.al.* 2000). As the editor and author of a spearheading anthology on international criminal justice (Nataranjan 2005), her present article,[37] reflecting the approach of that book, explains the component parts of the international criminal justice curriculum which is now applied to teach some 300 students.

---

36 See also Huggins and Coghalan 2004: 414-415; Reichel 2005.
37 See also Nataranjan 2002: 480-498.

Moving to the training arena, in the next article by Dick Ward and Joe Serio *("Opportunities and challenges in delivering a syllabus for international police training: The case of the International Law Enforcement Academy (ILEA) at Roswell, New Mexico (USA)")*, both authors describe the curriculum of the Academy and share their first-hand experience in training middle ranking foreign law enforcement officials. The Academy in Roswell is a part of a program of the U.S. Department of State, Bureau for International Narcotics and Law Enforcement Affairs. Speaking before the United Nations General Assembly at its 50th Anniversary on 22 October 1995, then-President Clinton called for the establishment of a network of International Law Enforcement Academies throughout the world to combat international drug trafficking, criminality, and terrorism through strengthened international cooperation.[38] ILEAs serve three regions: Europe (Budapest, Hungary), Asia (Bangkok, Thailand), Africa (Gaborone, Botswana). An Academy for the Americas (Salvador, El Salvador) is the last addition. The Academies' mission is to provide advanced criminal justice management instruction to mid- to senior law enforcement officials from around the world and expose them to American society and institutions.

The Academy in Roswell is interregional. It trains foreign visiting experienced middle-ranking law enforcement officials at its Advanced Management Course. So far 1664 participants from 60 countries from regions around the world, including Latin America, the Caribbean, Central and Eastern Europe, sub-Saharan Africa, and Asia, have been trained at Roswell. This large group of participants has undergone a four-module training seeking to accomplish several broad goals. Three of these goals are cognitive in nature (pertaining to learning concepts and procedures), two are affective (relating to a desired change in attitudes), and three are skill related. The article describes in detail these three elements and explains why the training has been so successful.

Carmen Solis *("Human Dignity/Human Rights and the police: training that manifests rule of law operations")* shares in this book another successful experience in imparting in the police work the human rights precepts, including dignity – "an innate quality possessed by all human beings" (Curran and Rothlein 1999). The training is conducted at the ILEAs, but also in the selected Caribbean countries. The author critically admits that despite the fact that the course fared well according to instructors' evaluations in each of the ILEAs, one of the major shortcomings has been the lack of follow-up programme evaluation. The paucity of systemic criminal justice teaching and training programme evaluations

---

38 The White House Office of the Press Secretary (New York, New York). Remarks by the President to the U. N. General Assembly, http://clinton4. nara.gov/wh/new/other/unspeech.html.

seems to be indeed a common problem for most of the entities, the work of which has been written about in this volume.

Within this limit, however, in another article by Emil Pływaczewski ("Making criminal justice transformation, teaching and training work: experiences learned from Central Europe") its author describes another successful initiative – the creation of the Central European Police Academy (in German Mittel-Europäische Polizei-Akademie – MEPA), located in (Vienna, Austria). Describing its activities since 1993 (the date of MEPA's establishment), the author emphasizes that the current focus of the program for trained policemen is not on technical skills, but on leadership, personnel and financial management of the investigative process, and other contemporary law enforcement issues. MEPA's establishment and work, as much as the ILEAs' contributions, can serve as good examples of international training effort which progresses throughout the world.

Andrew Millie and Dilip Das ("Police education and training in four countries: getting rule of law messages across") in their article looked into more detail into the teaching and training process of three MEPA countries (France, Germany and Switzerland) and one Asian country – Japan. The article describes trainee selection, the background philosophy of training, general organization and curriculum. The chapter draws largely from a series of interviews, observations and conversations conducted by one of the authors between 1998 and 2001 in each of the four countries. This has been supplemented by evidence from the research literature. The article concludes with the interesting finding that in the four countries under review there were three distinct teaching and training police philosophies: focusing on the rule of law (Germany), community (Japan and Switzerland) and human rights and multiculturalism (France).

James Finckenauer's article on "Culture of lawfulness training for police" explains this concept, which not only made its strides in France and the United States, but also in 2002, it has entered the agenda of the United Nations Crime Prevention and Criminal Justice Programme through the United Nations "Guidelines for the Prevention of Crime".[39]. There "culture of lawfulness" means "the rule of law and those human rights which are recognized in international instruments to which Member States are parties", and that "should be actively promoted in crime prevention" (ECOSOC resolution 2002/13, Annex, para. 12). However, the author's working definition is much more incisive. Culture of law is "a culture in which the great majority of citizens and the civil institutions of society (religious, educational, business, labour, cultural and social organizations) support the rule-of-law; and, where the average person believes that the laws and the system for creating, changing

---

39 http://www.un.org/docs/ecosoc/documents/2002/resolutions/eres2002-13.pdf.

and enforcing laws are fundamentally fair, and that the laws and the legal system operate in their best interest as well as in the best interests of the society". He then describes a project on culture of law curriculum, originally developed for secondary or middle schools in Mexico, then adapted also in similar schools in Colombia, El Salvador, Georgia, El Salvador, Peru, and, most recently, in Lebanon. This project (largely evaluated), now has been extended in Colombia to police training, hence the title of this article. The author presents the police curriculum, and drawing on his and other experts' opinion, concludes that such training curriculum, when administered, is in the best interest of the police forces which not only change themselves for the better, but also increases their effectiveness.

Next, Sheryl Van Horne in her article *("A content analysis of popular introductions to criminal justice textbooks")* investigated the amount of space allocated to international issues in five of the bestselling criminal justice introductory textbooks in the United States.[40] She hypothesized that very little space will be devoted to international issues in the primary introductory texts. Since this particular research has not been attempted in the past, the types and topics of international information in the main text were also examined. The results indicate that indeed a relatively small percent of space discusses international issues or international comparisons, though the results do vary by the text and subject matter, which is broken down as crime, police, courts, corrections and juvenile justice. She concludes that additional research needs to be conducted on the content, benefit, and perceptions of a more global focus of criminal justice material.

In this substantive sense, the limited interest in international criminal justice issues may be corroborated by other U.S. researchers, but the issue is far from unequivocal, if one takes into account that about one-third of the U.S. colleges have them in their course syllabi, as mentioned above. Substantively, those researchers argued that American academic criminology still strongly maintains its local focus on crime (McDonald 1995).

The review of the comparative research presentations (1991-1999) at the annual meetings of the American Society of Criminology revealed that they represented less than 20% of such presentations, while more than 80% indeed remained local (Barberet 2004). Just about that time (mid-90s) other researchers (Friday 1996) nonetheless postulated the need to integrate comparative and international criminal justice into a traditional curriculum in the USA. Nowadays, and as already documented by some other articles in this book, there appears quite a strong interest in genuinely internationalizing the teaching and training agenda, not only in the USA but in many other countries.

---

40 See also Wright 2002: 183-195.

The above may also be illustrated here with the next article *("Developing an agenda for international criminal justice teaching and training")* by Jay Albanese. The author, an academician and practitioner in one, argues that there are four ways in which a better effort can be made to provide useful criminal justice education, training, and technical assistance in the most appropriate way. These include: cataloguing training providers, organizing curriculum, documenting experience, capturing and disseminating best practices. He postulates increased professionalism in criminal justice agencies across the world. Emerging democracies, new crimes, negative incidents in all countries, and new legislation and international agreements have created the need for criminal justice training, education, and technical assistance on a broad scale through which that professionalism may be enhanced.

The topic of new crimes is addressed in two subsequent articles. First, Joon Oh Jang writes about "Criminal justice training in Korea – Korean Institute of Criminal Justice Policy and the development of training program for Asian developing countries". He emphasizes that the Republic of Korea has a long tradition of rule of law. Korean people see the modern idea of rule of law, or *Rechtsstaat*, as a standard of justice and human rights in a society. Among diverse criminal justice education and training programs, those related to cybercrime are prominent. Jang describes how the Korean Institute of Criminal Justice Policy, a government financed research institution, joined one of the newest initiatives of the United Nations Office on Drugs and Crime in criminal justice education and training - the Virtual Forum against Cybercrime. Its initial aim is to provide online anti-cybercrime training focused on law enforcement officers in Asia.[41] This aim well inscribes into "electronic governance"- government's use of information technology to exchange information and services with citizens,

---

41 Similar initiatives have started in other parts of the world. In Europe, the need for training programmes enabling criminal justice personnel to avail themselves of expertise in the field of prosecution and adjudication of cyber-crime has been recognized by Recommendation No. R(95) 13 of the Committee of Ministers of the Council of Europe on problems of criminal procedural law connected with information technology. The Council of the European Union (EU) and the European Commission (EC) have repeatedly emphasized their concerns about development of a comprehensive strategy on security of electronic networks and effective law enforcement of cyber-crime. In 2003, the EC commissioned RAND Europe to develop a *Legal Handbook of Legal Procedures of Computer and Network Misuse* in the EU Countries. The second edition of this handbook, now available, provides access to up to date information on rules and regulations concerning computer misuse and the collection and reporting of computer evidence currently in force in all 25 EU countries. We are grateful to Professor Andrzej Adamski (Poland) for his advice. See also http://www.lefis.org/ and the website of the Council of Europe (http://assembly.coe.int), for example on "Realising the full potential of e-learning at all levels of education", Teleconference of the Committee on Culture, Science and Education,, Strasbourg, 1 October 2007.

businesses, and other government bodies. Domestically, electronic governance is usually used by legislature, judiciary and administration to improve the internal affairs, the status of public services and the processes of democratic governance. It promotes transparency and trust in the activities of both government and administration. Internationally, it harmonizes various domestic concepts and brings them in line with a broader sense of justice worldwide.[42]

Next, in an article on *"Teaching cybercrime prevention: lessons learned from partnership with the academia"* by Roderic Broadhurst, this author further illustrates this ambitious justice aim in an academic context. A web-based pilot program and curriculum has been developed to help train first responders, investigators and forensic specialists. This pilot program will be delivered in to select developing jurisdictions. The on-line and off-line features of the training design include attention to evaluation and mentoring. A strength of the project is the involvement of industry, the academia and law enforcement showing that such partnerships can yield constructive responses to cyber-crime through international co-operation.

In the last article *"Why crime prevention is an essential component of international training and technical assistance: the experience of the International Centre for the Prevention of Crime"* by Margaret Shaw, she deals with the impact of recent global changes on training and technical assistance in the field of criminal justice. Referring to a long history of bilateral training and technical assistance, often characterized as disconnected and uncoordinated, and at times counter-productive, with countries or institutions offering competing models and paying little attention to the interests of needs of the recipient countries, this author from one of the PNI's institutes emphasizes the emerging trend towards a more coordinated and comprehensive technical assistance which is dynamited by crime prevention "explosion". Many developed countries now have well-entrenched national crime prevention strategies which began to take shape from the mid 1980s, including Denmark, Finland and Sweden, France, Britain, Canada, Australia, for example. Evidence-based crime prevention interventions have become a major component of many country policies. The article emphasizes four points. It is important for the future that crime prevention training and technical assistance has a strong focus on processes and implementation (not just good practice and knowledge); has a strong awareness of context – historical, cultural, political, economic and social realities and recognition of

---

42 In this context, see, *e.g.*, the forthcoming World Civic Forum. Building Just Societies. From Vision to Action. An initiative of Kyung Hee University and the United Nations Department for Economic and Social Affairs, Seoul, Republic of Korea, 2009, www.wcf2009.org.

complexity of all social institutions; is participatory – at the level of country or city or particular target groups; and focuses on human rights and inclusiveness.

Finally, this article like several other articles in this anthology, emphasizes also the role of new communication technologies in criminal justice and crime prevention teaching and training.

References

A/CONF.203/14, Eleventh United Nations Congress on the Prevention of Crime and Criminal Justice, *Measures to combat computer-related crime*, Working paper prepared by the Secretariat.

A/RES/55/2, United Nations Millennium Declaration.

A/55/305 - S/2000/809, *Report of the Panel on United Nations Peace Operations*.

Bufkin, Jana(2004). Criminology/criminal justice master's programs in the United States: searching for commonalities, *Journal of Criminal Justice Education*, Vol. 15, number 2 (2004): 240-262.

Chappell, Duncan and John Evans (1999). The Role, Preparation and Performance of civilian police in United Nations Peacekeeping Operations, *Schlaining Working Papers* 1/99.

Chawla, Sandeep and Thomas Pietschmann (2005). Drug trafficking as a transnational crime. In Philip Reichel (ed.), *Handbook of Transnational Crime and Justice*, Thousand Oaks-London-New Delhi, SAGE Publications, 160-180.

Cordner, A., Dammer, H., & Horvath, F. (2000). A national survey of comparative criminal justice courses in universities in the United States. *Journal of Criminal Justice Education, 11*(2), 211-223.

Corell, Hans (2002). International law and the law school curriculum, *International Law FORUM du Droit International* 4 (2002), 195–198.

Curran, J. T. & Rothlein, M. D. (1999). Course development and evaluation (in) Lynch, G.W.*, Human Dignity and the Police: Ethnics and Integrity in Police Work*. Springfield Illinois, USA: Charles C. Thomas Publisher, LTD.

Eskridge, W. Chris (2003). Criminal justice education and its potential impact on the socio-political-economic climate of Central European nations: a short essay, *Journal of Criminal Justice Education*, Vol. 14, number 1 (2003), 105-118.

Evans, Tony (2005). International human rights law as power/knowledge, *Human Rights Quarterly* 27, (2005), 1046–1068.

Flinterman, C. and Zwamborn, M. (2003). *From Development of Human Rights to Managing Human Rights Development: Global Review of the OHCHR Technical Cooperation Program Syntheses Report*. Utrecht: Netherlands Institute of Human Rights (SIM) & MEDE European Consultancy, September 2003.

Friday, Paul C. (1996). The need to integrate comparative and international criminal justice into a traditional curriculum, *Journal of Criminal Justice Education*, Vol. 7, No 2/November (1996), 227-239.

Gorard, S., Selwyn, N. (2005). Towards a le@rning society? The impact of technology on patterns of participation in lifelong learning, *British Journal of Sociology of Education* (2005), Vol. 26, Issue 1, 71-90.

Huggins, Denise Walker and Coghalan, Catherin, L. (2004). Social stratification and life chances: an interactive learning strategy for criminal justice classes, *Journal of Criminal Justice Education*, Vol. 15, number 2 (2004), 413-428.

Independent Evaluation Unit Brief, United Nations Office on Drugs and Crime, June 2006, http://www.unodc.org/pdf/ELearnBriefJune2006.pdf.

Jahan, Selim (2004). Human rights-based approach to poverty reduction – analytical linkages, *Practical Work and UNDP*, http://www.undp.org/poverty/docs/HRPR.doc, 2004.

Joutsen, Matti (2005). International instruments on cooperation in responding to transnational crime. In Philip Reichel (ed.), *Handbook of Transnational Crime and Justice*, Thousand Oaks-London-New Delhi, SAGE Publications, 2005, 255-274.

Kirkpatrick, D.L. (1994). *Evaluating Training Programs: The Four Levels,* San Francisco, CA: Berrett-Koehler.

Korean Institute of Criminal Justice Policy, United Nations Office on Drugs and Crime, on Drugs and Crime, *Expert Group Meeting on the Development of Virtual Forum against Cybercrime*, Report, June 28-30, 2006, Seoul, Korea (mimeographed).

Lanier, Mark M, (2006). Academic Integrity and Distance Learning, *Journal of Criminal Justice Education*, Vol. 17, number 2 (October 2006), 244-261.

McDonald, William F. (1995). The Globalization of Criminology: The New Frontier is the Frontier", *Transnational Organized Crime*, Vol. 1, Spring 1995:1-12.

Ministry of Interior, Turkish National Police, Department of Anti-Smuggling and Organized Crime, *Turkish Drug Report 2005*, March 2006, http://www.tadoc.gov.tr/ingilizce/Established.htm.

Nataranjan, Mangai (2002). International criminal justice education: A note on curricular resources, *Journal of Criminal Justice Education*, Vol. 13, number 2 (2002), 480-498.

Nataranjan, Mangai (2005). *Introduction to International Criminal Justice*, McGraw-Hill Primis Custom Publishing.

Palermo B., George (2004). Commentary: Globalization of knowledge, *International Journal of Offender Therapy and Comparative Criminology*, 48(6), 760-761.

Redo, Slawomir (2008). For a common language of justice: translating words into deeds, *Aktualne Problemy Prawa Karnego i Kryminologii* Wydawnictwo Temida 2, Białystok.

Redo, Sławomir (2003). New United Nations provisions against economic crime (in:) A. Adamski (ed.) *Przestępczość gospodarcza z perspektywy Polski i Unii Europejskiej*, Wydawnictwo Dom Organizatora, Toruń 2003, 33-53.

Reichel, Philip L. (2005). *Comparative Criminal Justice Systems: A Topical Approach*, Prentice Hall.

Rubiales, D., M. T. Steely, C. E. Wollner, J. T. Richardson, and M. F. Smith (1998). Distance Learning, *Academe* (May–June 1998),

S/2004/616, Report of the Secretary-General, *The rule of law and transitional justice in conflict and post-conflict societies.*

Schoenhaus, Robert M. (2002). *Training for Peace and Humanitarian Relief Operations. Advancing Best Practices*, United States Institute of Peace, Washington, D.C.

Snell, Clete and Penn, Everette (2005). Developing an Online Justice Studies Degree Program: ACase Study, *Journal of Criminal Justice Education*, volume 16, number 1, April 2005, 19-36.

Tomasevski, Katarina (2005). Globalizing what: education as a human right or as a traded service? *Indiana Journal of Global Legal Studies*, 12 (2005), 1-78.

United Nations Development Programme, Human rights cities program, Program document, mimeographed, 2003.

UNICRI: Trafficking in Human Beings and Peace-Support Operations. Pre-deployment/In-service Training Programme for International Law-enforcement Personnel. 1st edition 2004, 2nd edition 2006), available from UNICRI.

United Nations Office at Vienna, UNESCO Institute for Education, *Basic Education in Prisons*, (ST/CSDHA/25), 1995

United Nations Office on Drugs and Crime (2004). *Evaluation of Tools and Toolkits as a Modality of Programme Delivery by the United Nations Office on Drugs and Crime*. Vienna: UNODC - Independent Evaluation Unit http://www.unodc.org/pdf/Evaluation_04-Toolsandtoolkits.pdf.

United Nations Office on Drugs and Crime (2006), Independent Evaluation Unit, *Evaluation of UNODC's e-Learning initiative (with emphasis on Computer-based Training) as a modality of technical cooperation delivery and capacity building*, Vienna, January, 2006, http://www.unodc.org/pdf/Eval_E-learning_Jan06.pdf.

United States Institute of Peace (2006). *Progress in Peacebuilding. The Work of the U.S. Institute of Peace*, Washington, D.C.

Wright A., Richard (2002). Recent changes in the most-cited scholars in criminal justice textbooks, *Journal of Criminal Justice* 30 (2002), 183-195.

I. MAKING THE RULE OF LAW WORK: SECURITY AND JUSTICE REFORMS IN THE UNITED NATIONS

The United Nations in the International Security and Criminal Justice Politics: Making the Rule of Law Work

Jean-Marc Coicaud[1]

Introduction

At the international level, the dominating realist paradigm dissociates security from justice, by and large limiting justice to simply an idealist and moral matter marginal to the hard-core actuality of international politics. There is an urgent need to go beyond this approach to allow the world to move away from the overall insecurity trap in which it is now caught to a more constructive action for a common language of justice.

In this light, this article emphasizes the role of the United Nations as a major actor involved in developing the interrelated precepts of security and justice. This article contributes to that aim, by, first, explaining what makes security and justice in the United Nations optics and, how, through the rule of law criminal justice, transitional justice and transnational justice, that rule may operate in practice.

What is Security and Justice in the United Nations Optics?

Since 1990 much has happened in international security. This is a primary right[2] of States and other actors, from which all other rights derive (Rothschild 1995). Short of benefiting from security, States and other actors are impeded in their existence, in their ability to subsist, develop and flourish.

Unlike earlier, contemporary meaning of international security is anchored in the demands of justice[3]. For such demands, far from

---

1 Dr. Jean-Marc Coicaud is The Head of the United Nations University Office to the United Nations in New York (USA). The views expressed in this article do not necessarily reflect the views of the United Nations Secretariat.
2 The understanding of security in this chapter departs more from philosophy and political science in general than from the various schools of international relations.
3 Justice is conceived here in connection with recognizing and acting upon the rights with which individuals identify.

being external and marginal to security, are internal and central to it. While dovetailing the quest for security and justice may seem naïve, at least from a realist perspective, and is certainly a demanding task at the international level, as a whole it helps contain the dangers associated with the loss of legitimacy of the international system and the intertwining of geopolitics and negative effects.

This approach responds to a human rights-inclined version of security, with the emergence of notions such as human security[4] and the 'responsibility to protect'[5], which made some headway. What makes responding to the demands of justice so important to the quest for security? There is a short answer: as put in a modern United Nations parlance, there is no peace without justice and *vice versa*.

How this equilibrium between security and justice can be developed and maintained is a difficult question. Rousseau once said, that "(t)he strongest is never strong enough to be always the master, unless he transforms strength into right, and obedience into duty". But this implies no "tranquillity of spirit" (Montesquieu), neither among the powerful nor the powerless. As power assigns responsibility for the shortcomings (unfairness) of the political and social arrangements, the powerful is prone to be a target of resentment and acts of violence from those who feel cheated by the system. Consequently, the abusive concentration of power tends to become self-defeating for the power holder(s). It is, then, in a self-enlightened interest of even most powerful State, to take justice seriously, to look after people's rights. This is essential to ensuring security. Although at the national level, especially in democracies, the relation between security and justice has long been identified as an internal one, and one which, as such, has been epitomized in the value and institutions of the rule of law, this reality has still to enter the international realm.

The Rule of Law

That is why, I think, the rule of law is a concept at the very heart of the United Nations mission, even though, at a broader scale (internationally), this concept has not been adopted, shared and

---

4 See: the special issues of: Security Dialogue, 35:3 (September 2004) and, for a comprehensive account of what human security entails, see Andrew Mack (ed. in chief), The Human Security Report 2005: War and Peace in the 21st Century, Human Security Center (New York, Oxford University Press, 2006)
5 The document adopted on 16 September 2005 at the United Nations World Summit in New York, endorsed the acceptance of collective responsibility to protect civilians against genocide and other crimes against humanity.

followed to the same high extent. This became clear in the past century, when the rule of law became a focus of development projects. One conclusion resulting from their implementation was that, however hard it was to develop the theory of the rule of law with its social values and cultural beliefs, even harder was practically to pursue the rule of law with those values and beliefs (A/CONF. 187/3, para. 2). This concept, then, which is at the very heart of the United Nations, may now still be quite marginal elsewhere or may be interpreted in such a strict Western oriented supremacy fashion (let alone by one only powerful Western State), that it may be not acceptable to others, less powerful.

However, even within the most powerful States there are very substantial differences in the level of development of the rule of law, as shown on the table below.

Table Rule of law ratings (5 permanent members of the United Nations Security Council), 2006

Country	Percentile Rank (0-100)
CHINA	45.2
FRANCE	89.5
RUSSIA	19.0
UNITED KINGDOM	93.3
UNITED STATES	91.9

Source: Kaufmann D., A. Kraay, and M. Mastruzzi 2007: Governance Matters V: Governance Indicators for 1996-2006, http://info.worldbank.org/governance/wgi2007/

This table, with information drawn from the World Bank database, depicts the percentile rank on a rule of law indicator constructed on the basis of 2006 polls in the above countries. Percentile rank indicates the percentage of countries worldwide that rate below the selected country (subject to margin of error). Higher values indicate better rule of law rating.

This is a challenge for the rule of law makers and providers (*i.e.*, those who implement the concept in practice), and, obviously for the legal educators. Appreciating the difficulty in getting the concept across the wide spectrum of domestic and international actors, the United Nations advances the concept of the rule of law in operational rather than theoretical terms.

In the United Nations terms, the rule of law as a working definition, refers to a principle of governance in which all persons, institutions and entities, public and private, including the State itself, are accountable to laws that are publicly promulgated, equally enforced and independently adjudicated, and which are consistent with international human rights norms and standards. It requires, as well, measures to ensure adherence to the principles of supremacy of law, equality before the law, accountability to the law, fairness in the application of the law, separation of powers, participation in decision-making, legal certainty, avoidance of arbitrariness and procedural and legal transparency.

The above, taken from the report of the United Nations Secretary-General to the Security Council (S/2004/616, para. 5), can be complemented by another working definition of the rule of law, shared by the United Nations Secretariat at the Tenth United Nations Congress on the Prevention of Crime and the Treatment of Offenders (2000). According to that definition, "the rule of law is a system of interrelated principles that extend widely into social, economic and cultural and other structures in present-day societies" through several central principles: the law must be comprehensive; the law must be clear, certain and accessible; the law must be legitimate (consented and complied with); the law must balance stability and flexibility; equality before the law; institutional independence and the separation of powers; and a number of legal rights in criminal justice systems (A/CONF. 187/3, para. 5).

Criminal Justice and Transitional Justice

The latter central principle of legal rights, particularly relevant to criminal justice system (but also true of law in general), is indeed critical for penal law and penal procedure, because of the severity of the sanctions that can be imposed on an offender and the degree to which they can interfere with otherwise established human rights (*Ibidem*, para.7).

In the report of the Secretary-General to the Security Council, this criminal justice component of the concept of the rule of law, essentially serves to explain what justice means in the United Nations sense. The Secretary-General explains that for the United Nations, justice is an ideal of accountability and fairness in the protection and vindication of rights and the prevention and punishment of wrongs. Justice implies regard for the rights of the accused, for the interests of victims and for the well-being of society at large. It is a concept rooted in all national cultures and traditions and, while its administration usually implies formal judicial mechanisms, traditional dispute resolution mechanisms are equally relevant (S/2004/616, para. 7).

In the above context, one now needs to explain how that ideal of accountability and fairness can be advanced in practice through which one must balance out its various components in the criminal justice reform process. However, before we do so, we must first add and explain one more concept in the context of which this process is recently being pursued in the United Nations, namely that of "transitional justice". In 2005, this relatively new term, formalized in 2004 in the afore mentioned report of the Secretary-General, was discussed in working terms at the meeting on the "Rule of Law and Transitional Justice" organized by the United Nations University and the Legal Office of the United Nations Secretariat (A/61/31, para. 10).

Again, from the very essence of the term, "transitional justice" is a concept which applies to societies in transition. In the United Nations terminology they are also called "developing countries and countries with economies in transition", and conflict and post-conflict societies. In the latter group of countries such transition may only be first started by the humanitarian aid effort.

Since the above *explanandum* of transitional justice is tautological (for there is no *explanans*), and to cover a practical scope of this term, one may indeed define transitional justice as "the full range of processes and mechanisms associated with a society's attempts to come to terms with a legacy of large-scale past abuses, in order to ensure accountability, serve justice and achieve reconciliation. These may include both judicial and non-judicial mechanisms, with differing levels of international involvement (or none at all) and individual prosecutions, reparations, truth-seeking, institutional reform, vetting and dismissals, or a combination thereof" (*Ibidem*, para. 8).

From Transitional to Transnational Justice through Education and Training

Within this broad concept, legal education plays important role, for it is clear that transitional justice serves well when it extends beyond police, courts, prisons and the right of defence. A contribution to the legal education was provided by the United Nations University at another meeting, co-organized in 2005 with the Hague Academic Coalition (HAC)[6]. There, the question of

---

6 This is a consortium of academic institutions in the fields of international relations, international law and international development. The Coalition was established to promote collaborative efforts between the six institutions, based in The Hague: Carnegie Foundation (more specifically the Peace Palace Library), the Grotius Centre (Leiden University, Campus Den Haag), The Hague Institute for the internationalisation of Law, the T.M.C. Asser Instituut, the "Clingendael" Institute and the Institute of Social Studies. Specifically, the HAC promotes research, education and public debate in support of the development of international policy, law, governance and international negotiations towards

international criminal accountability and children's rights was taken up with a view to bridging the gap between two major conceptual and practical subjects: the protection of the rights of the child (as codified in international law); and the development of international criminal jurisdiction regarding crimes against children (A/61/31, para. 10).

In a UNU follow-up book on the same subject (Popovski and Arts 2006), that aim of bridging the gap was somehow narrowed, in the sense that the two fields – that of international criminal justice jurisdiction as a humanitarian law effort to extend the rule of law over children soldiers in conflict and post-conflict societies, and that of the protection of the rights of the child, as exemplified by the recently adopted *Guidelines on Justice Matters involving Child Victims and Witnesses of Crime* (ECOSOC res. 2005/20), have now been brought closer. This is because the *Guidelines* recommend a range of very specific legal instruments aimed at treating the victimized child and protect him/her from revictimization. This documents how relevant corresponding concepts of transitional and transnational justice have entered together into the realm of the rule of law, at least on paper.

While for the United Nations as the provider of criminal justice standards and norms this may be a very successful attempt, for the United Nations as the legal educator and trainer this is, however, only the very beginning of an effort to bring the message across the world to various addressees, including students and officials seized with this transnational subject.

What to Deliver and How to Deliver?

Except for a pioneering attempt of the United Nations Interregional Crime and Justice Research Institute (UNICRI) with its new Masters of Law Programme on "International Organizations, International Criminal Law and Crime Prevention", there should be other avenues to pursue global criminal justice and crime prevention education or training curriculae. This seems to be a potentially viable project with many possible specific topics.

This is due to the fact that over sixty years of existence of the Organization there has been altogether about sixty important United Nations crime prevention and criminal justice legal instruments (conventions and "soft law"), including the last one (the aforementioned *Guidelines on Justice Matters involving Child*

---

justice, peace and sustainable development. As part of this broad objective, the HAC in particular seeks to support the work of the various international courts, tribunals and other international organisations, based in The Hague.

Victims and Witnesses of Crime) which cover almost any issue in the crime and justice field. These Guidelines, serving here merely as an example for building up a broader United Nations curriculum on children's rights, show how interrelated they are with other standards and norms, *e.g.*, with Guidelines for the Prevention of Crime, Declaration of Basic Principles of Justice for Victims of Crime and Abuse of Power, and, obviously the Convention on the Rights of the Child (*Ibidem*, section II).

These various interrelationships create endless combinations in which the United Nations legal instruments may be taught about and used for training. And indeed, across the United Nations Secretariat and various agencies (*e.g.*, United Nations International Children Emergency Fund (UNICEF), United Nations Scientific and Educational Organization (UNESCO), but also beyond them, there have been many instances of and arrangements for international criminal justice teaching and training wherefrom one can draw enough experience on developing one or another course syllabus which may contribute to a more comprehensive and practically-oriented global criminal justice and crime prevention curriculae, or, let alone, recommendations for them.

For this purpose, the United Nations Secretariat may not have only the UNU in Tokyo (Japan) and UNICRI in Turin (Italy), but also located in Turin the United Nations Staff Training College, among many others. Although all these entities have their own scientific or advisory boards which guide their programmes, there is also an internal Policy Committee of the Secretary-General, with two working groups on Security Sector Reform and Rule of Law and Justice. Composed of the members of various offices involved in security and justice matters of the Secretariat, these groups are a kind of a relay enabling the field experience in implementing the security and justice issues to be shared for other field projects and work programmes, but also - potentially - projecting their recommendations into the course syllabi of the teaching and training institutions. Such recommendations will not be made soon, though, because the requisite relay between "bureaucracy/practice" and "academia/theory", has hardly ever been intentionally and successfully put in place, and when it was, at times, eventually to the detriment of the latter.

Conclusion

The question, then, of how to deliver the rule of law in practice? Although at some point may be better answered than above, it must still wait, until, at least, such a time when various international actors (those powerful and those powerless) will come to terms with their own limitations and see the benefits of acting in concert.

Acknowledging here that currently there is a disconnection between security and justice, *i.e.,* between their theoretical and practical aspects, one has to emphasize the need to pursue more comprehensive and balanced policy in the name of the international rule of law. The United Nations as a criminal justice provider and educator in the rule of law, can develop a common language of justice not only when there will be more viable avenues of communication between the theory and practice, but also more open-ended and pluralist discussion among Member States and the international criminal justice community at large.

References

A/CONF. 187/3, Promoting the rule of law and strengthening the criminal justice system, Working paper prepared by the Secretariat, Tenth United Nations Congress on the Prevention of Crime and the Treatment of Offenders, Vienna, 10-17 April 2000.

S/2004/616, Report of the Secretary-General, The rule of law and transitional justice in conflict and post-conflict societies, para. 5.

A/61/31, Supplement No. 31, Report of the Council of the United Nations University, January-December 2005, United Nations, New York, 2006

Guidelines on Justice in Matters involving Child Victims and Witnesses of Crime (ECOSOC resolution 2005/20, Annex).

Kaufmann D., A. Kraay, and M. Mastruzzi (2006). Governance Matters V: Governance Indicators for 1996-2005, http://info.worldbank.org/ governance/kkz2005/mc_chart.asp.

Popovski, Vesselin and Karin Arts (2006) (eds), International Criminal Accountability and Children's Rights, United Nations University, Tokyo.

Training and Effective Support of Comprehensive Justice and Security Reforms: Outcomes to Date and Lessons Learned

Yvon Dandurand[1]
Curt T. Griffiths
Vivienne Chin

Introduction

Technical assistance has become the new "mantra" in the context of renewed international efforts to develop effective justice and security institutions and to promote international cooperation in addressing various transnational crime problems. From a development perspective, justice and security sector reforms and institutional development initiatives are integral parts of an overall effort to promote good governance as a prerequisite to effective social and economic development. From a human rights perspective, technical assistance is needed to help institutions bring their policies and practices in compliance with international human rights and criminal justice standards. From the point of view of promoting international justice cooperation, bringing national systems into compliance with the requirements of a growing number of binding international criminal justice treaties presupposes the presence of a minimum basic capacity within existing institutions and the availability of specialized technical assistance. Whatever the perspective, technical assistance continues to be required to build core capacities even if, up to this point, investments designed to build these capacities in the sector have not always produced results commensurate with the levels of invested resources.

The current state of knowledge about "lessons learned" in capacity-building and reform initiatives is a consequence of at least two interrelated factors: what Carothers (2003:13) has referred to as a "disturbingly thin base of knowledge at every level",

---

1 Yvon Dandurand is a professor of criminology and criminal justice, and Dean of Research and Industry Liaison at the University College of the Fraser Valley, Abbotsford (B.C.). Professor Curt T. Griffiths, Ph.D., teaches at the School of Criminology, Simon Fraser University, Burnaby (B.C.). Vivienne Chin is a consultant and managing partner of DCA International Justice Consulting, Abbotsford (B.C.). All three of them have extensive experience with criminal justice reform and the delivery of technical assistance and are associates of the International Centre for Criminal Law Reform and Criminal Justice Policy, a member of the United Nations Crime Prevention and Criminal Justice Programme Network of Institutes, in Vancouver (B.C), Canada.

particularly with respect to how change actually occurs, how it can be supported, and what effects it tends to have on resistant systems; and, the failure of donor agencies and recipient jurisdictions to develop the capacity to evaluate and to develop a cumulative knowledge about "what works" and the specific factors that facilitate, or hinder, reform efforts. As Carothers (2003: 3) notes: "Although aid institutions engaged in rule-of-law assistance do attempt some 'lessons learned' exercises, many of the lessons produced are superficial and even those are often not really learned" (see also Channell 2005). Carothers (2003: 3) has also identified the obstacles to developing a cumulative knowledge about the factors that facilitate, or hinder, development assistance efforts in the justice and security sector:

"Several substantial obstacles to greater knowledge accumulation in this field persist, including the complexity of the task of promoting the rule of law, the particularity of legal systems, the unwillingness of aid organizations to invest sufficient resources in evaluations, and the tendency of both academics and lawyers not to pursue systematic empirical research on rule-of-law programming."

Notwithstanding these obstacles, the myriad of training and technical assistance projects conducted over the years in developing countries in support of law reform and capacity development in the fields of justice, crime prevention and security have nevertheless led to a fairly good understanding of the factors that typically facilitate or hinder the success of such initiatives. One may therefore ask why these "lessons learned" are so rarely incorporated into the design of new training programs.

Due to the absence in many developing countries of adequate institutional capacity in the justice and security sector in many developing countries, the focus of technical assistance activities is progressively shifting away from isolated reform projects to more holistic capacity building initiatives. Human resource development is generally a key component of these initiatives and it is often assumed that the success of the initiatives rests principally on training and education activities. However, the role of training and education activities within the broader context of capacity building, institutional reform and organization change has rarely been clearly defined.

In reality, building core capacities involves considerably more than the training of a few key personnel. Rather, it requires a number of inter-related support activities, including assistance with: the adaptation and transfer of new technologies; the development, recruitment and careful deployment of human resources; strategic planning and implementation of institutional reforms; the development of processes to guide, support, manage and monitor organizational changes; the modernization of existing structures and procedures; the development of organizational policies and regulations; the establishment of information systems, statistical databases, and performance monitoring tools to support sound management decisions and to provide timely feedback on the impact of various reforms; the implementation of simple yet efficient planning, budgeting, and case management systems; and, the building of necessary infrastructure and information systems.

All of these activities are important and the sequence in which they are undertaken can often affect their effectiveness and the nature and extent of their impact. From an in-depth study of reform initiatives in the justice and security sector (JSS) in Commonwealth Caribbean countries, Dandurand *et.al.* (2004: iv) concluded: "[T]he success of JSS programming initiatives cannot be taken for granted, no matter how critical the needs for a particular reform…[R]eform initiatives that do not adopt an integrated, multi-sectoral approach usually produce few sustainable results." It is instructive to consider the lessons that can be drawn from previous experience with respect to effective programming and assistance in the justice and security sectors. These lessons must be identified and integrated into future programming (Biebesheimer and Payne 2001; Dandurand 2005; Griffiths, Dandurand, and Chin 2005; Shaw and Dandurand 2006; World Bank 2000). Some of these lessons are now expressed in the forms of various programming guidelines (*e.g.*, OECD 2005).

In the extreme conditions that often prevail in a post-conflict or failed-state context, capacity-building initiatives that are part of a more ambitious institutional reconstruction effort are even more complex and even less likely to succeed when premised on hurried and improvised training efforts. Significantly, an effective capacity-building methodology adapted to such extreme conditions has yet to be fully articulated (Stromeyer 2001).

The following discussion briefly reviews some of the lessons that can be drawn from over a decade of technical assistance activities in developing countries. Using these materials, a framework could emerge that would assist in addressing a number of factors requiring attention during the design and delivery of technical assistance projects, in particular with respect to the necessary training and education activities. The discussion offers a preliminary overview of a number of practical considerations and principles that should be incorporated into future training and capacity building activities undertaken as part of justice and security sector programming and reform efforts.

Security sector reform is defined by the OECD as those measures designed "to increase partner countries' ability to meet the range of security needs within their societies in a manner consistent with democratic norms and sound principles of governance, transparency and the rule of law" (OECD 2004: 1).

Programming activities in this area typically include: 1. institutional strengthening and capacity-building activities in the justice and public safety sector in order to bring about organizational change; 2. activities to strengthen the governance of the justice and security sector and the various agencies operating within it; 3. activities to support strategy formation and consensus-building around the need for reforms and the nature of the changes to be promoted; 4. activities to promote law reform and the modernization of existing institutions as required; 5. activities to bring national laws and systems in compliance with international standards; 6. activities to promote the involvement of citizens and civil society organizations in the preparation, implementation and monitoring of reform projects; and, 7. activities to promote citizen participation in crime prevention, conflict resolution, and other aspects of the operation of the system.

In some cases, it may be appropriate to begin the process with a single point of entry. This can provide the basis for expanding the initiative, provided that the particular reform issue that is being addressed is part of a broader strategy to improve the functioning and governance of the system as a whole. Human resources development, training and capacity development projects can also offer a valid entry point; however, such initiatives are likely to fail unless they are part of a broader institutional reform and development process.

Capacity Building and Technical Assistance

Capacity development involves assistance directed toward reforming organizations and institutions so as to develop their capacity to efficiently and effectively achieve their function and their goals. However, assistance must be based on a careful assessment of the existing capacity of the organization or institution, the factors (political, organizational, psychological, financial, technical or technological) that may function to limit that capacity, the forces that can support and sustain the necessary reforms, and the obstacles or the resistance which could undermine the required changes. Moreover, it cannot be assumed that all stakeholders in a particular jurisdiction are in favour of improving the capacity, performance, or effectiveness of the system. There are often complex reasons why a system's relative "incapacity" has been tolerated or even cultivated. These reasons often involve a powerful group (or groups) benefiting in one way or another from the *status quo,* weak as it is.

One method that can be used is that of functional behaviour assessment, an approach developed by psychologists in order to better understand problematic individual or group behaviour. The method can be applied to an analysis of the conditions that prevail in justice systems and agencies that remain committed to dysfunctional and counter-productive modes of operation. Assuming that dysfunctional organizational behaviour is simply the result of a lack of training or know-how is, to say the least, very naïve. Prior to any attempt to introduce complex reforms, one should avoid simplistic assumptions and should first attempt to understand the forces of inertia at play within the relevant institutions and their resistance to change. In practice, however, training is the "solution" most often offered through technical assistance programs regardless of the outstanding organizational and system issues.

For example, a review of capacity development programs in the Caribbean justice sector by the Caribbean Group for Cooperation in Economic Development (CGCED 2000) noted how attempts at reform of justice sector institutions and organizations did not always produce the expected results. The report identified the difficulties encountered by Caribbean countries attempting to build a significant capacity in the justice and public safety sector and proposed a framework for sustainable reforms of Caribbean justice sectors that acknowledges the complexity of the task at hand. And, Dandurand and his colleagues (2004: 65) found in a study of attempts to reform the justice and security sector in the Commonwealth Caribbean that:

> "Priorities for action are frequently identified and reiterated, but the human and financial resources to address these priorities are often absent. Blame for the lack of progress is sometimes attributed to local inertia, incompetence, corruption, or even to political tribalism. However, there is the widespread perception that there are also issues with the kind of external assistance that is made available to countries of the region and how it is delivered. There are frequent complaints that that external assistance is too often offered in a piecemeal manner and for reform projects that are insufficiently integrated with the activities of other components of the system".

For many criminal justice and law enforcement agencies around the world, the concept of "technical assistance" has become associated with a number of unfortunate and inappropriate practices that often cause more harm than good. Project initiatives may, inadvertently, entrench existing institutional practice and result in only superficial, temporal changes, rather than substantive structural changes to policy and practice. Similarly, when the difficulty of altering institutional cultures is underestimated, the objectives of the reforms are often defeated. Even in the most ideal conditions, changing the orientation and behaviour of key personnel in the justice and security sector is a challenge, often of Herculean proportions.

The challenge is even more extreme in developing countries where human and infrastructure resources are scarce and where reform has historically been driven by external donors rather than by internal forces. Externally-driven attempts at reform will be unsuccessful because of the resulting absence of a dedicated cadre of senior officials within the system who are willing to take the risks associated with departing from status quo practice and who are committed to long-term, rather than short term change and gains. The experience of efforts at reform in the justice and security sector in some jurisdictions is that development assistance is readily accepted in the absence of any capacity, or even intent, to engage in substantive reforms.

Whenever issues of technical assistance are discussed, a number of recurring questions resurface: Is the assistance offered genuinely responsive to the needs of the recipient countries? Does the assistance contribute to the development of sustainable capacities? How are specific capacity development initiatives relating to the broader development assistance objectives? What is the normative basis for capacity-development activities and how relevant are international human rights and other justice norms to various capacity building initiatives? And, finally, what evaluation mechanisms can be embedded in the project so as to provide accurate information on the outcomes and success of the initiative in terms of its stated goals and objectives?

Program Design and Delivery

Implementing reforms in the justice and security sector requires interventions over the long term that will encourage and support structural, organizational and technological transformation. In his work on governance for the World Bank, Kaufmann (2003: 24) concluded that it is necessary to move beyond the traditional approach to public sector reforms and to rethink orthodoxy on legal and judicial reforms:

"Although donor programs supporting the traditional and largely unsuccessful legal and judiciary technical assistance projects of the past is yet to be fully abandoned, a salutary move away from narrow support for hardware, study tours, traditional training, focus on marginal improvement in narrow organizational issues such as caseload management, and the like is beginning to take place - even if slowly. In the next phase it will be important to face up to the enormous difference in the nature, performance, and vulnerability of legal and judiciary institutions across emerging countries. These vast differences have major strategic and practical implications."

The manner in which assistance is offered and delivered in the justice and security sector is often as important as the type of assistance offered.

In most developing countries, this sector is not easily amenable to accept reforms. It is an essentially conservative element of society which typically offers fierce resistance to any change, particularly when the latter is perceived to threaten its power and autonomy under the *status quo*. In many countries, this problem is compounded by the absence of a tradition of democracy and due process and by popular support for a "get tough" approach to crime and security. Finally, these difficult dynamics are further complicated by the pervasive corruption which reigns through the whole justice and security sector.

In many jurisdictions, there are neither the processes nor civil society involvement that could provide support for the proposed reforms or a source of accountability. Government ministries and, more specifically, elements of the justice system may be resistant to outside input or influence. In such cases, cooperation by governments and agencies should not be taken as reflecting an interest in, or capacity, to engage in significant reforms or to develop structures of accountability and transparency. The interrelationships between the various agencies in the justice and security sector mean that any attempt to use development assistance to address specific security problems in a piecemeal manner, without addressing broader systemic and structural issues, or without sufficient sector-wide buy-in and coordination, will generally fail to improve system capacity, efficiency and governance.

Training

Training is often viewed as a key component of capacity development and is generally a key component of assistance projects. Training activities can also provide an entry point that can lead to further collaboration between agencies and organizations in a jurisdiction (Protic 2005). Training alone, however, rarely produces appreciable results. The potential and limitations of training have been examined in relation to the technical cooperation programs in human rights in the administration of justice delivered by the United Nations Office of the High Commissioner on Human Rights (OHCHR). A recent global review of the OHCHR activities regarding the administration of justice reveals the need to put training activities into a wider perspective, e.g., the need to "get under the skin of the institutions." As Flintman and Zwamborn (2003: 41) note:

> "Requests for assistance in the field of training are interesting because they provide access to an organization. Knowledge of Human Rights law is a primary and central condition for compliance with these laws. As such it is of vital importance, but it is no more than a primary condition. If changing police conduct is the goal, as some of the evaluations indicated, much more has to be done. Institutional development is the next concern. Efforts have to become directed towards changing the culture and structure of the police and prison system, the quality and training of police and prison leadership, the improvement of operational practice, the selection and training of police officers and prison staff and the improvement of system of accountability. If the behaviour of the police and in prisons is to be changed, support for the institutional development of the police is unavoidable."

It should also be evident that the continued reliance on external "experts" who fly in, deliver a training program, and then fly out, does little to build local capacity or effect meaningful change for either the short or long term. The same holds true for retired experts who often are not current in their field, lack appropriate knowledge and skills, and may have little or no understanding of the cultural, political, social, or economic context in which they are attempting to provide assistance (Griffiths et.al. 2005: 109).

Too many experts/trainers arrive in jurisdictions without a full understanding of local needs, institutions, and context. Yet, in most technical assistance projects, insufficient funds and time are allocated to the preparation of the trainers and to the development of curricula and programs. Channel (2005: 12) advises that, before sending a trainer to a new assignment, extensive preparation should take place for the new conditions, cultural variations, and demands on the otherwise qualified specialists who will be involved in the training. The absence of pre-deployment training may lead to the experts making unsubstantiated assumptions as to the usefulness and transferability of knowledge, skills and technology to a different jurisdiction.

Study tours can be useful learning and training methods, provided that they are designed so as to offer more than a "perk" for would-be reformers or a disguised form of tourism. A study tour can offer an opportunity for firsthand observation and meaningful discussions with front-line personnel in the host jurisdiction. Unfortunately, the method has a tendency to neglect addressing issues of "transferability of techniques and models" and to implicitly present the system that is observed as model to be imitated. Furthermore, the full benefits of this method are often not realized because the people would benefit the most from the tour are not necessarily selected for participation. That privilege tends to be reserved for higher ranking individuals who tend to carry the right title, as opposed to the actual responsibility, for bringing about the reforms or building the system's new capacity.

Another approach to training that is of questionable efficacy is to send individuals who hold key positions in the justice and security sector to overseas conferences, seminars and training courses. There are a number of difficulties with this strategy. Personnel from developing countries are often placed in large classes with students from many countries. In this situation, no one student is afforded class time to have his or her unique issues and questions addressed in any detail or depth. In addition, training often takes place in isolation, meaning that there is no plan, process or support for local context. Many courses in policing, for example, do not provide pre-course reading materials or activities to prepare the participant for the learning experience. The same holds true after the experience where most students are not supported, equipped or challenged to implement the lessons learned once back in their workplace. The only tangible evidence of participation in the training program may be a photo album and fond memories.

The so-called "training the trainers" approach is also one that is valued by donors. They see in it an element of added "sustainability" as well as a means to multiply the impact of the assistance they provide. In practice, those who are identified as "trainers" are not necessarily individuals who will actively be involved in training others. Their capacity to conduct that additional training is rarely measured. In the absence of local institutions and mechanisms that can actually support that training function, the "train the trainer" approach is unlikely to amount much more than expensive window-dressing.

Training courses do provide participants with access to a network of professional contacts, insights into potential options, and some appreciation and level of understanding of new technologies and systems. While there is value to this, what is often lacking is a method or strategy for ensuring that this new knowledge finds fertile ground in the home jurisdiction and an understanding of the requirements that will increase the likelihood that the training will have an impact in the short and long term. The most common experience is that the individuals return from training overseas and there is no opportunity or strategy for sharing their new learning amongst their peers or to integrate the knowledge and skills they have gained into the policy and practice of their particular organization or agency.

Another attribute of training in technical assistance and capacity development projects is that it is most often directed toward the most senior personnel in the relevant agencies. While these individuals may have the interest and/or capacity to facilitate substantive, long-term change, this should not be taken as a given. Rather, there may be a hesitancy to initiate, and sustain, the process of reform. And, it is at the middle-managerial level that any proposed changes in policy and process will be implemented or, conversely, blocked.

Insufficient attention tends to be paid to leadership training and training in organizational behaviour, systems theory, and change management. This is because the capacity development projects are too often based on simplistic assumptions about what is required in order to bring about some effective institutional and organization changes. For example, changing the legislative framework is a necessary, but not sufficient, component of facilitating long-term reform. There is a need to develop methodologies, including training and human resource development methods, which can address the resistance to change that is invariably encountered.

Noticeably absent in most training program is provision for representatives from community-based organizations, non-governmental organizations, and civil society groups that can, potentially, play a major role in the reform process. Although there is an increasing recognition that non-governmental organizations and community-based groups must collaborate with the reform process, donors are sometimes reluctant to offer the kind of leadership training that could empower community leaders and others outside of national government.

Transferability

A deplorable attribute of many training programs for justice and security personnel in developing countries is that little consideration is given to how, to what extent, or whether the various models or techniques that are presented during the training apply to developing countries. Course materials are often heavily biased toward the North American or western European justice and security models. The difficult task of assessing the *transferability* of techniques, structures, procedures, strategies, and legislation requires far more attention than it has received to date. However successful a particular practice or strategy may have been in Canada or other North American or European jurisdiction, it does not necessarily follow that it will be useful or effective in a different development context. Comparative evaluations of various practices and the identification of the conditions and specific features responsible for their success in a given context can assist in identifying and addressing the issues related to transferability.

Few of the "experts" involved in capacity development and training activities actually have expertise in comparative law or in comparative analysis of criminal justice systems. It is even more difficult to find professionals with field experience in these areas. In the absence of such expertise, project personnel have a limited ability to move out of the methods and processes used in their home country. As a result, project personnel may be poorly equipped to assist countries in developing solutions that have at least a fair chance of succeeding in the local context.

With respect to legislative reform, for example, a key lesson learned is that simply transplanting legislation from one country to another is not an effective strategy for promoting reform. Even the promotion of "model legislation" is likely to have limited success unless it is accompanied by the expertise required to adopt these generic instruments to local circumstances. Rather, local solutions, including relevant legislation, must be developed. While foreign legislation can be considered for ideas and examples, it needs to be understood that it likely will not operate in the same fashion in the recipient jurisdiction.

One way to increase the transferability and sustainability of information and options presented in training sessions is to have trained experts paired with local experts and future managers in order to facilitate the development of talent and the transfer of skills and responsibilities to local management (Stone *et al.* 2005:25). Another strategy to address transferability and sustainability issues is to ensure that they are taken into account at the very beginning of any initiative, when the needs for assistance are being assessed.

Training Tools

Manuals, handbooks, and toolkits can be appropriate, effective and efficient delivery mechanisms of technical assistance. In recent years, the United Nations and various other organizations involved in technical assistance have sponsored the development of such tools. In addition, there has been an increased emphasis on developing training curricula and materials that are designed to be relevant to the jurisdictional contexts in which they will be offered as well as to the learning styles of the trainees. The Rule of Law Section of UNODC has developed a number of practical assessment tools that provide a more solid basis upon which to develop training programs.

These various tools can support capacity-building initiatives in relevant institutions provided that they are adapted to local circumstances. As was noted in a recent evaluation, adapting these tools to the circumstances that prevail in the countries that will use them is crucial (UNODC 2004: 32):

> "The relevance and effectiveness of tools will be enhanced when they are based on the experience of resource-poor developing countries, which are the primary users of tools. To develop tools largely on the basis of the experience of resource-rich developed countries makes them less effective in operational terms. A long-term effort to organize the experiences of developing countries to provide a basis for tool development is therefore vital."

Performance Indicators and Independent Evaluation

Another disappointing attribute of many development assistance projects in the justice and security sector is the absence of measurable performance indicators. Most often, intended outcomes are couched in very general, bureaucratic language, *e.g.*,. "to improve transparency," "to contribute to the development of good governance and civil society." It is the rare project that contains specific, measurable objectives. As well, most projects do not include provision for independent evaluation of the extent to which the assistance initiative achieved the goals that were set out by the donor agency.

To this end, the development of performance indicators to measure the impact of training initiatives, capacity-building programs and institutional reforms should become a priority. These indicators should be simple, appealing, and useful to national and local governments. In the area of policing, for example, these indicators should attempt to assess the extent to which the development assistance initiative has contributed to public safety and access to justice. Performance indicators should also be designed with reference to applicable international human rights and justice standards (Broome and Inman 2005), including indicators for assessing the capacities of rights holders and duty bearers (UNDP 2006). As well, donor agencies should build in an evaluative component, ideally providing for an independent assessment of outcomes, particularly in larger, longer-term initiatives. A key requirement is that there be strong linkage between the training offered and the reform goals that are contemplated.

Alternative Methods

It is time perhaps to consider more effective methods of integrating training and capacity development activities within the overall technical assistance framework in the justice and security sector. It may be worthwhile to explore institutional mentoring and development methods such as those that have been involved in the education sector. This could involve, as part of a broader reform and capacity development program, empowering some key personnel from the recipient country and offering them an opportunity to participate in "job-shadowing" their counterparts in the donor country. Then, the mentors from the donor country can accompany the personnel back to their home country and continue the mentoring process as the personnel put into practice the skills and strategies that have been learned.

It may also be important to pay more attention to the development, within recipient countries, of educational institutions and programs that can engage in sustainable, longer-term capacity development activities. It is of crucial importance to develop an institutional capacity, perhaps within local colleges, academy and universities, to develop local expertise and talents and limit the future reliance of local institutions on outside assistance. International cooperation among these educational institutions involved in justice and security sector capacity development should be supported.

The development of graduate and undergraduate programs in the fields of justice, security and crime prevention that are accessible to students and officials from developing countries is long overdue. Similar programs have been developed in the field of human rights through international cooperation between academic institutions. The same is clearly possible in the field of justice and security. Innovative training programs (*e.g.*, a virtual criminal justice academy, special international institutes focused on practical justice and security issues), accredited by various colleges and universities, could offer a welcome substitute to many of the present *ad hoc* and expensive activities which produce little appreciable results.

Conclusion

The need for reform in the justice and security sectors in developing countries is acute and the interest among donors in sponsoring reform initiatives is high. The frameworks within which technical assistance projects have been designed and implemented, however, have produced a record that is less than stellar. The absence of an overall framework with clearly defined, measurable goals and objectives, ineffective training and human resources development models, a lack of attention to transferability and sustainability issues, and the failure of donors to compile evaluation and outcome data are among the factors that have undermined the potential efficacy of technical assistance and reform efforts. These factors must be addressed in order to enhance the likelihood that assistance projects in this sector will have significant, sustainable, long-term impacts. Many of these factors run counter to the prevailing technical assistance models and require a re-think on the part of both donors and recipients. The pressing need for reform in the justice and security sector dictates that new models of development assistance, including training be developed.

References

Biebesheimer, C. and Payne, J.M. (2001). IDB Experience in Justice Reform. Washington: International Development Bank.

Broome, J. and Inman, M (2005). "Using International Standards as Tools for Judicial Reform", in EBRC, Law in Transition 2005 – Courts and Judges. London: European Bank for Reconstruction and Development, pp. 80-87.

Carother, T. (2003). Promoting the Rule of Law Abroad – The Problem of Knowledge. Working Paper No. 34. Washington (D.C.): Carnegie Endowment for International Peace, Democracy and Rule of Law Project, January 2003.

Caribbean Group for Cooperation and Economic Development (2000). Toward a Caribbean Vision 2020: A Regional Perspective on Development Challenges, Opportunities and Strategies for the Next Two Decades. Washington, D.C.: World Bank, June 2000.

Channell, W. (2005). Lessons Not Learned: Problems with Western Aid for Law Reform in Postcommunist Countries. Working Paper No. 57. Washington (D.C.): Carnegie Endowment for International Peace, Democracy and Rule of Law Project, January 2003.

Dandurand, Y. (2005). Enhancing Criminal Justice Reforms. Workshop 2: Enhancing Criminal Justice Reform, Including Restorative Justice. Eleventh United Nations Congress on Crime Prevention and Criminal Justice Bangkok, Thailand, 18-25 April 2005. http://www.icclr.law. ubc.ca/Publications/Reports/1 1_un/Dandurand% 0Final%20Paper.pdf

Dandurand, Y., Chin, V. Griffiths, C., Lalonde, M., Montgomery, R., and B. Tkachuk (2003). Programming Opportunities in the Justice and Security Sectors in the Caribbean. A report to the Canadian International Development Agency. Vancouver: ICCLR.

Flinterman, C. and Zwamborn, M. (2003). From Development of Human Rights to Managing Human Rights Development: Global Review of the OHCHR Technical Cooperation Program Syntheses Report. Utrecht: Netherlands Institute of Human Rights (SIM) & MEDE European Consultancy, September 2003.

Griffiths, C. T. (2003). "Implementing International Standards in Corrections: Challenges, Strategies, and Outcomes". Expert Group Meeting. The Application of United Nations Standards and Norms in Crime Prevention and Criminal Justice, 10-12 February 2003, Burgenland, Austria. Vienna: UNODC.

Griffiths, C.T., Dandurand, Y. and Chin, V. (2005). "Development Assistance and Police Reform: Programming Opportunities and Lessons Learned", The Canadian Review of Policing Research, Issue 2, pp. 101-113.

OECD (2004). Policy Brief - Security System Reform and Governance: Policy and Good Practice. Paris: Organisation for Economic Co-operation and Development. (www.oecd.org/ publications/Pol_brief)

OECD (2005). Security Reform and Governance - DAC Guidelines and Reference Series. Paris: Organisation for Economic Co-operation and Development.

Shaw, M. and Dandurand, Y. (2006). "Effective Technical Assistance in Crime Prevention and Criminal Justice " in Shaw M. and Y. Dandurand (Eds.). Maximizing the Effectiveness of the Technical Assistance Provided in the Fields of Crime Prevention and Criminal Justice. No.49., pp. 19-34. Helsinki: HEUNI - European Institute for Crime Prevention and Control, affiliated with the United Nations.

Protic, D. (2005). "Judicial Reform in Serbia: Enhancing Judicial Performance through Training", in EBRC, Law in Transition 2005 – Courts and Judges. London: European Bank for Reconstruction and Development, pp.75-79.

Stone, C., Miller, J.; Thornston, M., and Trone, J. (2005). Supporting Security, Justice, and Developement Lessons for a New Era. New York: Vera Institute of Justice.

Stromeyer, H. (2001). "Collapse and Reconstruction of a Judicial System: The United Nations Missions in Kosovo and East Timor". The American Journal of International Law, Vol. 95, no. 46, pp. 45-63.

UNDP (2006). Indicators for Human Rights Based Approaches to Development in UNDP Programming – A Users' Guide, New York: NDP, Bureau for Development Policy, Democratic Governance Group.

UNODC (2004). Evaluation of Tools and Toolkits as a Modality of Programme Delivery by the United Nations Office on Drugs and Crime. Vienna: UNODC - Independent Evaluation Unit. http:// www.unodc.org/pdf/Evaluation_04-Toolsandtoolkits.pdf.

World Bank (2000). Challenges of Capacity Development: Towards Sustainable Reforms of Caribbean Justice Sectors Volume II A Diagnostic Assessment. Washington, DC: World Bank, Caribbean Group for Cooperation in Economic Development.

II. INTERNATIONAL CRIMINAL JUSTICE THROUGH DISTANCE LEARNING

Distance Learning: An Alternative Service Delivery for Criminal Justice Training and Higher Education

Jacqueline L. Schneider[1]

Introduction

Degrees conferred from institutions of higher education are an eagerly sought commodity. Demands in both the private and public workplaces are encouraging, if not forcing, employees to seek more advanced levels of training. However, access to traditional colleges and universities can be limited to those who live and work in remote areas of the world and to those whose work schedules preclude the attendance in traditional classrooms. Employers are also being forced to reconsider how training opportunities are offered to their employees. Both education and training is expanding beyond the traditional modes of delivery into the electronic media so that information can be shared across distance.

The idea behind the concept of distance learning is admirable to the point that colleges, universities, as well as employers are developing programs at record pace. No one can deny that expanding educational opportunities to a new population is a positive development. However, the rapid expansion of educational products and changes associated with them may have unanticipated negative consequences for faculty and staff. Distance learning is being touted as the new and improved way. It is proposed here that university administrators may possibly be getting lulled into a false sense of financial security with the fast adoption of distance learning programs, which can be extremely lucrative.

---

1 Dr. Jacqueline L. Schneider is an Assistant Professor with the Department of Criminology, University of South Florida, St. Petersburg, Fl., USA. Before moving to the United States, she had been teaching and conducting research in the United Kingdom. Her work on stolen goods markets (The Market Reduction Approach), has been put forward as best practice in England and Wales (UK) and has attracted interest by policy makers in Chile. She was the first recipient of the UK Home Office's Innovative Research Challenge Grant. Prior to her work in the United Kingdom, Dr. Schneider taught undergraduate courses at universities in the United States, receiving an outstanding teaching award. She has authored several papers and chapters in books on gangs and stolen goods markets.

This article examines general definitions of distance learning. It then progresses into a discussion as to why distance learning is seen as the crowning jewel in education for the new millennium. Existing standards for distance learning are reviewed and followed by a discussion of advantages and disadvantages. The article concludes with a brief commentary from personal experience, having been a staff member of one of the UK's largest providers of distance learning.

Distance Learning

As early as 1986, Keegan offered a definition, stating that distance learning is:

> "...the delivery of a program of education using a wide range of methods of delivery, not solely confined to text or the Internet, and in which students rarely meet face to face with a teacher. The key feature of such programs is that students themselves, in their engagement with the curriculum, decide their own pace of study" (Keegan 1986:232).

Distance learning is, very simply, a modern day re-formulation of the correspondence courses popular many years ago. This mode of educational delivery is the process of learning where the teacher and the student are separated for the vast majority of the time. They are, however, united by media or technology, which includes phone, fax, closed circuit television, CD-ROM, webcams, blackboard, listserves, among others. Students are evaluated by the school that confers final degrees, or the employer in the case of training. The main idea behind distance learning is that it is an independent process.

It is important here to distinguish between education and training. McKenzie (2002) provides a very useful delineation between the terms. Education is the provision of contextualizing knowledge by the development of broad understanding. In other words, education addresses the 'why', whereas training pertains to the 'how'. Training, according to McKenzie (2002), deals with procedural rules and enhancement of information relevant for the goals of the organization.

There exists a complete body of literature that tells us that effective learning, in general, is that which is: as independent as possible; self directed and personal; results in the discovery of information and relationships; and done in small groups (see Sullivan 1995; Dance 2000).

Distance learning is decentralized and flexible. In large part, it proffers individuals, who may have never been afforded the opportunity to gain advanced learning, the chance to bring education into their home at a pace they can manage effectively. Dance (2000) sees distance learning as an agent of change in which, "[s]tudents can see, read, hear, repeat as needed, learn by doing, and students can interact with faculty with their convenience" (Dance 2000:1).

While Dance (2000) outlined the general characteristics of non-specific learning, he also observed the implications of distance learning as related to learning effectiveness. Teachers and students are, obviously, separated, thus making the learning process independent. The problem of geography is solved by technology, so the teacher and student are, in essence, joined in the learning process. There remains a one-to-one relationship between the learner and the instructor—no matter how many miles or what circumstance separates them. The separation is really paradoxical. On the one hand, separation aids in the student's feeling of independence, which is desired. However, McKenzie (2002:232), in his review of UK programs, notes the "loneliness of the long distance learner," which can result in negative feelings of isolation and detachment.

The Expansion

Each provider of education or training has its reasons for developing programs. Generally speaking, there are a number of prevailing reasons why institutions of higher education develop distance learning programs. These programs expand, with relative ease, existing activities. The numbers of paying students increase rather quickly when distance learning programs are implemented. The programs attract students not only from the school's host country, but if advertised properly, students from the most remote places where educational opportunities are lacking or unavailable may enroll. This is an important point to stress. Tuition from leading universities worldwide can be provided to students who might never have been able to leave their home country in order to attend, thus providing them with not only quality instruction, but with a desirable and extremely marketable degree from an prestigious institution. Additionally, individuals who reside in the same country where the degree is offered but who cannot attend traditional classes due to work or family obligations can pursue a degree without ever having to leave their home. Universities are under increasing demands in terms of inadequate physical facilities, so distance learning relieves the pressure of repairing or building new buildings/classrooms. Finally, distance learning programs are less expensive to run than traditional, classroom based courses (See Yarcheck, Gavazzi and Dasoli 2003).

While there is no current way to track the actual rate of expansion in programs worldwide, the Peterson's Guide to Distance Learning Programs[2] listed 77 schools offering criminal justice and/or criminology programs in the USA (Mayzer and DeJong 2003). A more recent review of the Peterson's Guide reveals the type of degree programs currently available (see Table 1). While it is unclear as to how many universities offer these programs, we can be sure that the numbers have grown and will continue to grow in future.

Table 1: Distance Learning Programs, USA

	AD	BS	UG Cert	Grad Cert	Grad MS	Grad PhD
Criminal Justice/ Corrections	17	17	4	0	8	1
Criminal Justice/Law Enforcement	17	21	2	1	10	1
Criminal Justice/Police Science	4	2	3	1	2	0
Criminal Justice/Safety	29	41	7	3	23	2
Criminal Justice Studies	29	41	7	3	23	2
Criminology	3	9	3	1	5	0
Criminalistics	1	0	0	0	0	0

Format

What a distance learning program consists of and how it is actually delivered varies by institution, as well as subject matter. For example, delivery of a clinically based subject will be different than a social science like criminology. Obviously, the material produced must meet the standards of the accrediting body (*i.e.,* the

2 See http://www.petersons.com/distancelearning/code/search.asp?sponsor= (accessed 16 October 2005).

university). According to McKenzie (2002) material must be well written, informative, properly structured distance learning texts. The design, development and updating of material lies at the heart of a successful program. The material (known as modules in the UK) falls somewhere in between pure academic textbooks and converted lecture notes. McKenzie further explains that effective distance learning material must be interactive—stimulating the student to engage with the concepts so that they are motivated to read outside the provided course material. Because of the dynamic aspect of criminological literature, updates are necessary at least every 18 months. This according to McKenzie (2003: 258) is "to ensure [that] the new policy, practice, legislation...is taken into account."

The University of Portsmouth is one of the UK's leading distance learning providers in criminal justice and criminology. Their modules contain 80 text-based units that pay particular attention to design, using stoppers (text boxes that offer additional advice and instruction) and checklists that help the students evaluate their in-take of vital material. A single course unit contains approximately 80 thousand words and costs are estimated at $1,500 USD. Additionally, the university provides an array of student support services such as telephone and email access to tutors, as well as web-based support. (See McKenzie 2003 for further details). Portsmouth also holds regional seminars with their students at various locations outside the UK.

Hopkins Burke and Gill (2000) provide an historic overview of another distance learning provider in the UK. The program at the University of Leicester requires six substantive modules, containing approximately nine modules in each. The rate at which these modules are reported to be updated is unclear from Hopkins Burke and Gills' account—only stating that they are done "regularly". They describe the modules as being "designed to provide a comprehensive background to theoretical, substantive, and methodological issues that have an academic coherence of their own" (Hopkins Burke and Gill 2000: 286). The university also has various forms of student support and provides weekend study schools within the UK twice a year.

The administrative function or support service component of distance learning is often under-emphasized. Yet, it is crucial. Non-academic staff is responsible for coordinating the printing of materials, disseminating it, as well as collecting student assignments for grading. These staff often time serve as an initial filter between students and academic faculty so that non-academic questions are answered, thus not impinging on the faculty's time. Additionally, arranging on-campus tutorial sessions, if part of the program, generally falls under the responsibility of support staff members. Finally, some programs have support offices or liaison staff operating at remote locations. These staff help facilitate the running of the course, advising students and other related issues.

Distance Learning Guidelines: The UK's QAA

In the UK, an independent body, Quality Assurance Agency for Higher Education, works to monitor, as well as to encourage improvements in, standards of higher education. The agency reports to the Higher Education Funding Council for England (HEFCE) its review findings of academic departments and programs of higher education. HEFCE uses the finds of the agency to assess departments, which can affect funding strategies and opportunities. Therefore the standards of the Quality Assurance Agency are admittedly high, thus giving academic bodies guiding principles within which departments must work to develop programs of academic excellence.

The agency's guidelines for distance learning are broken down into six thorough[3] sections, which include: system; program; delivery; development/support; communication; and assessment. The aforementioned programs contain elements that will be discussed here, no doubt because of the QAA's influence over educational service and delivery. System reviews examine how the distance learning program fits into the overall university system of delivering higher education. The program element of the review looks for assurances that the distance learning program meets the same or similar standards with traditional classroom-based degrees. The delivery aspect is, to some degree, a continuation of the program component of the review. However, it expands to determine whether or not the distance learner has an equivalent opportunity to that of the traditional student to achieve academic standards needed in order to complete successfully the degree. In order to determine the degree to which the distance learner has an educational experience that promotes autonomous learning, development and support mechanisms of the program are examined. Instruments for communicating course expectations, avenues of assessment and academic progression are subject for QAA review, as well as the way in which the school monitors the communication with the distance learner. Finally, forms of assessment are reviewed in terms of their appropriateness and reliability.

---

3 For all the details pertaining to this rather complete description of standards, see the website: http://www.qaa.ac.uk/academicinfrastructure/codeofpractice/ distancelearning/ default.asp.

Many of the advantages associated with the development and implementation of distance learning programs are the same as the fundamental reasons for adopting it in the first place. Distance learning programs are less expensive to run than are traditional classroom-based courses. These courses widen the pool of potential students, which leads to the potential for increasing the knowledge base in countries and regions where advanced degree programs may be lacking. Given the way that distance learning courses are written, students can read original pieces written by the world's leading experts in various fields—all contained within a module or unit. Students can, therefore, be provided a wealth of information that would not necessarily be contained in a single textbook.

The disadvantages, unfortunately, are underreported[4]. The distance learning faculty/student ratio is much larger than with traditional students. The number of students accepted can grow well beyond the capabilities of existing staff. Not much is written on this issue; it is mentioned, but not monitored. In some instances, faculty members who contribute to distance learning programs also contribute to traditional classroom programs. The issue becomes balancing the totality of responsibilities with those of a growing student base. Some programs have one faculty to hundreds of students. The 'knock-on' effect is that course materials are not updated regularly or entire units are reported within modules on the same course. Quality control is key to a successful and satisfactory distance learning course. In fact, because of the fundamental nature of distance learning, the pool of candidates can choose an excellent program anywhere in the world. Therefore for a program to remain competitive internationally, the attention to detail must be precise. The fact that technology aids in connecting remotely students to teachers becomes important. The goal is to bring education to those who cannot necessarily get to the classroom. For those students who live and work in an industrialized nation, technology is probably not a constraining issue. However for those students who do live in countries where technology is not available universally, distance learning courses become irrelevant. Therefore, the ideal of widening the net may be just that—an ideal.

The distance the net can be spread is only as far as the technological support mechanisms are operational and available.

---

4 As a former distance learning course director at an institution in England that provided a wide arrange of criminological distance learning courses, I can speak, albeit anecdotally, about the manner in which institutions and management oftentimes become immune to hearing negative aspects of these types of courses. I can only surmise that my experience is not unique or an aberration.

For example, if Internet access, computers, CD-ROMs or DVD readers are either unreliable or unavailable primary technologies actually facilitate keeping distance between students and information. Similarly, adequate libraries or access to print material may be problematic in these remote areas. Therefore, distance learning education may have built-in stratification issues that need to be evaluated. When local agencies are contracted to assist in the delivery of programs at remote sites, problems of competency, efficiency, and continuity become relevant. Unreliable postal service, untimely distribution of materials, poor advertisement of course/institutional information, or improper assessment assistance at remote sites can damage the distance learning course. When these problems are encountered, more stress is applied on the providing institutions. Hidden costs such as long distance telephone and fax charges, along with postage and travel can overrun budgets if the administration of the course is not managed properly. Finally, distance learners can feel isolated and detached during the course of their study. Trying to provide pastoral support and counsel for these students can present specific problems for those who are experienced educators of the traditional classroom setting.

Conclusion

The standards set forth by the UK provide an exemplar for distance learning units worldwide. Independent evaluations of programs are the only sure way that consumers will know how well a program meets the goals and objectives it sets forth. Far too often evaluative research is being conducted by faculty members within academic units who sponsor the program under scrutiny. The results read more like propaganda or course advertising rather than a properly conducted evaluation conducted by an independent source. Until such time that evaluations like those conducted in the UK become more commonplace, the shortcomings of programs may be hidden. Additionally, academic faculty members must be surveyed in order to assess the impact in the change in service delivery. University administrators may be blinded by the financial benefit that a distance learning program can undoubtedly bring. However profits must be weighed against the other potential problems that may underline the new system of delivering higher education.

References

Dance, M. (2000). The Promise of Distance Learning, www.interweb-tech.com/nsment/doc/dance_htm. Accessed 1 October 2005.

Hopkins Burke, R. and Gill, M. (2000). The Experience of Distance Learning at the Scarman Centre: The Realities and the Prospects, Innovations in Education and Training International, 37(3): 286-289.

Keegan, D. (1986). The Foundations of Distance Learning Education. London: Croom Helm. In Ian McKenzie, Distance Learning For Criminal Justice Professionals in the United Kingdom: Development, Quality Assurance and Pedagogical Properties, Journal of Criminal Justice Education, 13(2): 231-249.

Mayzer, R. and DeJong, C. (2003). Student Satisfaction with Distance Learning Education in a Criminal Justice Graduate Course, Journal of Criminal Justice Education, 14(1): 37-52.

McKenzie, I. (2002). Distance Learning For Criminal Justice Professionals in the United Kingdom: Development, Quality Assurance and Pedagogical Properties, Journal of Criminal Justice Education, 13(2): 231-249.

Spitzer, D.R. (1998). Rediscovering the Social Context of Distance Learning, Educational Technology, 7: 52-56.

Sullivan, M. (1995). Needed Now: A New Model for Pedagogy, Technos, 4(3): 8-11.

The Peterson's Guide to Distance Learning Programs (2005) http://www.petersons.com/distancelearning/code/search.asp?sponsor =. Accessed 16 October.

The Quality Assurance Agency for Higher Education (2005), http://www.qaa.ac.uk/academicinfrastructure/codeofpractice/distancele arning/default.asp/ Accessed 16 October 2006.

Distance Learning as a Tool for the Effective Dissemination of United Nations Criminal Justice Instruments to Future Law Enforcement Officers: The Case of Ethnic and Gender Issues

Rodrigo Paris-Steffens[1]

Introduction

The United States has been a pioneer in the creation and development of university programmes in the field of criminal justice. This is reflected in the fact that the overwhelming majority of such programmes are to be found at American universities. The emergence of those programmes is a relatively recent phenomenon, taking place mainly in the second part of the twentieth century in response to a number of social trends, some of which will be examined in more detail below.

In many countries, even in the industrialized, democratic West, the idea of a university-imparted course of studies in criminal justice is not easily accepted or understood. Attempting to explain the rationale or the content of such a course of studies to criminal justice practitioners - predominantly graduates of police academies or schools of law - in countries that have not yet introduced them, is a difficult task. This is the case essentially because the idea of criminal justice as an integrated course of studies at an institution of higher learning conflicts with established beliefs concerning the nature of the criminal justice process itself as well as with the traditional structures, traditions and philosophies of educational institutions. At the universities one studies law, in all its aspects. And the training of police officers takes place in police academies. And that is that.

By contrast, the United States academic culture is comparatively more open to innovation, new programmes of study in every imaginable field appear with considerable frequency and, if they

---

1 Dr. Rodrigo Paris-Steffens is currently a Senior Lecturer at the Department of Criminology and Criminal Justice at the University of Texas, Arlington Campus, USA. He was a Visiting Scholar at the College of Criminal Justice at Sam Houston State University, Huntsville, Texas. In the past, Mr. Paris-Steffens has been Director-General of the United Nations Institute on the Prevention of Crime and the Treatment of Offenders (ILANUD) headquartered in San José, Costa Rica, and before that was a Senior Officer with the United Nations Crime Prevention and Criminal Justice Branch (Vienna, Austria). He has taught social sciences at universities in Costa Rica, the United States, and Austria (Vienna).

respond to a need, they are rapidly copied by numerous institutions of higher learning. In the case of criminal justice, it was the growing emphasis on professionalization of law enforcement personnel that provided some of the initial impulse to the creation of criminal justice programmes of study.

It is in this context that the emergence of electronic communication is rapidly perceived as a means of reaching a larger number of students who, for a variety of reasons, cannot attend classes in a campus. More and more academic disciplines are creating the possibility of obtaining university degrees without the students having to be physically present in the classroom, and criminal justice has certainly not been an exception to this development.

Such online training in criminal justice provides in principle an excellent opportunity to disseminate the basic concepts of human rights, as contained in a number of United Nations documents, among future practitioners such as police officers, criminal investigators, probation and parole officers, prison managers and guards, including graduates who may go into the booming private security business.

The first step is found in the preparation of a syllabus that spells out the structure of the course, with specific tasks and readings, as well as the core text, all of this easily accessible by computer, to online students. Thus, the cooperation of the professionals who prepare those teaching programmes is crucial, since they need to be persuaded of the importance of conventions, rules, and guidelines that the United Nations has elaborated since its inception, starting with the Universal Declaration of Human Rights. This point will be further elaborated below.

This article attempts to examine all the points listed in the previous paragraphs. Specific documents are brought to the attention of the reader. At the conclusion, the author describes his personal experiences in teaching a specific course online, namely, ethnic and gender issues in criminal justice, taught at the Department of Criminology and Criminal Justice at the University of Texas at Arlington, one of the institutions in this state that jointly offer a programme in criminal justice leading to the acquisition of a Bachelor's Degree.

The Rationale for Academic Criminal Justice in One Country

Criminal Justice, as a field of academic endeavour, is a relatively recent development in universities across the United States. It emerged, at least in part, in response to the growing awareness that law enforcement needed professionally trained personnel in order to acquire not only a higher level of efficiency, but also social recognition. In this connection, the training normally provided by police academies was perceived as too focused upon law enforcement in the narrow sense of the term, *i.e.*, the use of force, if needed, to maintain and/or reestablish public order in public or private areas. It was felt that, if law enforcement was to be more effective, while avoiding errors leading to social tensions as well as mistakes leading to the dismissal of charges, law enforcement officers had to acquire at least some knowledge normally associated with other academic disciplines, such as law, psychology, sociology, and other relevant fields. This led gradually to the establishment of programmes of study tailored to the specific needs of law enforcement.

Very gradually, such programmes have found acceptance in a number of campuses across the United States, as well as to the refinement of the programmes themselves, which have grown to include a large variety of courses in a number of fields, such as, *inter alia,* techniques of criminal investigation, police management, social science research methodology, corrections, and constitutional law, to mention only a few. As a result of this trend, such programmes are found at dozens, if not hundreds of universities across the country.

But, as the field developed, the content of the programmes was also oriented towards the increasing sophistication of criminal activity and its transnational dimensions. As a result, many of the programmes now include courses addressing the variety of criminal justice systems to be found in the world, as a means to provide a better understanding of the obstacles to international cooperation as well as to facilitate efforts at coordination and common action in the struggle against crime.

As mentioned above, criminal justice studies are to be found currently in a very large number of campuses, starting at the level of community colleges, sometimes as isolated courses, as well as fully integrated programmes leading to bachelor's degree as well as master's degrees, offered at departments of criminal justice. There exist also some programmes leading to a Ph.D. degree in criminal justice. It should also be mentioned that some universities have created, within the traditional academic structures, colleges of criminal justice, an administrative arrangement which, in the United States, implies an organization higher than the department level.

Distance Learning

The recent boom of distance learning, a result of the innovations brought about by the electronic revolution in global communications, has been a welcome development for the academic criminal justice programmes. This is, in part, because a large percentage of the persons interested in furthering their training in criminal justice happens to be people who are already working full-time in law enforcement, such as police officers, probation and parole officers, and corrections personnel, and in private security companies, among others. For such potential students, the opportunity of obtaining a degree without having to disturb their employment status, is a great opportunity for acquiring knowledge and skills that, quite naturally, will improve their chances for advancement in their professional status. This is particularly true in view of the widespread accessibility of computers in the population, from personal computers to laptops, as well as the availability of terminals at work or in internet cafes.

As a result, programmes have emerged through which several universities cooperate in offering a complete course of study leading to an online degree in criminal justice. This phenomenon is bound to grow rapidly, as the technology improves and the interest of potential students is stimulated by the availability of such programmes.

Positive Aspects

Almost all criminal justice courses, online or otherwise, lend themselves optimally for the dissemination of human rights concepts and instruments. Be it courses on basic criminal justice structures and procedures, on international cooperation, comparative criminal justice, corrections, victimology, criminal law, ethical issues in criminal justice, to mention only a few, the specific content of those courses present the possibility of including important considerations and information concerning the history and implementation of human rights in the daily practice of law enforcement and criminal justice.

The first step is necessarily the inclusion of all that information in the syllabus of the course and, of necessity, in the online text provided by the programme to the students. Such information, however, seems to be very rarely provided in, or emphasized by, existent online courses in the field of criminal justice. To obtain a radical change in this connection would require a concerted effort on the part of relevant entities, such as several instances within the United Nations, to raise awareness of the relevance of human rights to the teaching and practice of criminal justice. The faculties and administrations of those programmes should be targeted, so as to provide them with relevant information concerning the existent conventions, guidelines, and standards in the field of criminal justice, or in relevant areas thereto, that have been adopted by the Organization. In addition, this effort should be accompanied by a variety of ideas on how to persuasively explain the relevance of such instruments for the practitioners of criminal justice. Even a modest beginning could, within reasonable time limits, result in an increase of the amount of relevant material being included in syllabi and on-line texts.

The structure of the online courses in criminal justice in the particular programme discussed here includes, as part of the tasks to be performed by the students in the course of the semester, such as taking multiple-choice tests aimed at testing the students' mastery of the on-line text, a number of Discussion Boards, by means of which students are expected to comment, through postings, on different sections of the online textbook, and to comment on the comments posted by their classmates. If, depending on the material being covered, at least one of such discussion boards addressed matters of human rights, an additional amount of information on such rights would thus become a component of the training the course is censed to provide. In addition, students are asked to write at least one project and one book review, a practice which, again, could provide the opportunity to make much relevant information an integral part of the course and thus accessible to a larger constituency. This is why recruiting the faculty for such an endeavour is a critical, *sine qua non* goal of an effective strategy of dissemination.

The Case of a Course on Ethnic and Gender Issues in Law Enforcement

The course on ethnic and gender issues in criminal justice is thought at the online criminal justice programme of the University of Texas System, a programme enlisting the cooperation of five campuses of the System, namely, University of Texas at Arlington (UTA), University of Texas at Brownsville, University of Texas at Permian Basin (Midland/Odessa area), University of Texas at El Paso, and University of Texas at Dallas.

The author was not responsible for the online text, which had been prepared some time back by one of his colleagues at UTA, who kindly allowed him to teach 'his' course. This means that, in addition to the online text, the reading assignments and the book to be reviewed and commented upon by the students, were already established and outside of the author's power to change. These circumstances no doubt radically limited the author's effectiveness in providing information, information that undoubtedly would have been relevant to the course thereby helping to disseminate human rights concerns and concepts.

Further, one may point at the 'double-barrel' nature of this course. As the title clearly indicates, the course is expected to handle the relationship of criminal justice practices to ethnic/racial minorities, and to women of all races, ages, and social statuses. This provides a double opportunity to bring to bear human rights principles upon the contents of the course. And also makes commenting on a variety of topics covered by the course sort of a minefield both for the instructor and the students, insofar as, in view of the history of the United States and the situation of minorities in the country, there exists an extreme sensibility to any disparaging remarks uttered by a participant in postings, as the author had the opportunity to learn. The crucial fact is the perception of a particular remark. Thus, a well-intentioned remark may be perceived as, for instance, patronizing, and, consequently, elicit an offended reaction.

This fact notwithstanding, part of the author's responsibility was to monitor in this particular course and to comment on the postings and to guide the discussion around each one of the three discussion boards, as well as to direct the elaboration of the project. The author used these limited opportunities to mention, rather sparingly, relevant human rights documents, in particular, and almost exclusively, the Universal Declaration of Human Rights's Articles 1: "All human beings are born free and equal in dignity and rights. They are endowed with reason and conscience and should act towards one another in a spirit of brotherhood", and Article 2: "Everyone is entitled to all rights and freedoms set fort in this Declaration, without distinction of any kind, such as race, colour, sex, language, religion, political and other opinion, national or social origin, property, birth or other status," insofar as they, *i.e.*, the two articles, are of great relevance to the content of the course.

A source of concern was that more than a few students were totally unaware of these few lines, and, the author is sorry to say, some reacted negatively to the mere mention of the United Nations, a reaction brought about by a systematic negative publicity the Organization has received in the United States for a number of decades. It seems that the way to neutralize such distrust is to use every opportunity to indicate that many, if not most, principles to be found in the Declaration had their origin in very similar principles contained in such fundamental American documents as the Declaration of Independence and the Constitution, in particular the Bill of Rights of 1791, as well as the so-called Civil War Amendments - Thirteenth, Fourteenth, and Fifteenth - which abolished slavery, reinforced the concepts of equal treatment and due process, and extended voting rights to all citizens, without distinction of race.

Although the author did not do it in this occasion, for reasons he has no possibility of discussing here, it would be possible for the instructor of this course, throughout the semester, to direct the students to other documents, pointing at the fact that they are, first of all, logical derivations of the statements contained in the Universal Declaration, and secondly, that they are highly relevant to what is being discussed. The author could not, however, formally assign those documents as part of the reading material, insofar as they were not part of the original syllabus. But one can see that the instructor could bring into the discussion a number of human rights documents, such as, in particular, the United Nations Declaration of Basic Principles of Justice for Victims of Crime and Abuse of Power and the Convention for the Suppression of the Traffic in Persons and of the Exploitation of the Prostitution of Others, as well as the Inter-American Convention on the Prevention, Punishment and Eradication of Violence Against Women of the Organization of American States, to mention only a few.

It is quite evident that criminal justice programmes, taught online or in the classroom, lend themselves particularly well to the dissemination of human rights concepts and instruments, as mentioned in the introduction. The problem, as indicated above, is, in part at least, the ignorance of such instruments on the part of criminal justice faculties. To that, the author would like to add a certain degree of opposition to anything and everything that could remotely suggest a limitation of sovereignty and possible foreign interference with criminal justice practices and procedures.

But the negative stance among certain segments of the population notwithstanding, it is worth pointing out some other obvious links of specific criminal justice courses with specific United Nations initiatives. In this article, a personal experience with a course on ethnic and gender issues in criminal justice has been already described. Nonetheless, some conclusions may be helpful.

Conclusion

Insofar as students in the course, and, in particular, those who belong to a racial or ethnic minority, often mentioned in their postings in the Discussion Board, the issue of police brutality and excessive use of force by law enforcement officers, behavior seen by the victims as being motivated by some form of racial bias. The discussion of this topic could be fruitfully used to direct the participants' attention to, for instance, Article 5 of the Declaration, "No one shall be subjected to torture or to cruel, inhuman or degrading treatment or punishment", Article 7, "All are equal before the law and *are entitled without any discrimination to equal protection of the law*", as well as Article 9, "*No one shall be subjected to arbitrary arrest, detention or* exile" These few illustrations should already have made my point quite clear. Other linkages that come readily to mind, in the same context, are Article 11 (presumption of innocence), Article 12 (arbitrary interference with privacy), as well as Article 29.2: "*In the exercise of his rights and freedoms, everyone shall be subject only to such limitations as are determined by law solely for the purpose of securing due recognition and respect for the rights and freedoms of others."*

Equally important was the discussion concerning domestic violence and the reaction thereto by law enforcement agencies. In this connection, rape and sexual exploitation are issues that have gained high profile as a result of both the feminist and victims movements. Although perhaps less explosive than the issue of race, the number of postings in the Discussion Board reacting to the assigned readings indicates the perceived importance of this topic. In fact, the topic of women's rights is again one of the crucial issues in contemporary American society, as witnessed by the lively debate around abortion, as well as around affirmative action, sexual harassment, and the treatment of women who have broken the law. Recent increases in the rate of female crime have alerted the public and brought much needed attention to women as offenders and victims of crime. The conventions and guidelines elaborated by the United Nations that directly relate to this topic could be integrated without much effort both in the online text and in the Discussion Boards.

Other courses in criminal justice programmes, online or in the classroom, that could lend themselves to the dissemination of human rights principles and instruments, are, to mention only a few, criminal procedure, juvenile justice, victimology, corrections, terrorism, women and crime, capital punishment, and, particularly, comparative criminal justice systems and ethics in criminal justice. Currently, not all these courses are offered online, at least in the programme the author is directly acquainted with. But the dynamics of the programme are such, that there is no question that these and other courses will in the near future form part of the curriculum. A concerted plan of action could gain the cooperation of the professionals that will be developing and teaching these and other relevant courses.

Education via Satellite Technology Applied to Promotion of Non-custodial Measures

Damásio de Jesus[1]

Introduction

This article discusses the promotion of alternative, that is non-custodial, measures to imprisonment in Brazil. Two specific experiences will be reviewed underway: one in a post graduate law school in São Paulo, capital of the State of the same name, and the other in a non-governmental organization with its head office in Bauru, an important middle-size city in the same State, in Brazil.

The first experience involving the promotion of alternative measures by satellite fits well the application of modern technologies, like distance education, virtual schools, *etc.* The second experience involves the support for the called third sector – that is support for the judiciary mechanisms of the State and to the society in general, in the application of penalties that are an alternative to imprisonment for less serious transgressions and for non-dangerous criminals, following a trend prevailing in the criminal justice systems of many countries.

In this article, both experiences will first be analyzed separately and then combined for the purpose of conclusions.

Preparatory Course via Satellite for Admission into Judicial Careers (Complexo Jurídico Damásio de Jesus)[2]

The educational institutions presently incorporated in the "Complexo Jurídico Damásio de Jesus-CJDJ" had a very modest origin 35 years ago. This preparatory course, which gradually enlarged, now contributes to the programme of a big criminal

---

1 Damásio de Jesus is the chairman and professor at *Complexo Jurídico Damásio de Jesus* (São Paolo, Brazil). He has published more than 50 books, edited 5 volumes and authored about 670 articles and reports. He is the founder of *Patronato Professor Damásio de Jesus* for alternative penalties, and General Director of *Faculty of Law Damásio de Jesus*. He is 'Invited Professor' at Austral University (Buenos Aires/Argentina) and University of Salerno (Italy), from where he also received his honorary doctorate. He is actively involved in the international events organized by the United Nations. He has also provided his expertise as individual observer to many congresses hosted by the United Nations.
2 See also http://cdsat.damasio.com.br.

justice teaching institution, with dozens of professors selected among the best in Brazil and educating thousands of students.

During these 35 years thousands of students have attended the CJDJ courses. Among them there have been judges, chief judges, prosecutors, attorneys, state attorneys, attorneys-general, police officials and even ministers of the Federal Supreme Court, not to mention an undefined number of politicians, ambassadors and other high ranking officials. As years elapsed, former students of the course spread over many States in Brazil in the exercise of their careers, maintaining liaison with the CJDJ and significantly contributing for the promotion of its didactic methods.

As a result, following on many suggestions and requests from the alumnis, the CJDJ expanded its preparatory course to the whole country, based on the re-evaluated methodology and with the same core staff of professors.

The task of enlarging the area covered by the course maintaining the same tuition level was not an easy one. From the inception of the idea up to its accomplishment, a long and laborious maturation process took place, while the CJDJ kept on pursuing various technical solutions for broadening the outreach of the course. Besides being too expensive, those solutions did not correspond to the required quality standard, nor did they assure complete reliability in image transmissions. While major importance was given to the state-owned company more capable of assuming the technological part of the project (Embratel), its feasibility was depending on the adequate and accurate selection of partners. Maintaining in the course via satellite the same student-service philosophy, which is based on respect, complicity and on the strong commitment of providing the best study and apprenticeship conditions was a must. Thus, the CJDJ could not run the risk of airing a weak image, or what was worse, of keeping a student waiting in vain for such image, or allowing an inadequate execution of services in any department involved, anywhere in the country, because of a technical failure in the transmission or of an erroneous selection of a partner.

As a means of promoting a careful selection of the interested parties, the CJDJ managers thought first about utilizing the franchise system. However, after several studies, the managers concluded to opt for the licensing system, which besides strengthening the brand preserving its values and principles, has proven to be economically more feasible for the licensed partners. The adopted system merges two objectives: the licensor's, who assures his principles and know-how are reinforced beside the client, and the licensee's, who expects return on investment in the lesser period possible.

Finally, in 2002, after a long testing period, it was possible to initiate live transmissions of classes administered in a studio specially designed for the course, via satellite and in a closed channel, providing access to high-quality images and perfect sound, as if the student was inside a class in the CJDJ São Paulo. From this point the first licensed units were created. Presently, they are in 32 cities across Brazil and the number is growing. What is important is that the achieved results level remains the same of that achieved by the attendance tuition practiced in the head office in São Paulo, further achieving the same student satisfaction levels.

In order to achieve this goal, the course via satellite relies on the support of TV specialists, technicians and advertisers who always discuss with the professors the methods and alternatives to be pursued in the class. The major technical and methodological challenge is reconciling the course syllabus with the need of rendering the transmission more attractive and user friendly for those who are kilometers far, in front of a screen.

The education via satellite is already considered as of a very high level. The CJDJ continues to enhance it.

Execution of a Community Service Order

There is a vision still prevailing in the legal apparatus of the State that penal law is the best instrument to control crime and offender. In the system's simplified logic, acting punitively the State acts preventively as well, hence educating the society. This point of view has lately been the object of criticism among legal experts. It is inefficient, to start with: it does not prevent crime, does not rehabilitate criminals, it also does not satisfy and indemnify victims. Additionally it is extremely onerous at a public expense, and most of all, it does not reconstitute the social tissue torn by crime.

In case of Brazil, there is a penitentiary system which is, both, oversized and inoperative. Prisons are already overpopulated often with offenders who should not be imprisoned. Moreover, there are thousands of warrants issued by judicial authorities that are still not executed, great part of which concern dangerous criminals who really represent a risk for society.

Juvenile delinquents imprisoned with dangerous adults criminals learn what they should not learn. When released from prison they do not return to social and community life, but remain within the criminal underworld. Our sad reality is that prisons were transformed in real "crime universities". And the imprisoned individuals who had the bad luck of passing through such "universities", even if for a short time, will bear for the rest of their lives a sad stigma that shall prevent them, even if willing to, from a full reintegration in social life and in the job market.

This is what is happening in the Brazilian penal system. Unfortunately, however, this occurs not only in Brazil. To a lesser or greater extent, the same terrible problem occurs in numerous other nations. Even in highly developed countries, with model penitentiary institutes, there is a high recidivism rate. In view of this, a common sense reaction has been to pursue alternative sanctions, which allow convicted individuals with prospect for rehabilitation to pay their debts to the society and the victims in a useful and effective manner, without grave imprisonment inconveniences. In fact, alternative penalties such as fines, execution of community service and temporary restriction of rights, besides many others, may substitute with advantages imprisonment in the case of less serious offences, when applied to offenders whose imprisonment would be not advisable because of low prospect of re-socialization.

The Seventh United Nations Congress on the Prevention of Crime and the Treatment of Offenders (Milan, Italy, 1985) emphasized the need of reducing the number of imprisoned individuals through expanding alternatives to imprisonment. In 1986, the United Nations Asia and Far East Institute for the Prevention of Crime and the Treatment of Offenders initiated the development of the Standard Minimum Rules for Non-Custodial Measures (the Tokyo Rules), later adopted on the recommendation of the Eighth Congress (Havana, Cuba, 1990) by the United Nations General Assembly on December 14th 1990 (resolution 45/110, Annex).

Within this international legal context operates the Brazilian criminal justice system. In Brazil, alternative penalties are a substitute, that is, the judge first determines the liberty restriction penalty and then may substitute it for one or more alternative sanctions. They cannot be applied directly, nor cumulatively with penalties involving restriction of liberty. Substitution is obligatory once the admissibility conditions are met, thus not being the case of a mere judicial faculty.

Alternative penalties are executed conditionally, that is subject to offender's compliance with them. In case of non-compliance, imprisonment is imposed.

The Patronage Professor Damásio de Jesus, a private non-for-profit organization established in the city of Bauru in 1997, pursues the aim of assisting justice in the application of alternative penalties. The Patronage, which receives no governmental support, belongs to the "Complexo Jurídico Damásio de Jesus - CJDJ". It executes, implements and monitors alternative measures. The Patronage was established by a group of professionals from several areas, who studied, planned its structure and elaborated its

Statutes[3]. Its present President Dr. José Roberto Moraes dos Santos works directly with criminal justice organs of the County of Bauru.

The Patronage has as its objectives:
- rendering a feasible re-socialization process of sentenced individuals;
- providing its beneficiaries, by means of reflections, the conditions for the rescue of their values, thus contributing for the improvement of their quality of life, by means of individual/community relations;
- orientation for sentenced individuals on their duties regarding execution of the alternative penalty;
- allowing sentenced individuals the access to an institution in accordance to their profile, qualification and capacity level, where they shall execute services as any other employee, not subject to distinctions;
- contributing for their valorization, by their insertion in the community and in the family core.

The Patronage is invested with a task of a huge social importance: preventing the re-imprisonment, thus keeping away the offenders from recidivism. Through free workmanship it provides as a community service, the Patronage benefits various entities which receive assistance of offenders trained in computer science, medicine, engineering, law, *etc*.

In addition to the educational aspect, community service implies for sentenced individuals an excellent opportunity for the recovery of their social status, allowing their reintegration in the job market, while the interaction between the community and the services executor makes room for more stable bonds between them.

Statistically, from 844 sentenced individuals who at the time of analysis (2003) underwent or are still undergoing alternative penalties, only nine (9) cases of recidivism were registered. Many sentenced individuals, after having met the conditions of the sanction, continue to work as collaborators and volunteers in schools and crèches. They identified themselves with the

---

3 Participated in the Patronage's creation: Dr.ª Ana Luzia de Campos Morato Leite, Dr. Aniel Chaves, Dr. Bruno Henrique Gonçalves, Dr. Cirineu Antônio Bonete, Dr. Damásio Evangelista de Jesus, Dr. Eder Serra de Campos, Dr.ª Elci Aparecida Papassoni Fernandes, Dr. Elyseu dos Santos, Dr. Francisco Bento, Dr. Freddy Gonçalves Silva, Dr. Daniel Gonçalves Silva, Dr. Jerônymo Crepaldi Júnior, Sr. José Octavio Guizelini Balieiro, Dr. José Roberto Moraes dos Santos, Dr.ª Lia Clélia Canova, Sr.ª Luciana Raquel Gonçalves Silva Bergamini, Dr. Luiz Toledo Martins, Dr.ª Marta Adriana Gonçalves Silva Buchignani, Dr. Ranolfo Alves, Dr.ª Rosana de Jesus Reis de Souza e Silva e Sr.ª Rosângela Santos de Jesus Romano Mattos.

concluded programmes, established friendships, and received recognition, hence regained their self-esteem. In this way, sanctions became pleasant activities.

Beneficiaries of the "Patronato Professor Damásio de Jesus", all of them above 18 years old, were sentenced for community service in the city of Bauru and in other cities of the region, and were accepted independently of their educational and social-economic background, ethnic group origin, political or religious beliefs, *etc*. Community service consists of gratuitous tasks rendered to assistance entities, hospitals, schools, and other similar establishments, either in State or in communitarian programs.

In Bauru, the Patronage works with several beneficiary entities, including public organs, among which one may cite hospitals, crèches, asylums, religious or philanthropic associations and public organs of the neighboring cities of Agudos, Arealva, Avaí, Bauru, Pederneiras and Piratininga.

The procedure for contracting community service starts with summoning the sentenced individuals by means of a warrant stating date and time they shall come for an individual interview and evaluation by a social worker. The said interview is intended to check capabilities of sentenced individuals, their professional experience, education level and professional qualification, in a way to subsidize their conduction to the execution of communitarian services. Then, the entity in which the sentenced individual shall undergo his penalty is selected. A presentation and conduction official letter is made to the person responsible for the benefited entity, stating identification data, address, crime, and the term to undergo the execution of services. The monthly report on the individual's activities is also remitted with the official letter. However, acceptance by the entity of the sentenced individual is not obligatory (school, factory, *etc.*). Execution of the service amounts to eight hours a week (on Saturdays, Sundays and holidays), on basis of one hour per day of imprisonment foreseen in the court sentence.

The sentenced individual attends the place where he or she shall undergo the alternative penalty. The Patronage is in charge of notifying the judge about the adopted procedure. The institution reports on a monthly basis accounting for all the activities accomplished by the sentenced individual and remits said report to the Patronage, allowing the Social Service to effect control upon the hours already completed. At the end of the service, the sentenced individual is notified upon such fact and is then discharged from the entity. The reports on the execution of services are registered in the competent register office by means of official letters remitted to the sentencing judge, for process filing purposes.

As of this writing, in 8 years of activities the Patronage has already assisted 1453 sentenced individuals, whereas 600 were assisted in 2005.

A sentenced individual undergoing his penalty in penitentiaries of the State of São Paulo costs in the average R$ 767.00 (about US$ 340.00 or € 281.00) per month at public expenses. Whereas, sentenced individuals rendering communitarian services under supervision of the "Patronato Prof. Damásio de Jesus" have a cost of approximately R$ 25.00 (about US$ 11.00 or € 9.00) for the institution.

The Patronage is a non-governmental organization accredited by the Tribunal of Justice of the State of São Paulo. On October 31st 2001, the Municipal Law No. 4.753, of the city of Bauru, declared the Patronage of public utility, thus recognizing its merit and social value.

New Project under Development (Patronage's work via satellite)

The experience of the Patronage was always considered as a pioneering one. Since it succeeded, the time has come for another project.

This next project aims at countrywide dissemination via satellite of the method applied by the Patronage, with a view to adopting it on a broader scale, especially as far as the execution of community service order is concerned.

This includes opening a free-access television channel ("Canal Jurídico Damásio de Jesus"[4]), with a weekly one-hour programme on alternative penalties intended to encourage the execution of community service via Patronage all over Brazil. The programme involves lectures, news and information.

Conclusion

We do not want to impose the concrete model of the "Patronato Prof. Damásio de Jesus" to countries with different conditions. Even in Brazil there are alternative methods for the application and promotion of non-custodial measures different from those adopted by the Patronage.

---

4 See further http://cdsat.damasio.com.br.

However, the experience of and the advice from the work of the Patronage may be made available free of charge to every interested party in order to achieve the same common objective: broadening the scope of application of non-custodial measures, allowing a fairer penal justice, more effective and more humanized.

III. TEACHING INTERNATIONAL CRIMINAL JUSTICE IN A REAL CLASSROOM

Teaching Criminal Law in its International Dimension – Where to Start?

Frank Hoepfel [1,2]

Introduction

Since criminal law has been put, also for a broader public, on the world agenda in the recent past, the field is well apt to deepen the understanding of globalisation also in law. For law students international criminal law can be an eye-opening experience, comparable to the diachronic view they used to be offered in earlier days, as a tool to grasp the relativity of a given legal system.

But to get the message through to the students, it needs to be an attractive subject at law schools. That will only work, when it is not too complex. Given the continuous developments in this field of law, it may be less feasible to teach it in the traditional sense, and to pre-process it in terms of introducing it into textbooks.

---

1 Professor of Criminal Law and Criminal Procedure at the University of Vienna; *Ad litem* Judge at the International Criminal Tribunal for the Former Yugoslavia (ICTY), The Hague, The Netherlands.
2 The author would like to thank Slawomir Redo for the opportunity to share his thoughts with this group of experts who participated in the panel of the American Society of Criminology in Toronto (Canada, 2005). It was not only the meeting of specialists from the different disciplines but, as Slawomir Redo has been promoting already for a number of years, the dialogue needs to be underpinned by a common understanding of the practical challenges. These are fueled not only by the usual bipolarity between theory and practice, but to a large extent by the need to include regional differences in respect of historical and cultural background. In the criminal law context this is as indispensable as the international community has learned to see it in the field of human rights. Here I need to mention Manfred Nowak, United Nations Special Rapporteur on Torture, and yet so often present and prepared to co-teach our annual seminars on the individual criminal responsibility for serious violations of human rights and humanitarian law. I am including my thanks to Gerhard Hafner, head of the Austrian delegation at the negotiations which resulted in the 1998 Rome Statute of the International Criminal Court. Gerhard Hafner has become the backbone of these seminars by having introduced the criminal law into the regular teaching of public international law.

International Criminal Law: a Subject Matter in Flux

Legal history which keeps shifting into the background in most curricula, used to be a more appropriate means to demonstrate the relativity of human laws. As the subject – for example Roman law as crystallised in the *Corpus Juris Civilis* – stays unchanged, its presentation have reminded of the anatomy lessons in medical school. In contrast, the international dimensions of criminal law and of law in general have not yet satisfyingly fallen into place. For example, at Vienna University a vivid discussion has resulted in a draft issued in winter 2005/06 which has provided for an introductory phase on "European and International Fundaments of Law". However, it appears to be highly questionable how far such an undertaking may, or shall, include the specific international dimensions of criminal law.

The Interdependence of Different Legal Disciplines

One may be of the opinion that international criminal law is a compound matter. Therefore it should be taught only when students have been acquainted with the single components. In fact, international criminal law merges two legal disciplines that are fundamentally different in their focus, and in their methods: international law, which basically deals with the legal duties and rights of equal sovereign states, and criminal law, where the focus is on the criminal responsibility of individuals (Höpfel and Angermaier 2005: 310 *et seq*.). At least in Europe where they typically start their studies at a faculty of law right after high school, these students on the average will be too young.

That has to do both with the compound structure in terms of a legal subject and with its interdisciplinary character. This matter should be first discussed in the interdisciplinary context, and then as interrelated within the law.

Once students have an advanced understanding of world politics and international relations in light of globalisation both on the institutional level and in terms of civil society, they will be extremely interested and better motivated to acquire and exchange views on this matter. From frequent discussions with young colleagues it can be seen that in spite of the high degree of acceptance of criminalisation through the statutes of international courts and tribunals, the idea of direct enforcement by such international bodies is nevertheless a controversial one – not only in the United States. It is difficult to have a productive discussion on these issues before there is a rather profound understanding on all sides. But at the same time a different problem may arise as soon as they have acquired a "sense" for this matter. As soon as this big step seems to lay behind them, they often will be reluctant to question their position as openly as less advanced students are ready to do. Without doubt that is the advantage of starting earlier in addressing international criminal justice. However, this requires a great deal of didactical competence.

In this regard it seems useful to include some remarks of a more personal nature. By close contacts with my friend and colleague Gerald S. Reamey from St. Mary's University School of Law, San Antonio, Texas (USA), I think I can tell the difference. I met him in 1986 when they started their Innsbruck program ("Institute on World Legal Problems") and he contacted the criminal law department of the Innsbruck University to discuss extradition law.

Over the years, I had the pleasure to participate in his classes and seminars, as silent guest, discussion partner, guest lecturer, or sometimes co-teaching, first in the field of comparative criminal procedure and later also in international criminal justice. These experiences have made me understand better what the teacher of law in general, and of comparative and international criminal law in particular, *can* accomplish. However, they have left in me the impression that this nearly insoluble issue which I chose to address here is not to be answered solely on a rational level. Rather it is the matter of an art, maybe comparable to psychoanalysis. An example, and to me still a bit of a mystery, is how Geary succeeded in summer 2005 when he at the end of a course on "International Criminal Justice", which he had offered together with Richard Goldstone, proposed to students who had in general just finished their first or second year at an American law school to prepare for a debate on the pros and cons of a country like the United States participating in the Rome Statute of the International Criminal Court. Although this is a highly political issue, it was possible to look through the surface to the ground with its important legal perspectives. The secret of this success was not easy to catch. It is not only the teacher's charisma. At the same time, it appears to lie in a special ability to draw lines which give a picture which is more differentiated than in a woodcut, but still not carrying every nut, bolt and screw; and which is a still life and yet lively.

The Need for Basic Understanding of Legal Principles

Including criminal law in its international dimensions into law curricula by default will remain a questionable idea also for another reason. The point is to pay attention to the context within the whole legal order. It does not make much sense to only then teach the fundamental principles of criminal law, normally assembled under the heading of the "General Part". Whether it is the chapter of the theories justifying any punishment, as it has been the concern of legal philosophy for ages, or any specific issue, *e.g.,.* the legislative and doctrinal methods to assemble the elements of a given crime, it causes unnecessary challenges when these issues are not being taught before their arising in the context of international criminal law. A case in point is the notion of "inchoate offences" (crime of preparing for or seeking to commit another crime) which is relevant both for international criminal law (Cassesse 2003: 190-191) as well as a fundamental concept in the "General Part" of most domestic criminal justice systems. Another topical issue is the meaning of justification and excuse (*Ibidem*: 219 *et seq.*). It seems much more rewarding to teach the subject in separate programs and specialisation courses, including Master studies with a special orientation. They either may have their emphasis in human rights law[3] or they also may take the route via criminology and criminal justice.[4] Again a different way is to undertake a "vertical" comparison between international law on a universal level – both in terms of jurisdictional issues of national laws and cooperation between states culminating in direct enforcement models – and on the European level.[5]

European Law vs. International Law

The ongoing Europeanisation of criminal law has led to a high level of integration – a case in point is the Framework Decision on a European Arrest Warrant – which raises the question whether criminal law has become an instrument of integration, or whether it is merely following some imagination of a degree of unity which in fact still is lacking. This problem demonstrates the peculiar aspects of so-called European criminal law. Within the goals defined in the draft European Constitution Treaty, the various meanings of what a "harmonisation" of criminal law and procedure may turn out to be will be the subject of a deeper analysis before making it a teaching subject. It is therefore important to distinguish this issue from the questions pertaining to international criminal law. By all means it is

---

3 An example is the successful "European Master's Degree in Human Rights and Democratisation – EMA" organised by the European Inter-University Centre for Human Rights and Democratisation in Venice and run in a quite unique cooperation of some 40 universities in the 27 Member States of the European Union.
4 These aspects are the focus of the M.A. program in "European Criminology" offered at famous Leuven University (Belgium).
5 An example is the summer program we jointly developed in our "Beccaria Academy on European and International Criminal Law", a specialisation course which we could start at the University of Turku (Finland) in 1999 (with Ari-Matti Nuutila, Jo Dedeyne-Amann and Peter Van der Auweraert) and continue in Vienna in 2003 (Damian Korosec from Ljubljana University (Slovenia) and Pedro Caeiro, Universidade de Coimbra (Portugal), being additionally on board).

important to challenge the approach whereby the two levels are combined. Further reflection may produce a consensus that European and the international criminal law have become even two different disciplines. They will profit from each other. And they may, or even have to, be addressed in teaching and research by the same professors. It is as though one would be starting from a domestic perspective and see two roads leading to different levels: the regional level and the universal one. In which of these two fields of law the persons concerned will specialise may differ – between colleagues and also between phases of one's own life.

This difference is also reflected by separate (but usually interconnected!) associations and networks. Fledgling groupings like the "European Criminal Law Academic Network – ECLAN", based at Université Libre de Bruxelles, which are adding to the network of associations devoted to European criminal law issues (originating from the idea of criminal law instruments being needed as accessory to classical EC law) demonstrate this. A first, and sustainable, crop of this ECLAN network is an own "Summer School on the European Penal Area". On the other hand there exist leading scholarly non-governmental organizations which play their role on the international level, including a strong interest, and a considerable influence, in the work of the United Nations.

Good examples are the International Association of Penal Law (AIDP) and the International Society of Social Defence and Humane Criminal Policy (ISSD), both having consultative status with ECOSOC. Courses which they have initiated – such as the annual "specialisation course in international criminal law" at the renowned *Istituto Superiore Internazionale di Scienze Criminali* (ISICS) in Siracusa, Italy, contribute to a reasonable concept of continuing legal education which produces its fruit in the form of promising offspring in the academic environment.

This process of evolution in respect of organisational diversification can be fed back to the discussion on the future of legal teaching. The theory is: letting the two avenues (the "European" and the "international" roads) cross again does not at all have to be an ambition within regular law studies. It will suffice, but be indispensable at the same time, to show students where the roads go. The rest will be up to postgraduate education.

Possible Solutions

A look into recent editions of textbooks in Austrian legal education illustrates this approach. For instance, in a textbook on the "General Part" of criminal law (Kienapfel and Höpfel 2007) a concluding chapter on the international dimensions of criminal law was added, while a leading textbook of public international law

(Neuhold 2005) appeared with a chapter on the penal dimensions.[6] The authors of these textbooks agree there should be at least some acquaintance every law student has to make with this extraordinary dimension of international, and of criminal, law. The approach taken at the Vienna University is to bring these dimensions together in a series of co-taught[7] seminars for advanced graduate as well as post-graduate students. It appears to be more realistic to distinguish between basic aspects and such content which is more appropriate for postgraduate education.

To whom else should one explain or with whom debate over, *e.g.*, the impact which the International Court of Justice (ICJ) Judgment of 14 February 2002 in the case between the Democratic Republic of the Congo and Belgium (ICJ Judgement: 2002) – including Christine Van den Wyngaert's outstanding Dissenting Opinion – concerning the lawfulness of an international arrest warrant issued by an investigating judge of a Belgian court of first instance against the incumbent Minister for Foreign Affairs of another country might have on the position of ex-dictator of Liberia Charles Taylor in the criminal proceedings instituted against him before The Special Court for Sierra Leone (SCSL),[8] or, to take another example, the relevance of an extradition request of country A to a country B which is located in the territory of the former Yugoslavia and has surrendered the person concerned to country C (the Netherlands, hosting the ICTY), were the person was charged and subsequently convicted for war crimes, the sentence having to be served in a country D? The tricky mix between classical extradition issues and the direct enforcement model represented by these Tribunals will be something for a Ph.D. student – maybe!

The opinion has often been expressed that issues of extradition and mutual assistance will be learned early enough in practice, *i.e.*, when working as an intern or clerk, or young judge. But that may be a little too late to lay foundations. And not encountering these modern challenges during the graduate studies at all also means

---

6 The author of this chapter is Gerhard Hafner whose above-mentioned role as the head of the Austrian delegation during the States' Conference on the Statute of the International Criminal Law in Rome in July 1998 coincided with the time when Austria had taken over the EU presidency.

7 As to possible strategies from a common law perspective, compare Stacy Caplow and Maryellen Fullerton, "Co-Teaching International Criminal Law: New Strategies to Meet the Challenges of a New Course" (*Brooklyn Law School Legal Studies Research Paper* Nr. 45, Oct. 2005), *Brooklyn Journal of International Law*, 2006.

8 SCSL, *Decision on Immunity from Jurisdiction, Prosecutor v. Taylor*, Case no. SCSL2003-1-I, A. Ch., 31 May 2004. In: André Klip and Göran Sluiter (eds.), Annotated Leading Cases of International Criminal Tribunals, Vol. 9, The Special Court for Sierra Leone 2003-2004, p. 187 *et seq.*; with Commentary by Claus Kreß, *ibidem*, p. 202 *et seq.*

not understanding what problems have to be mastered today: cooperation being the key word for this, and therefore requiring, but also enhancing, one's teamwork skills. This appears to be highly symptomatical for the challenges we are unequivocally facing when following the goal to continually improve teaching and research at our universities.

Top-down vs. Bottom-up Approach

What flows from these few reflections? The specific challenge posed by the recent materialisation of a new (directly enforced) "International Criminal Law" raises the question in which way to approach this field in law school and in continuing legal education. Two approaches may seem to be competing: a top-down and a bottom-up design. When starting from the sources of law, this modern international criminal law first would have to be looked at in terms of the framework of Security Council measures within Chapter VII of the United Nations Charter or of international conventions, like the Rome Statute of the International Criminal Court. This primarily includes the perspectives of International Relations (*e.g.*, issues of sovereignty as raised esp. by the US Administration in regard to the Rome Statute). However, when delving deeper into the contents of the statutes and into the jurisprudence of international or internationalised criminal courts, it will be recommendable to teach these issues in a way which can build on the fundamentals of classical criminal law doctrine. Actually, one ought to make a distinction between substantive and procedural law. The case-law of international criminal tribunals shows that there are considerable problems contained both in respect of substantive and procedural issues.

While the issues of substantive law can be addressed very well by building on the understanding of a single domestic legal order, the procedural questions additionally would require a good foundation in comparative law. For the purposes of teaching comparative procedural systems it even will be useful to require, or at least to recommend, an education in Latin. For jurists from a continental European system it usually is a surprise to see how little the shift of the emphasis from legal history to comparative and international law would change in this regard.[9]

---

9 While the editors of famous *Black's Law Dictionary* (8th edition, p. 1703) argue the legal maxims collected in their Appendix B would, without replacing legal arguments, often add an element of fun, it is important to note the bridging role of Latin maxims and expressions for international tribunals which are, while predominantly using English as their working language, supposed to blend legal methods of the major systems of the world.

The recommendation to first be extremely familiar with a domestic criminal law regime will be relevant for both the substantive law and the procedure. However, the differences – if not contradictions – between the two main legal systems of the world, common law and civil law, are mainly to be found in the procedural models and maxims. Without going into too much detail, the view of nearly everyone involved in the trial, from the defendant to the judges, but in particular the philosophy behind the professional role of counsel, differ greatly and partly irreconcilably between the methods of common law and civil law. It does not immediately transpire from the aim to connect the cultures of the "representation of the principal legal systems of the world", as invoked by the rules concerning the qualification and election of judges in this field,[10] but appears to remain a challenge for the near future to understand better how to bridge the gaps between these traditions, or occasionally find some "third way".

Although this international justice is a direct fruit of the work of the United Nations, another vast part of its work in the field of criminal law is often overlooked, at least in ordinary law schools: A field of growing importance for domestic legislation, the rich *aquis* of treaties and of principles developed as United Nations standards and norms in crime prevention and criminal justice should incrementally also become part of the teaching of international criminal law.[11] This, however, does not pose any technical problem to the drafters of curricula. It is rather up to the single professors to integrate these standards and norms into their teachings.[12] The same is true for the most central international treaties, such as the 2000 Convention against Transnational Organised Crime and its Protocols and the 2003 Convention against Corruption, not to mention the anti-drug instruments, in particular the 1988 Vienna Convention against Illicit Traffic in Narcotic Drugs and Psychotropic Substances.[13]

However, the role of the Crime Commission and of the services of UNODC, regarding the preparation and implementation of these instruments is just one example of the work of international as well as regional organisations, including the Council of Europe, to which more attention should be directed. Here the competition between a

---

10 See, Article 36 (8) (a) of the Rome Statute; compare Statutes of the International Criminal Tribunal for the former Yugoslavia, Articles 13 *bis* (1) (c) and 13 *ter* (1) (c), and for Rwanda, Articles 13 *bis* (1) (c) and 13 *ter* (1) (c).
11 Vienna University is in the privileged position to be in a fruitful contact with UNODC, and it is hoped this cooperation will be further developed.
12 To give an example, for the various models of victim-offender-mediation it may be useful to discuss the United Nations basic principles on the use of restorative justice programmes in criminal matters (ECOSOC Resolution 2002/12 of 24 July 2002, Annex).
13 For the legal background see Chawla and Pietschmann 2005, p. 310 *et seq.*; as to the legal methods, compare Joutsen 2005, p. 255 *et seq.*

top-down and a bottom-up approach will not play the same role as in respect of the teaching of international criminal justice.

Conclusion

As not only different disciplines of law, but also these different legal cultures are merging, there is an ever growing need for the ability to think in different "worlds". It cannot be the goal of legal education to make the students fit *in* both worlds. But they need to be made fit *for* these different worlds.

What can be aimed at in this regard? It will be helpful in any case to first make the regular student fit in their own system.

There is no question that this can be taught best in the home country. But mobility programs are mushrooming, fortunately already during the regular law studies. Although it is popular to do "neutral" subjects when abroad, it would be a real chance to make comparative law a blossoming subject (also beyond family law and similar sectors in which comparative teaching already has more tradition!). This can, as we all have experienced, be of great assistance to even understand the own system better. However, that is not the primary concern in comparative law. Rather it is a frequent by-product, already when comparing systems which are not as foreign one to another, and seem to follow similar approaches.[14]

Talented students of course should always be encouraged to go abroad and learn about foreign systems, and in particular to try to get an understanding of the way of legal thinking in the opposite legal system and their cultural, linguistic, and maybe philosophical background. Such a principal understanding imports by far more than any rich knowledge in details of the law and the doctrine. By the way, can't we learn from that again for our own system? I am not so much referring to the legal, rather to the educational system.

But, to repeat, as far as the law is concerned, intimate understanding of the own law and procedure, *i.e.,* of one national criminal justice system, will always be a good starting point. It seems to be no matter which one – be it a system with a common law or with a civil law tradition. Both have their place in the global family of nations. Both have their peculiarities. And we will be more and more aware of that, the "smaller" the world is becoming.

---

14 As the author has had many occasions to learn in a series of seminars which were fathered by Hans-Heinrich Jescheck and Robert Hauser, the doyens of German and Swiss criminal law and procedure, and masters of comparative law.

To conclude, the developing of curricula is presently a challenge all over. And it therefore is rewarding to be in the position to compare views about this international issue from a truly adequate viewpoint, within an appropriate scene. And the scene of crime is not meant here. It is rather the global perspective. For me that perspective has gained so much by this wonderful contact before, at, and after Toronto.

References

Arrest Warrant of 11 April 2000 (Democratic Republic of the Congo v. Belgium), ICJ Judgment of 14 February 2002.

Cassese, A. (2003). International Criminal Law, Oxford – New York: Oxford University Press.

Chawla, S. and Pietschmann T. (2005). Drug Trafficking as a Transnational Crime. In P. Reichel, Handbook of Transnational Crime and Justice Thousand Oaks, CA: Sage.

Höpfel, F. and Angermaier, C. (2005). Adjudicating International Crimes. In P. Reichel, Handbook of Transnational Crime and Justice, Thousand Oaks, CA, Sage.

Joutsen, M. (2005). International Instruments on Cooperation in Responding to Transnational Crime. In P. Reichel, Handbook of Transnational Crime and Justice, Thousand Oaks, CA, Sage.

Kienapfel, Diethelm and Frank Höpfel (2007). Grundriss des Strafrechts. Allgemeiner Teil, 12th edition, Wien, Manz.

Klip, André and Göran Sluiter (eds.). Annotated Leading Cases of International Criminal Tribunals, Vol. 9, The Special Court for Sierra Leone 2003-2004.

Neuhold, Hanspeter et.al. (eds.) (2005). Österreichisches Handbuch des Völkerrechts, 4th edition, Wien: Manz.

Using the Topic of Torture for Interrogation to Teach about International Standards and the Rule of Law

Philip L. Reichel[1]

Introduction

In late 2002 and early 2003, media reports began suggesting that persons being held in the CIA interrogation center at Bagram Air Base in Afghanistan were being tortured or subjected to practices very close to torture ("Ends, means and barbarity" 2003; Priest & Gellman 2002). A Fox News opinion poll in March 2003 asked Americans if they favored or opposed allowing the government to use any means necessary, including physical torture, to obtain information from prisoners that might protect the United States from terrorist attacks (FOX News/Opinion Dynamics Poll 2003, March 11-12). Forty-four percent of the respondents were in favor compared with 42 percent who opposed, 5 percent said it depends and 9 percent were unsure. It seemed without any basis for comparison, that 44 percent of the American public favoring the use of torture in any circumstances was remarkably high. Would students have opinions similar to or different from the national perspective?

In March 2004, while teaching a Comparative Justice Systems course at the University of Northern Colorado (a seniors only capstone course for criminal justice majors), this author decided to administer an opinion poll that would ask the same FOX News question, and a few others, related to torture and government powers. At the time the students were asked the question, the course was covering the topic of terrorism as a transnational crime and having class discussions on substantive and procedural law changes in the United States since September 11, 2001. All the students indicated they were aware of the allegations of abuse and torture by Americans of persons being held at places like Guantánamo Bay. The results of the class poll (administered electronically using the course web site) showed 52 percent of the students favored allowing the government to use torture. Thirty-

---

1 Philip Reichel is professor of criminal justice at the University of Northern Colorado (USA). His teaching and research interests are in the areas of comparative justice studies and in corrections. He is the author of a textbook on comparative criminal justice systems, has edited a handbook on transnational crime and justice, and is actively involved in the international sections of both the American Society of Criminology and the Academy of Criminal Justice Sciences.

three percent were opposed and 15 percent chose a "not sure" option.

Those results, quite honestly, were surprising. One could assume (hope?) that persons interested in criminal justice careers would be appalled at the prospect of using torture to extract information. During class discussion, students were asked why more than half of these criminal justice students were more willing to accept torture techniques than was the general public? The interesting, if not enlightened, responses included such points as:

- torture could provide valuable information that would not be gathered using other techniques;
- techniques being identified in the media at the time as being torture by American personnel (e.g., sleep deprivation and keeping prisoners in awkward and painful positions for long periods of time) were not viewed by some students as their idea of torture. So, they interpreted the poll question as asking if they favored allowing the government to use those techniques to obtain information;
- some criminal events rise to such a high level of importance that otherwise unacceptable response-techniques become acceptable.

A lively discussion ensued with one group of students forcefully disagreeing with an equally adamant other group of students. By the end of the class period, opinions on either side seemed unchanged and remarkably parochial. This situation required a focus on what type of international education the students should have and what specific topics were of particular importance for that international education. This chapter explains how the topics of "international standards" and "rule of law" came to be the focus of several class periods.

Goals of an International Education

There is a need to both "educate internationally" and to "provide an international education." The former is accomplished, in part, when international institutes and academies provide a common educational experience for students from many countries. The latter is accomplished, in part, when students anywhere are educated about issues of international importance. Many contributions in this anthology describe efforts to educate internationally by reviewing training courses on the importance of human dignity and human rights, strategies for fighting organized crime, and identifying best practices. Fewer of the contributions focus on providing an international education. Both goals are important in today's global village and typically when one is the focus, the other is included as well. After all, what would be the point in providing common training in law enforcement techniques to police from several countries (*i.e.*, educating internationally) without noting the benefits derived from cross-national cooperation in combating transnational crime (*i.e.*, providing an international education)? Despite that overlap, it is desirable to sometimes discuss the goals independently. For purposes of this entry, focus is on providing an international education, specifically, to university-level criminal justice, criminology, and law students.

Contributions in this volume show us that international issues are being covered in criminal justice textbooks. It also appears that an increasing number of universities are including international criminal justice issues in their curriculum. Cordner *et.al.* (2000) found that about one third of the criminal justice programs at American universities offered some international or comparative courses. Beyond just course offerings, degrees in comparative or international criminal justice are being offered at the bachelor's (*e.g.*, John Jay College of Criminal Justice, City University of New York, New York, USA) and post-graduate (*e.g*, University of Wales, Bangor, United Kingdom) levels.

The growing academic interest in comparative and international criminal justice has been accompanied by professional journals devoted to the topic (*e.g.,*, *International Criminal Justice Review*, *International Journal of Comparative & Applied Criminal Justice*, *International Journal of Comparative Criminology*) and by textbooks specifically on comparative criminal justice (*e.g.*, ,Dammer, Fairchild and Albanese 2006; Ebbe 2000; Reichel 2005; Sheptycki & Wardak 2005; Terrill 2002). Clearly, the field of comparative/international criminology and criminal justice is gaining recognition and acceptance, yet, as with so many emerging fields, significant attention must be paid to justifying its existence. Following a brief review of the benefits derived from taking a comparative and international perspective, we return to the efforts at providing students with an international education regarding torture, international standards, and the rule of law.

Benefits of Comparative and International Perspectives

The terms *comparative* and *international* are related, yet distinct. Both are important and relevant to criminal justice, but for different reasons. Natarajan (2005) explains that international criminal justice is a broad term that covers crime and justice from a global perspective. It includes the topic of international crime (*e.g.*, genocide, war crimes, crimes against humanity), but also considers transnational crime (*e.g.*, money laundering, terrorism, trafficking in humans), human rights issues (*e.g.*, forced sterilization), and international justice efforts (*e.g.*, transnational cooperation in law enforcement and prosecution). Comparative criminal justice, on the other hand, considers similarities and differences in how countries attempt to maintain social order and accomplish justice (Dammer, Reichel, & He 2004). The focus is on how countries respond to domestic crime individually, but also how each country participates in a global response to international and transnational crime. In this sense, international criminal justice is the broader term that encompasses comparative criminal justice studies.

For present purposes the distinction between international and comparative criminal justice is important because of the perspective each hopes to accomplish. Specifically, a benefit of comparative and international studies is to help students replace the traditionally parochial view of the world with a global perspective. Doing so has always been important, but today it is essential. That is because, as *New York Times* columnist Thomas Friedman's book title declares, "the world is flat." By that, Friedman means the people of the world today are able to do business, communicate, entertain, or engage in almost any other activity, instantaneously with billions of others around the globe. Several technological (digital, especially) and political forces have converged, and that has produced a global playing field that allows for multiple forms of collaboration without regard to geography or distance, or soon, even language (Friedman 2005: 176).

Importantly, just as the world is flat for legitimate enterprises and lawful people, it is flat also for illegal endeavors and criminals. Efforts to contain illegal behavior in a flat world require that criminal justice practitioners move about on the playing field as easily as do the criminals. That skill is acquired, in part, by providing those practitioners with an international education that helps them understand: (1) similarities and differences in social control mechanisms at domestic and transnational levels, (2) how countries can work together effectively to combat "flat world crime," and (3) how one's own justice system might benefit from understanding how another country's system operates.

With the goals of an international education in mind, the professor returned to the classroom exercise that asked students in a comparative justice course their opinions about the use of torture as an interrogation technique. As explained at this chapter's start, three particular reasons were presented in class discussion for favoring the use of any means necessary, including torture, to obtain information from prisoners that might protect against a terrorist attack. Briefly, they were:

- torture allows the gathering of information not otherwise gotten;
- techniques known to be used did not rise to the level of torture; and
- an acceptable means given the desired end.

All three of those explanations are worthy of class time, but the last two seemed to be especially relevant for purposes of providing an international education to students in the comparative justice class. Specifically, the "doesn't rise to the level of torture" argument was chosen to discuss *international standards*. The "end justifies the means" explanation seemed appropriate for discussing the *rule of law*.

International Standards

When students were asked in Spring 2004 whether torture should be used to extract information from terrorist suspects, the examples of torture being given in media reports were of the "sleep deprivation," and "awkward and painful positions," type. This suggested that students may not be aware that the international community has actually identified standards to be used when confronted with questions such as "What constitutes torture?" It was determined that a review of such standards, with necessary background information, must be included in the course material.

When one thinks of international agreements in the broadest sense, one can include actions by some principal organs of the United Nations (General Assembly, Security Council, Economic and Social Council International Court of Justice) or United Nations functional commissions. For example, resolutions from the General Assembly relate to a wide variety of topics concerning the international community. Declarations emanating from the United Nations Commission on Human Rights are more specifically focused on human rights topics and those from the United Nations Commission on Crime Prevention and Criminal Justice deal specifically with criminal justice issues. A review of instruments from these sources results in many documents on issues ranging from the use of force and firearms by law enforcement officials to protection of prisoners against torture. The treaty especially relevant for current purposes is the *Convention against Torture and Other Cruel, Inhuman or Degrading Treatment or Punishment* (CAT).

The CAT considers torture to be "any act by which severe pain or suffering, whether physical or mental, is intentionally inflicted on a person for such purposes as obtaining from him or a third person information or a confession...". The CAT became effective in 1987 and was ratified by the United States in 1994. The Convention essentially bans torture under all circumstances and establishes the United Nations Committee against Torture to monitor convention compliance. Countries that have ratified the CAT are required to make torture illegal and to provide appropriate punishment for those engaging in torture. Many of the Committee against Torture's activities are directed toward claims of torture used as an interrogation technique rather than as punishment.

Using the CAT to exemplify an international standard for what constitutes torture is helpful but not without problems. For example, the CAT does not include examples of techniques that represent torture. That problem can be responded to (even if not resolved) by using some of the teaching aids mentioned later in this chapter. The point to make here is that it is possible to show that there are international standards regarding the use of torture as an interrogation technique. Therefore, students who express a favourable opinion about allowing the use of certain interrogation techniques simply because they do not reach the student's concept of torture is an untenable opinion. When international standards exist, especially when one's own country has agreed to them, individuals should be willing to defer to those standards rather than holding to personal opinions. (Although, admittedly, that argument can also make for interesting class discussion).

Rule of Law

The idea that saving innocent lives overrides a person's right not to be tortured has a certain appeal. However, neither international human rights law, nor U.S. law, has any exceptions to the prohibition against torture (Human Rights Watch 2004). And that point provides a good opportunity to present the topic of rule of law, again, with background.

The phrase "laws change but the Law must remain" is commonly used to express the concept of rule of law. That point reduces to the question of whether a country views its law, or its government, as supreme. Achieving rule of law requires a nation to first recognize the supremacy of certain fundamental values. Those values may have either secular or divine origin as long as they are understood to reflect basic and ultimate principles. After being recognized, the fundamental values must be reduced to written form. A country's constitution often accomplishes this task. Finally, the trek to rule of law requires a nation to provide procedures that hold its government to the tenets of this higher law. If citizens cannot challenge laws made by the country''s legislature or ruler, the concept of a higher law is lost. Similarly, if government officials find situations wherein they believe the law does not apply—and thereby effectively ignore it—the rule of law is absent.

When students (or anyone) favour the use of torture as an acceptable means to achieve a laudable end (*e.g.*, thwarting terrorism), are they rejecting the rule of law? An argument can certainly be made that they are, but it is not as easily accomplished as pointing to a document (such as the CAT) that expresses an international standard. The rule of law principle seems straightforward, no one is above the law; but persons wishing to avoid the constraints imposed by the rule of law may make claims the law is not what it appears or is not relevant in a particular situation. Providing students with an international education can help them make an informed decision regarding when, and by whom, the rule of law may be compromised.

Encouraging an International Perspective

Having decided that students in the comparative justice class would benefit from class time spent on international standards and rule of law—and believing the topic of torture for interrogation was an appropriate vehicle for that coverage—it was decided to have a Spring 2005 class respond to the same "favour or oppose" question asked of the Spring 2004 class. This time, however, lecture and class discussion on the topics of international standards and rule of law would precede the administering of the questionnaire. As seen in Table 1, students in the Spring 2005 class were less likely to favour the use of physical torture against terrorist suspects.

Table 1:

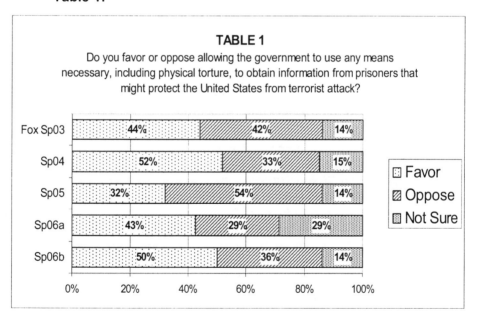

TABLE 1

Do you favor or oppose allowing the government to use any means necessary, including physical torture, to obtain information from prisoners that might protect the United States from terrorist attack?

	Favor	Oppose	Not Sure
Fox Sp03	44%	42%	14%
Sp04	52%	33%	15%
Sp05	32%	54%	14%
Sp06a	43%	29%	29%
Sp06b	50%	36%	14%

Importantly, however, that decrease in persons favouring, and increase in persons opposing, cannot be attributed solely (maybe, at all) to the class-time coverage of international standards and rule of law. As noted above, about one month after the Spring 2004 students responded to the poll question, the previously unverifiable allegations of former detainees, from Iraq or Afghanistan or in the detention camp at Guantánamo Bay, were substantiated. First in a report by Major-General Antonio Taguba that detailed incidents "of sadistic, blatant, and wanton criminal abuses" of detainees by American troops in an attempt to "set favourable conditions for subsequent interviews" (NBC News 2004). Then, most forcefully, when photographs appeared in media around the world showing Iraqis held at Abu Ghraib prison being subjected to abusive practices that many argued were examples of torture. It would be difficult to argue that the photographs from Abu Ghraib prison played no role, even a year later, in the decreased number of students who favored the use of torture.

Class discussion after the Spring 2005 poll suggested that many of the students truly believed there were international standards that made reasonably clear what acts constitute torture for interrogation—and that Americans had used such techniques at Abu Ghraib. However, some students held to the "end justifies means" argument and suggested (with reference to comments by officials in the Bush Administration, including the President himself) that extraordinary events required extraordinary measures. Obviously, the task of providing an international education was not yet complete.

Spring 2006

As this chapter was being prepared, the comparative justice class was being taught again. This time, several new pedagogical aids were used to bring the topics to life.

In January 2006, within a few weeks of the semester start, students in the comparative justice class were asked to respond to the same poll question asked of students in this class during Spring 2004 and Spring 2005. As always, the poll was taken via the class internet site. Table 1 (see Sp06a) shows that 43 percent of the students were in favour, 29 percent opposed, and 29 percent not sure. As the photos from Abu Ghraib fade in memory, it is not surprising that more students favoured the use of torture than had students in Spring 2005 (yet still fewer than in Spring 2004). It was, however, somewhat comforting that a rather large percentage of students were unsure of their position almost twice the number in preceding years. The classroom was set for coverage of international standards and the rule of law.

At the first class period after the poll was taken, the students discussed the results in class and were shown how students in their class and in previous semesters had answered. Responses to a query about reasons for favouring the use of torture centered on these arguments:

- whereas a few Americans may have engaged in acts that constituted torture of prisoners, the interrogation techniques officially authorized and more often used, do not rise to the level of torture (a "not really torture" argument);
- extreme crimes require extreme measures (an "end justifies the means" argument), and
- some crimes cannot be fought in traditional ways.

This last argument (put forward by one student but found appealing to several others during discussion), suggested that some crimes are peculiar enough that they cannot be responded to with standard techniques. The argument was a variation of the "end justifies the means" position, but its proponent cared little about the seriousness of the crime to which torture was responding. Instead, he argued that torture, as a non-standard technique, may be necessary for a crime like terrorism not because of the seriousness of the crime but because of the difficulty of preventing or responding to the crime. The first two arguments provided the base for class coverage of the topic and torture for interrogation.

The "not really torture" argument allowed coverage of international standards, and the "end justifies the means" allowed discussion of rule of law. Two specific items were used as pedagogical aids.

Two Pedagogical Aids

It is neither appropriate nor necessary to provide extended explanation of the two teaching aids used. The more important point is that it is possible to use an international education to affect student understanding of such topics as international standards and rule of law. Instead, the following discussion briefly notes how each was used, and how student understanding was increased through class coverage of the topic.

HRW website: *Human Rights Watch* has a very informative web site devoted to issues of torture (see Human Rights Watch 2004). Using the classroom's Internet access, students were shown the web page on a screen at the front of the class. With the help of the very cogent arguments and information provided at the web page, the class quickly read responses to such questions as "What is torture," "What laws prohibit torture," and "Shouldn't torture be permitted if it will save lives?"

Frontline, The Torture Question: On October 18, 2005, the program "The Torture Question" was aired on the Public Broadcasting Service program *Frontline*. The 90-minute program is available to watch online (see Public Broadcasting Service 2005). The documentary is quite powerful and includes photos from

Guantánamo Bay and Abu Ghraib as well as explaining how officials in the Bush administration struggled to create a legal framework that gave the President authority to aggressively interrogate enemy fighters in the war on terror. It provided excellent material for discussion of the rule of law.

Gauging Change

To gauge whether the course activities and/or discussion resulted in any change of position, students were asked to once again respond to the same "favor/oppose" question.[2] Of particular interest to the professor was whether fewer students took the "not sure" option as a result of class coverage of the topic. Another hope was that fewer students would select the "favor" response. However, students in this class are encouraged to express *their* supported opinion on topics rather than supporting what they perceive to be the professor's opinion. Table 1 (see Sp06b) shows that the course material was successful in reducing the number of students who were unsure of their position, but students moved, almost in equal number—away from the "not sure" response to both the "favor" and "oppose" responses.

After responding to the "favor/oppose" question, students were asked to respond to the following question:

Regardless of whether your opinion about the use of torture for interrogation changed since you were first asked the question, please explain briefly what information you believe was the most informative and potentially persuasive during our discussion of this topic. Why? Consider, (1) lecture, (2) class discussion, or (3) *The Torture Question* video.

Some of the interesting student responses (with spelling and grammar corrections made) include:

- [Student A] I still feel that if we have to do these things to be safe from others, then we should. I also feel that whether or not we do these things, the enemy will always continue to do them.

---

2 Students took the follow-up poll after spending two class periods covering the topic. Although the class website does not allow the professor to know how each student responded to poll questions, it does show who responded. For the follow-up poll, students who had not responded to the initial poll were blocked from accessing the follow-up poll. That meant the follow-up respondents consisted only of those who had responded the first time. However, not all students participated in the follow-up. Specifically, 28 students took the first poll and 22 responded to the follow-up.

- [Student B] I changed my mind because of the class discussion and the torture video. I think the government abuses their power.
- [Student C] Regardless of the method used, I strongly believed that in most cases the tool of torture is more often than not unsuccessful, resulting in wasted time and energy.
- [Student D] We are obviously getting some useful information that is helping us get the information we need. Otherwise, I seriously doubt we would continue our interrogation techniques.
- [Student E] When I first answered the question, I answered in favor of it. During class discussion I changed my position to opposing it because I began to question the effectiveness of torture.
- [Student F] I was in favor of using torture until someone in class said that they (the prisoners) are trained to die no matter what. So, why go and make the United States look like the bad guys. Unless we know for a fact that the torture will be beneficial we shouldn't do it.
- [Student G] I am opposed to using torture as a way to obtain information. The main thing that led me to this opinion was the class discussion. I believe that America is no better than any other country and if we don't want it done to our soldiers then we shouldn't do it to other countries.

It was especially interesting, and worrisome, that several of the students (*e.g.*, Students C, E, and F) indicated that they changed their opinion to be opposed to using torture because they didn't think it was effective at getting useful information—not because it was unethical, violated international standards, or was against U.S. law.

Conclusion

The search for a high profile subject that would provide an opportunity to cover issues of international standards and rule of law led to the topic of torture for interrogation. After several years of attempting to teach about these topics in a comparative justice course this author still searches for effective methods.

U.S. Supreme Court Justice Thurgood Marshall wrote in his opinion in a death penalty case (*Furman v. Geogria*) that an informed public generally would oppose the death penalty. This author takes a similar position regarding the use of torture for interrogation. Specifically, it is believed that students familiar with international standards regarding torture and with the concept of the rule of law, will not favor the use of torture to obtain from prisoners information that might prevent a terrorist attack. Also important, however, is that students gain an understanding and appreciation for the concepts themselves. In other words, an interest in providing an international education means that instructors should want students to know that international standards exist, to comprehend the value of the rule of law, and to recognize attempts to violate or circumvent either.

Accomplishing those goals is not easy. Certainly, it was frustrating to see that a greater proportion of students favored the use of torture for interrogation after we discussed international standards and rule of law in class than had favored it prior to discussion. However, it was gratifying that the proportion opposing it also increased. Also pleasing was the less parochial discussion in which the students engaged. After class coverage of international standards and rule of law, students—whether favouring or opposing the use of torture for interrogation—provided arguments that drew on those concept. As arguments were presented, students used the concepts to challenge the positions that others were taking or to support their own position.

This author will continue to incorporate international standards and rule of law into the comparative justice systems course because they are integral concepts when providing an international education. Even if positions are unchanged after class coverage of the concepts, it is hoped that the basis upon which arguments are built will be less parochial and that is another valuable objective of an international education.

References

Cordner, A., Dammer, H., & Horvath, F. (2000). A national survey of comparative criminal justice courses in universities in the United States. Journal of Criminal Justice Education, 11(2), 211-223.

Dammer, H. R., Fairchild, E., & Albanese, J. S. (2006). Comparative criminal justice systems (3rd ed.). Belmont, CA: Wadsworth/Thomson Learning.

Dammer, H. R., Reichel, P., & He, N. (2004). Comparing crime and justice. In P. L. Reichel (Ed.), Handbook of transnational crime & justice (pp. 20-42). Thousand Oaks, Calif.: Sage Publications.

Ebbe, O. N. I. (2000). Comparative and international criminal justice systems: Policing, judiciary, and corrections. Boston: Butterworth-Heinemann.

Ends, means and barbarity. (2003, January 11). The Economist, 18-20.

FOX News/Opinion Dynamics Poll. (2003, March 11-12). Do you favor or oppose...? Retrieved July 27, 2003, from www.pollingreport.com.

Friedman, T. L. (2005). The world is flat: A brief history of the twenty-first century. New York: Farrar, Straus and Giroux.

Human Rights Watch. (2004, June 1). The legal prohibition against torture. Retrieved January 22, 2006, from http://www.hrw.org/press/2001/11/ TortureQandA.htm.

Natarajan, M. (2005). International crime and justice: An introduction. In M. Natarajan (Ed.), Introduction to international criminal justice (pp. xv-xxiii). Boston: McGraw-Hill.

NBC News. (2004, May 4). U.S. Army report on Iraqi prisoner abuse. Retrieved January 20, 2006, from http://www.msnbc. msn.com/id/4894001/.

Office of the High Commissioner for Human Rights. (1984). Convention against torture and other cruel, inhuman or degrading treatment or punishment. Retrieved January 22, 2006, from http://www.unhchr.ch/tml/enu3/b/h_cat39.htm.

Priest, D., & Gellman, B. (2002, December 26). U.S. decries abuse but defends interrogations [Electronic version]. Retrieved June 1, 2003, from http://www.washingtonpost.com/ac2/wp-dyn/A37943-2002Dec25.

Public Broadcasting Service. (2005). The torture question. Retrieved February 5, 2006, from http://www.pbs.org/wgbh/ pages/frontline/torture/view/.

Reichel, P. L. (2005). Comparative criminal justice systems: A topical approach (4th ed.). Upper Saddle River, N.J.: Pearson Prentice Hall.

Sheptycki, J., & Wardak, A. (2005). Transnational & comparative criminology. London: GlassHouse Press.

Terrill, R. J. (2002). World criminal justice systems: A survey (5th ed.). Cincinnati, OH: Anderson Pub. Co.

New Ways of Teaching Students about International Criminal Justice

Michael Platzer[1]

Introduction

Teaching has changed greatly in the last decade. New, more realistic textbooks have been published[2]. Course materials are now available on sophisticated web sites and are downloadable. Libraries offer journals and entire books to students online[3]. E-

---

1 Dr. Michael Platzer served 34 years in the United Nations Secretariat in a variety of capacities, in Human Rights, Office of the Secretary-General, Department of Technical Cooperation, Habitat, United Nations Development Programme, Reconstruction and Development Support Unit and the United Nations Office on Drugs and Crime. In the last Office, he was Head of the Rule of Law Section and Criminal Justice Reform Unit. Dr. Platzer is currently involved with the Austrian United Nations Association and with the Academic Council for the United Nations System. He teaches the United Nations, Global Media and International Criminal Justice in Austria and Australia. His recent research has been on foreigners in prison, which he has carried out for the Austrian Ministry of Justice and the Institute of Criminology of the University of Vienna. He has republished in English, German, and Spanish, the United Nations and European Union recommendations on the treatment of foreigners in prison for the International Commission of Catholic Prison Pastoral Care and run workshops on this topic. Dr. Platzer has written articles on the Secretary-Generals of the United Nations, human rights, the rule of law, HIV/AIDS, development, the environment, maritime law, peacebuilding, ethnic minorities, as well as poetry and book reviews. His most recent effort has been the organization of a colloquium on "The United Nations and New Media" (Wels, Austria, 16 November 2007) and the new technologies that can be used for networking, research, human rights, peacebuilding, societal development, and communicating with youth. He has also written and produced two short films on prisoners' rights and victims' rights. He has received a Doctor of Law with specialization in International Affairs from the Cornell University and an M.A. from the Columbia University.
2 Cryer, R., An Introduction to International Criminal Law and Procedure, Cambridge, 2007; Arnold R., G.T-J.A. Knoops, Practice and Policies of Modern Peace Support Operations under International Law, Hotei Publishing, 2006; Reychler, L. and Paffenholz, T., Peacebuilding: A Field Guide, Lynne Riemer Publishers, 2001); Fulton, J.(ed.) Achieving Peace with Justice: Five Case Studies (Centre for Peace and Conflict Studies, Sydney 2001; Krasno, J. (ed.) The United Nations: Confronting the Challenges of a Global Society, Lynne Riemer, Boulder, Colorado, 2003.
3 ASIL Guide To Electronic Resources for International Law: International Criminal Law http://www.asil.org/resource/crim 1.htm; LLRX.com:International Criminal Law http://www,llrx.com/features/int_crim.htm; SOSIG: International Criminal Law and War Crimes; WORLDLII: International Criminal Law, http://www.worldlii.org/catalog; Electronic Information System for International Law (EISIL), http:www.eisil.org; HeinOnLine-full text journal articles; AGIS Plus Text; Lexis- International Law Section; Index to Foreign Legal Periodicals; Foreign and International Law Resources: An Annotated Guide to Web Sites

learning is now provided by the most prestigious universities, and even by the United Nations[4]. Students need hardly even come to a classroom. Moreover, today's students are more demanding, as fee paying is much more common and tuition at private universities has greatly increased. Good lectures are no longer enough. The *PowerPoint* presentations and lecturers' notes are routinely posted on the class web sites. Lectures are videotaped and streamed. Exams can be written electronically, and teacher feedback takes place online. Multimedia stimulus education – short films, the discussion of current cases, popular movies, the preparation of briefs, moot courts, legal clinics, and role playing – have been highly developed in North America and the Antipodes. As Chris Eskridge has argued, criminal justice education must "stay ahead of the curve", develop a spirit of inquiry, and promote an interdisciplinary understanding of the social, psychological, philosophic, economic, behavioural, historical, legal, and political aspects of crime, deviance and justice[5].

Learning by Mistakes

Bond University (Robina, Queensland, Australia) prides itself on the practical, hands-on education it provides. In addition to small class sizes with world-renowned criminologists, forensic scientists, and practitioners, there are visits to prisons, courtrooms, police stations, and forensic laboratories, as well as internships in a variety of criminal justice, victim support, hospital, and offender programs. The students have even worked with risk assessment teams as part of the profiling course.

However, the most innovative course, for which university Professor Paul Wilson[6] has received the prestigious *Carrick*

Around the World, http://www.law.Harvard.edu/library/services/research/guides; United States Institute of Peace, (http://www.usip.org, International Peace Academy, http://www.ipacademy.org, International Crisis Group, http://www. crisisgroup.org.
4 United Nations Institute for Training and Research (UNITAR, Geneva, Switzerland) through its Programme of Correspondence Instruction in Peacekeeping Operations (POCI) provides distance learning to peacekeepers, potential peacekeepers, police and humanitarian workers worldwide through e-learning, audio and video materials, and online interaction with course authors, http://www/unitarpoci.org.
5 Chris Eskridge, The impact of criminal justice education on the socio-political-economic climate of transitional and developing nations, Journal of Criminal Justice Education, Vol. 14 (1), Spring 2003:105–118.
6 Paul Wilson was the Director of Research at the Australian Institute of Criminology in Canberra. He has authored or co-authored 32 books, including the textbook, *The Australian Criminal Justice System*. He has been a Visiting Professor at the University of California (USA), Rutgers University (New Jersey, USA) and Simon Fraser University in British Columbia (Vancouver, Canada).

Teaching Award is a multi-sectoral learning experience about Miscarriages of Justice. The course examines causes of miscarriages of justice, institutions for correcting them, and mechanisms for preventing them or minimizing their incidence. Rather than looking from a top-down, positive-law approach about how things should be, Paul Wilson looks at the mistakes.

This makes the course more realistic and retains the students' interest. The course involves team-based examinations of specific cases where verdicts may have been "unsafe". Students look into police investigative culture and practices; forensic evidence including DNA testing; the role of the media in both generating and correcting miscarriages; the significance of the rules in respect of the admissibility and use of potentially unreliable evidence; the need for good legal representation; the importance of competence and fairness in prosecutorial agencies and the judiciary; the appeal structure and pardoning system; and the development of innocence projects and special review commissions.

Particular attention is paid to high-profile cases that have undermined confidence in the criminal justice system. Judges, prosecutors, police investigators, defence attorneys, defendants, and released prisoners talk with the students. In the end, the students have a excellent understanding of the criminal justice system as a whole. Moreover, they can become more effective in their career upon leaving university. The course is consistently highly valued by students from different faculties (Law, Criminology, Public Health). Professor Wilson is a very popular and excellent teacher; Moreover, the approach is also replicable and provides an excellent way of learning how criminal justice works in the real world.

Global Criminology – Learning from the Aborigines

Global Criminology at Bond University is taught by Robyn Lincoln, who is an expert on aboriginal justice.[7] She takes students out of their comfort zone by showing them that crime and criminal justice problems are being tackled under different systems in different parts of the world often better than under the Commonwealth

7 Robyn Lincoln has lectured at Bond University since 1994 as well as at other universities in Queensland (University of Queensland, Queensland University of Technology, Griffith). She conducted research at Simon Fraser University in Vancouver (British Columbia, Canada) and Rutgers University (New Jersey, USA). Her projects have focused on the treatment of marginalized groups within the criminal justice system, runaway and homeless youth, violence in Aboriginal communities, peer influences on juvenile offending, fraud by medical practitioners, and the careers of white collar offenders. She was Managing Editor of the Journal of Sociology; Editor of *The Australian Journal of Social Issues*, and Senior Editor at the Aboriginal Studies Press in Canberra for five years.

model. Global Criminology takes a critical and comparative look at the various justice systems throughout the world and provides students with a comparison to their own systems. It is designed for those students interested in criminology, international relations, journalism, business, law, forensic psychology, and other related disciplines to provide an understanding of what is believed to work in theory and practice, in specific social and cultural contexts. It is not true that even the best-made laws and criminal justice systems will work in all countries and stages of development. Often there is less crime and deviance under less sophisticated systems of justice.

The course also deals with emerging crime topics such as human trafficking, drug networks, and terrorism, as well as non-traditional forms of justice and reconciliation. The course covers concepts such as punishment, prevalence of specific types of crime in certain societies, and the relevance of social and political structures in both the committing of crime and the application of justice. On completion of this subject, students are expected to be able to demonstrate an appreciation of the breadth of issues covered in the contemporary criminological literature as well as have an understanding of aboriginal justice in Australia. Extensive use of films and non-judgmental classroom discussions are favoured by Dr. Lincoln.

The Media as a Major Component of Criminal Justice

The other subject which Robyn Lincoln teaches is Media and Crime. She believes the media plays an integral role in criminal justice processes and yet is often overlooked in criminal justice studies. For her, the media as social institutions are just as imperative to understand as police, courts, and prisons in justice systems. The course examines the way journalists and media organisations report and construct news about crime and criminal justice, compared to the actual reality and statistics. It covers the relationships between police and journalists; media coverage of the courts; laws relating to contempt and defamation; representations of prisons and prisoners; investigative reporting; and the psychological and sociological issues relating to the effects of high-profile crime reporting. The course also analyses how particular groups or specific crime categories are dealt with by the mass media. Attention is paid to the future of crime journalism in an era of media concentration and globalisation, and to changes that may result from new technologies (Internet, e-mail, video games). How high-profile crime stories, popular films, TV shows, detective novels, docudramas, and the new trend of reality police and courtroom shows influence public perceptions is also examined. Students are asked to be self-critical as consumers of crime media and to engage in lively class discussion on their views about the presentation of crime cases in the media.

Diverse Notions of Prevention and Control of Crime

Professor Duncan Chappell teaches Criminal Justice: Developments in Prevention and Control at the University of Sydney[8]. His aim is to examine contemporary debates in criminal justice policy, the shifting notions of responsibility for crime, crime control and crime prevention, and the influences on the current crime control agenda. He raises as many questions regarding the commonsense assumptions about crime as well as the different ways in which one can understand the term "criminal justice" rather than providing straight answers. He raises issues about restorative justice in regard to due process, as an alternative to conventional criminal justice, and the context for which restorative justice is best suited. What are the contemporary criminal justice practices that seem to have a primary concern with managing risk? What is actuarial justice? What is the relationship between criminal justice and culture? What renders some criminal justice policies desirable and others unthinkable? Which offenders are more likely to be diverted? When can compulsory treatment be justified in criminal justice? What are the implications of the increased resort to private

---

8 Professor Chappell was a Research Fellow at the United Nations Interregional Crime and Justice Institute (UNICRI, Italy), 1994-1995. He wrote on *The Role, Preparation and Performance of Civilian Police in United Nations Peacekeeping Operations* for the International Centre for Criminal Law Review Reform and Criminal Justice Policy, Vancouver (British Columbia, Canada), which was coauthored with John Evans and published by the Austrian Center for Peace Studies, Stadtschlaining. He was Chair of the Commonwealth Observer Mission to South Africa (COMSA) in 1992. Dr. Chappell was the Director of the Australian Institute of Criminology for many years. In addition to being a faculty member at the University of Sydney, he has taught at the School of Criminal Justice at the State University of New York at Albany (USA). Professor Chappell has published widely on a range of crime and criminal justice issues, His publications include *The Police and Public in Australia and New Zealand* (with Paul Wilson), *Australian Policing Contemporary Perspectives* (with Paul Wilson), *The Australian Criminal Justice System* (with Paul Wilson), and *Preventing and Responding to Violence at Work*, published by the ILO. Professor Chappell was President (2001–2006) of the New South Wales Mental Health Tribunal, member of the New South Wales Law Reform Commission (2002–2006), member of the Australian Law Reform Commission (1978–1979), Deputy President of the Australian Federal Administrative Appeals Tribunal (1996–2001), Chair of a National Committee on Violence, appointed by the Prime Minister (1987–1990), Commissioner in Charge of a reference on Sentencing, and member of the Commonwealth Secretarial Arbitral Tribunal based in London (United Kingdom, 2001–2005). He was also Director of Battelle Memorial Institute's Law and Justice Study Centre in Seattle, Washington (USA).

security, and for whom? What are the implications for community engagement in crime control and prevention? To what extent is crime an urban problem? Is there a consensus as to what constitutes crime prevention? What are some of the key ethical issues that arise in situational crime prevention? How have recent technologies such as closed-circuit television (CCTV) changed the regulation of space? He presents the different models of crime prevention, encourages critical analysis, and pushes inter-disciplinary research. Each student is expected to give a verbal presentation on a topic related to the weekly themes, such as social exclusion, no space for young people, violence against women, criminal justice privatisation, and private dispute resolution. Students must also submit a paper of 2,500 words which reviews the key literature and identifies the major debates in their chosen topic.

Mental Illness and the Criminal Justice System

The other course developed by Professor Duncan Chappell deals with mental illness and the criminal justice system. A significant proportion of the persons who come into contact with the criminal justice system suffer from some form of mental illness, retardation, or mental disorder, often in association with alcohol/drug abuse, "unemployability", discrimination, homelessness, and material deprivation. Many such persons now find their way into prisons because of the lack of treatment options for the mentally ill in the community, resulting in the correctional system becoming a substitute for the large closed mental hospitals. Duncan Chappell has established an innovative course at the University of Sydney Faculty of Law together with the School of Public Health for practitioners in this area and persons concerned about this growing phenomenon.

Psychiatrists, judges, and prison managers are brought into the classroom. The difficult areas of mental health law and practice, contemporary diagnosis and treatment options, the types of medications provided, involuntary treatment and review mechanisms, electroconvulsive therapy, guardianship, responsibilities of medical officers, and the different approaches in Australia, the United Kingdom, and Europe are covered in the course. The overlapping issues of intellectual disability and victimization in the criminal justice system are also discussed. The draft of a reform proposal is examined at the end of the course. Students are required to complete a research paper of 4,500 words on a topic of their choice to be agreed with the teacher, in addition to a two-hour open book examination. It is a popular course because it deals with real issues and problems in the criminal justice system[9].

International Criminal Law through Case Studies

International criminal law is taught by Eric Colvin and Jodie O'Leary at Bond University[10]. Team teaching and involvement of guest lecturers are becoming the norm. The courses cover contemporary issues relating to crimes of aggression, war crimes, and crimes against humanity, the special tribunals on Rwanda and Yugoslavia and the International Criminal Court, the cases of Slobodan Milosevic, Saddam Hussein and Charles Taylor, Truth and Reconciliation Commissions, responses to international problems such as terrorism, people smuggling and money laundering, and the relationship between international and domestic criminal jurisdiction/prosecution. The complicated dilemmas about granting amnesties, genocide and sovereignty, following orders and criminal liability, terrorism control and civil liberties, as well as the practical problems of the investigation, prosecution, and punishment of international crimes are discussed in the class. Films such as *Out of the Ashes – the Founding of the United Nations*, describing the importance that the Holocaust has had on the development of the United Nations and international law, as well as films on the responsibility to protect, Rwanda, Darfur, the Congo, and United Nations peacekeeping are in the library for students to view and to inform classroom discussions. Students must select a particular topic (with approval) for a research paper (7,000 words) and lead a discussion in the classroom on their research paper.

International Conflict Resolution

Dr. Wendy Lambourne[11] of the Centre for Peace and Conflict Studies[12], teaches The United Nations and International Conflict

---

9 See further: United Nations Principles for the Protection of Persons with Mental Illness and for the Improvement of Mental Health Care (General Assembly resolution 46/119 of 17 December 1991, Annex), available at: http://www.unhchr.ch/html/menu3/b/68.htm).

10 Assistant Professor Jodie O'Leary's research interests are transitional justice, international criminal law, humanitarian law, and sentencing. She has worked at Legal Aid, Queensland, dealing with juvenile offenders and at a Community Legal Centre in East Timor.

11 Dr Wendy Lambourne is the author of the section "Peacekeeping and Peacebuilding" in the report *Australia and the United Nations,* published by the United Nations Association of Australia. She writes on peace, conflict, and development, reconciliation as a political process, and has edited a book on *National and International Perspectives on Violence against Women.*

Resolution at the University of Sydney. She uses Kofi Annan's report "In Larger Freedom" – freedom from want, freedom from fear, and freedom to live in dignity – as the structure for examining past United Nations operations. She looks at the gap between mandates, resources, and political will; national interest versus collective security; the ethical, political, and legal dilemmas of balancing respect for state sovereignty with protection of human rights and maintenance of peace and security; the relationship between the United States and the United Nations; the perceived dilemma of peace versus justice in conflict settlements; questions of the neutrality and impartiality of the United Nations; manipulation of information and intelligence to serve political and strategic interests; a geopolitical analysis of the functioning of the United Nations Security Council; as well as the measurement of "success" of United Nations peacekeeping. In addition to examining the role of the media in determining the political will of member states to act, her class studies the logistical and operational challenges of peacekeeping, such as the use of force and training, and the composition of peacekeeping forces; the cooperation and coordination between civilians and military, the United Nations and non-governmental organizations and among the various parts of the United Nations; and the need for reform of the structure and functioning of United Nations peace operations.

The students discuss United Nations intervention as a form of neo-imperialism and imposition of the Western democratic model, the relationship between the United Nations and regional organizations and interventions; and the United Nations emphasis on consensus and "soft law" and their implications for enforceability of United Nations decisions. The course deals with current crises such as Darfur and Iraq and is highly valued for its *realpolitik* analysis.

---

12 The Director of the Centre of Peace and Conflict Studies is Jake Lynch who has developed the concept of peace journalism (the author has used his textbook in his other course on Global Media), and teaches a course "Conflict-Resolving Media" with actual examples. Dr. Frank Hutchinson teaches a unique course on "Peace and the Environment" which brings together hitherto separate disciplines with guest lecturers concerned with environmental issues and the origins of conflict. Dr. Lynda-Ann Blanchard is the convener of a course "Non-Violence and Social Change" which involves training in non-violent intervention by Peace Brigades International – Australians protecting human rights defenders in conflict zones. The Centre is also promoting the realization of a United Nations Emergency Peace Service, a stand-by force of 15,000 personnel including civilian police, military, judicial experts, and healthcare professionals. It also cooperates with AusCare (Multicultural Home & Community Services) in training humanitarian protection officers who are assigned to the United Nations agencies operating in crisis regions.

The author has taught "Concepts in Global Governance - the United Nations" for two years at Bond University. He has learned that, in order to get across the basic principles of the United Nations Charter, the Universal Declaration of Human Rights, international humanitarian law, the responsibility to protect, the Convention on the Rights of the Child, and the United Nations crime prevention and criminal justice standards and norms, these must be made real by examining concrete situations and working backwards to the principles.

Students are concerned about injustice in the world and what can be done about it. They expect the United Nations to intervene and establish peace, justice, and the rule of law. Therefore, the author has incorporated messy cases to be studied – sometimes hypothetical, sometimes real situations (the intractable ethnic conflict in Darfur, the violent break up of Yugoslavia) – involving civil war, massive human rights violations, terrorist acts, irregular combatants, child soldiers, and a United Nations peacekeeping operation.

The students are asked to prepare a Security Council resolution and design a United Nations operation comprising peacekeepers, civilian police, human rights officers , and child protection officers, with appropriate terms of reference. The students are assigned, at the beginning of the course, to take on the roles of a representative from one of the Permanent Five Security Council Members, a traditional troop-contributing country, one of major financial contributors, the recipient country (the country in crisis), neighbouring countries, as well as countries representing different regions and with ideological positions on sovereignty and the responsibility to protect. (Usually the current Security Council members are representative enough; however, one wants to ensure a vibrant discussion).

Without much teacher assistance, what quickly becomes evident to the students is the difficulty of designing an intervention to overthrow a murderous tyrant or to finance a mission in a failed state. Historical models of the United Nations Security Councils have also been useful to see if alternative strategies and operations might have been viable. In all the case studies that have been set, the discussions have been lively and the insights gained long-lasting.

Country X is divided into a northern, predominantly Muslim area and an equally large southern region, dominated by Christians. The federal government is weak and is trying to hold together the country through the military. Widespread human rights violations have occurred and women are discriminated against under the Shari'a law in effect. The southern Christian Liberation Army (CLA) is attacking government police stations and Muslim shopkeepers in the south, saying their people are being oppressed. In the north, the Christians are being harassed by their Muslim neighbors. The CLA has resorted to terrorist attacks not only in neighboring countries but also in Muslim countries believed to be supporting country X. They have also threatened to blow up the *Petronas* twin towers in Malaysia, as well as public buildings in China, Japan, Europe, and the USA if the human rights violations and their demands for independence are not brought formally before the United Nations. Country X borders with country Y which is Muslim and country Z which is Christian. Country Y has threatened to invade country X if order is not established in country X. Country X is prepared to receive a United Nations mission under certain conditions. Several countries are prepared to consider humanitarian intervention on the side of the Christians. Others are not ready to violate the sovereignty of country X and there is no great enthusiasm for a large-scale peacekeeping operation among the traditional troop contributors or large donors. The Secretary-General is ready to offer his good offices and send a fact-finding mission. The task is to design a multi-component United Nations mission comprising peacekeepers, police, mediators, human rights officers, child protection officers, election officers, and criminal justice personnel (law reformers, judges, penal officers).

If there are 20–30 students in the class, the Security Council model is usually appropriate, taking the current membership plus the Secretary-General, a representative of the Organization of the Islamic Conference, country Y, and country Z. Depending on how many students remain, usually representatives of troop-contributing countries (Argentina, Brazil, India, Nigeria, Pakistan, Nigeria) and donors (Germany, Japan) can be added. If there are still students who remain, an equal number of countries who advocate the "responsibility to protect" such as Canada and those who are reluctant to launch humanitarian intervention (*i.e.,* Cuba) can be added. Students are reminded to stay close to their "chosen" countries' position in the United Nations.

It quickly becomes apparent how difficult it is to achieve a consensus and to launch a mission with agreed terms of reference (particularly if China and the United States remain true to their usual positions). Discussions have usually been lively about "peace *versus* justice", rights of secession, responsibility to protect, terrorism prevention, rights of victims, ethnic/religious conflicts, rule of law in a lawless state, abuse of power, tyrannical majorities, and the obligations of the international community. The students should concentrate on what types of assistance might be most useful – peacekeepers, police, election officers, refugee officials (for displaced persons), human rights officers, child protection officers, civil affairs/political officers, administrative/logistics officers, development specialists, forensic specialists/major crime investigators, and criminal justice personnel (law reform lawyers, judges, and penal officers).

If the discussions become stalemated, one can add new developments which might stimulate Security Council action: documented massacres in villages in the south, widespread rape and ethnic cleansing in border regions, the assassination of the prime minister of country X, the discovery of oil, the invasion of country X by country Z, the bombing of the *Petronas* towers or public buildings in China and Japan, or use of gas, biological weapons, missiles, or weapons of mass destruction by one of the parties. The action appropriate to each of the new developments should be discussed in light of United Nations principles as they have evolved in recent years. The readiness to intervene may become greater as the atrocities reach the international media and the country stumbles into civil war and lawlessness. Taking the authorizations of recent United Nations missions – to deal with war in former Yugoslavia, Sudan, Somalia, and the Congo – into account, the students are expected to suggest the manpower and resource requirements for both peace keeping and peacebuilding in country X, focusing particularly on law and order.

At this point, the homework assignment is to prepare the Secretary-General's proposal for the mission, including the types of personnel he would be seeking (the order of magnitude) and the justification. Students are graded for their accurate representation of their countries' positions (the written opening speech in the model Security Council), their participation in the Council's deliberations, and their efforts in drafting an acceptable resolution. Of course, such a scenario can be discussed over several sessions. However, a two-hour model Security Council as described in the previous paragraphs is usually sufficient plus a subsequent one hour to analyze any resolution that may have emerged, as well as the Secretary-General's proposals viewed against existing United Nations principles and recent authorizations to see how realistic the students' proposals might be.

In this situation, the student is asked to imagine him/herself as a civilian police officer (or a human rights officer) as part of a United Nations operation, who is expected to deal with grievous violation of human rights on the spot. A trainer's Guide for Child Protection Training for United Nations Peace Operations Personnel, prepared by the UNICEF, the Office of the Special Representative for Children and Armed Conflict, Save the Children (Sweden), and the Department of Peacekeeping Operations has a number of good examples ranging from encountering child soldiers, sexual exploitation of girls, and children involved in illicit activities.

The manual contains relevant normative instruments and standards as well as outlining the expected/encouraged behavior of United Nations personnel. The author has used two suggested activities in courses at the Austrian Study Center for Peace and Conflict Resolution. The first, a police advisor, is confronted with the problem of 30,000 child soldiers (many preferring to remain in illegal gangs) and is asked to propose realistic strategies to deal with young people who have been involved in the fighting forces (who cannot go home because they have committed terrible crimes in their own communities).

The second suggested activity that has been used successfully involves a civilian police officer stationed at the police headquarters of the national police force of a country emerging from a devastating civil war. Most of the top posts in the police force have gone to loyal ex-fighters from the faction that brought the President to power. They have little understanding of international policing practices and standards.

During the first visit to the headquarters (HQ), the United Nations police officer is given a tour and sees two boys, aged 12 and 14, held with 14 adults in a small cell. The boys say they were picked up for making fun of a drunken soldier, were beaten, and then made to stand with 25-liter buckets full of water on their heads for hours at a time. The detaining officers have told them that they will be charged with treason. The United Nations officer also notices that two of the young officers guarding the entrance to the HQ are children and both are armed (the peace agreement only allows for adults to be trained and retained in the new Armed Forces; no one else is to carry arms). The United Nations officer tries to raise his concerns about the boys in the cells, but the police chief tells him they are hardened juvenile offenders and suspected of killing an old woman in the course of a robbery. There is no juvenile court or judge in the country; nor are there facilities for detaining juveniles separately. What issues are there to consider? Realistically, what steps can the United Nations officer take? What issues can he include in his report to his superiors? These questions could be considered by the class in an open discussion or it could be a homework assignment examining the Optional Protocol to the United Nations Convention on the Rights of the Child and other relevant normative instruments and standards. Moreover, the Geneva Conventions should not be forgotten.

This case study is an excellent example of a situation where little can be done directly (as the facts of the boys' previous criminal career are not clear). There are no local institutions that the police officer can refer the boys to, and the mandate of the officer is limited to training and advising. Nonetheless, he can make specific medium-term and long-term recommendations.

Case Study 3: Darfur

The horrific situation in Darfur has been used several times for classroom discussion. On different occasions, the films, *Darfur Diaries*, *The Lost Boys of Sudan*, and *Soldier Child* (as well as *Hotel Rwanda*) have been shown and the class has subsequently discussed notions of Genocide, Responsibility to Protect, and what the United Nations can do.[13] They have examined the succession of actual resolutions pertaining to peace in Sudan and the crisis in the Darfur region as well as the problems of obtaining agreement in the Security Council.

The students have re-enacted a model Security Council, followed closely the efforts of the Secretary General, and drafted their own resolution. They have noted the difficulty of delivering even humanitarian assistance and that a harsh critique of the host government can jeopardize any expanded United Nations operation. The worst crimes imaginable – murder, rape, robbery, destruction of homes – are being committed with seeming impunity. Discussions have focused on granting immunity in order to obtain a cessation of hostilities, the difficulty of capturing and extraditing war criminals, and the track record of the International Criminal Court, the Hague Tribunal, the Rwanda Tribunal, and the Sierra Leone court. The international instruments that prohibit crimes against humanity and the obligations to collaborate, extradite, and prosecute such transnational criminals were reviewed. Classroom discussions quickly led to questions about what can be done in cases such as those (*e.g.*, in Myanmar (Burma) and Zimbabwe). Excellent movies are available from the organization Witness,

---

13 The author has produced two films on prisoners' rights and victims' rights which have been used for stimulating classroom discussions at the University of Vienna, Bond University, and the Austrian Study Center for Peace Studies, downloadable from the website www.two handsfree.org.

Human Rights in Burma and *A Duty to Protect* with discussion guidelines.

Case Study 4: Torture and Prevention of Terrorism

In order to ensure a balance of perspective, two classes are devoted to the Abu Ghraib (Iraq), viewing the films *Ghosts of Abu Ghraib* and the extraordinary rendition film, *Outlawed*, and to discussing Guantánamo , the secret detention facilities and torture as practiced by the United States, as well as the violation of relevant international laws. It is queried whether in times of terrorism, human rights protection measures can be loosened. It is interesting that in all the classes that the author has taught, there is initially a feeling that security has priority. However, when the students are asked to judge whether 200 persons dying in an exploded airplane is really worse than 200 innocents dying when a missile, directed at a supposed military target, explodes in a settlement, the response is not as categorical. Some students have an understanding of the denial of basic social and economic rights and the systemic violations of human rights being linked to terrorism.[14] Poverty, after all, is the basic issue in the first three cases above. Without sufficient resources, a basic system of justice – courtrooms, paid judges, humane prisons, and alternatives to prison – cannot be implemented. The issue of rampaging youth gangs with no detention facilities or functional juvenile justice system is focused on. The denial of basic rights, whether political or economic, leads to the only redress open to the oppressed – further violence[15]. This spiral of violence can be stopped only if there are adequate protections for minorities, a rule of law, and democracy. However, often, dictators and tyrants are supported so as to keep order and stability in a region or for more overt political reasons (to combat their "terrorists").

Learning by Doing

Practical seminars have been running for two years at the Karl Franzens-Universität in Graz Austria together with the two prisons

---

14 Two other excellent courses, Peace and Environment, taught by Dr Frank Hutchinson and Conflict-Resolving Media, taught by Professor Jake Lynch (author of *Peace Journalism*) are available at the University of Sydney, Centre for Peace and Conflict Studies.
15 Mahnood Mamdani, *When Victims Become Killers: Colonialism, Nativism, and the Genocide in Rwanda*, Princeton University Press, 2001.

in Graz[16]. Over four semesters, law students have studied the penal systems, the rights of prisoners, and "experienced" the actual reality through direct discussions with prisoners and the wardens. They subsequently prepared a brochure and a web page for dependents and anyone interested in the prison regulations and practice, with answers to frequently asked questions[17]. The prison administration organized an "open house" for 300 students who had been unable to take part in the course. The students appreciated the direct experience with the prison system (which is rare in Austria). The prisoners appreciated the contacts with the outside world. The families of the prisoners were grateful for the practical information. The web site was given an award and the Ministry of Justice would like to expand such information to other prisons in Austria[18]. It is also hoped that such practical courses might be expanded to other law schools.

Conclusion

At the end of my courses at the Bond University in Australia, I received the teacher evaluations. What I particularly valued were the comments: "allowed detailed discussions...encouraged debate and student input....letting us get involved in having conversations about the subject...loved everything, especially the controversial movies... extra-curricular assignments...prompted us to find extra information".

If the larger political and moral issues are not discussed, few students will feel that learning international criminal justice standards will seem real or meaningful. This important expanding field of justice must be contextualized so that the students may make realistic judgments as to whether to pursue careers in this field. Working on concrete situations will also make them more useful practitioners when they begin to work in international organizations, non-governmental organizations, or national institutions concerned with an aspect of transnational criminal justice.

---

16 Rechtsambulanz in Strafvollzug, Strafrechtliches Risikomanagement, Internationales and Europastrafrecht, Institut für Strafrecht, Strafrecht, Strafprozessrecht und Kriminologie, www.uni-graz.at
17 Richard Soyer and Silvia Hauser, Rechtsambulanz in der Justizanstalt Graz Karlau, (in:) *Österreichische Juristenkommission. Kritik und Fortschritt im Rechtsstaat*, Vol. 28 (2007):95.
18 A new course is being offered by the University of Vienna, School of Law on "Violence in Prison" which involves student interviews with prisoners in four Vienna prisons. For further information, contact ireen.friedrich@univie.ac.at

John Jay's Bachelor's Degree in International Criminal Justice

Mangai Natarajan[1]

Introduction

As in many universities, the existing criminal justice and criminology programs at John Jay College offer courses on comparative criminology and criminal justice and the many instructors teaching general courses in the area do make an effort to provide cross-cultural examples. However, comparative criminal justice or criminology is not the same as international criminal justice. This encompasses comparative studies but it covers a much broader set of topics:

- International crimes including genocide, war crimes and crimes against humanity such as terrorism, murder, extermination, enslavement, deportation or forcible transfer of population, imprisonment or other severe deprivation of physical liberty, torture, rape, sexual slavery, enforced prostitution, forced pregnancy, enforced sterilization, sexual violence, persecution, enforced disappearance of persons, apartheid, other inhumane acts;
- Transnational crimes including trafficking in humans and commodities such as drugs, arts, *etc.*, money laundering, computer hacking, *etc.*;
- Conventional crimes such as core crimes (homicide, rape, robbery, aggravated assault; burglary, larceny-theft, motor vehicle theft and arson) at the national level (*i.e.*, U.S. index crimes);

---

1 Mangai Natarajan is a professor in the Dept. of Sociology, John Jay College of Criminal Justice. She has an MA in Criminology and a Post graduate diploma in Indo-Japanese Studies (University of Madras, India) and obtained her Ph.D. in Criminal Justice from Rutgers University, USA in 1991. She is an active policy-oriented researcher who has published widely in three areas: drug trafficking; women police and domestic violence. Her latest article on "Understanding the Structure of a Large Heroin Distribution Network" uses wiretap data collected in New York and is awaiting publication in the Journal of Quantitative Criminology. Dr. Natarajan is the founding coordinator of the International Criminal Justice Major at John Jay College, one of the fast growing and popular majors at John Jay. She recently published a text for use in the major titled "International Crime and Justice" (McGraw-Hill 2005), consisting of 50 short chapters that she commissioned from national experts.

- Human rights issues at local, national and international level including treatment of women and children, atrocities, torture and legal rights of illegal immigrants;
- International criminal law and international relations;
- International law enforcement and criminal justice;
- Rules of procedure and evidence of the International Criminal Court;
- The role of the United Nations and other international agencies in preventing crime and establishing criminal justice standards.

International Criminal Justice (ICJ) education therefore is geared to providing knowledge on a wide range of criminal justice related topics from a global perspective. It is not confined solely to global issues. However, since to be effective it must make benchmark reference to local criminal justice. In summary, ICJ education can be characterized as providing a vehicle to understand both local and international aspects of crime and ways to control them.

The ICJ major at John Jay College kicked off with just few students in January 2001. Currently, more than 300 students are enrolled, making it one of the fastest-growing and popular undergraduate majors at the college. At the College, the major has been defined as interdisciplinary and three departments (Sociology, Law and Police Science, and Government) have joint responsibility for the program. The coordinator for the major assumes the position for three to five years. The "newness" of the field demands a great deal in terms of curriculum and of the preparation of students for graduate studies and careers in international criminal justice. These demands are discussed in this paper together with recommendations for the future, both short and long term.

ICJ Curriculum

Though ICJ students can take courses from a wide selection of those offered at John Jay College, eleven of the courses were created specifically for the major. Of these, two (Introduction to International Criminal Justice and Capstone Seminar in International Criminal Justice) are specifically geared to International Criminal Justice. Consistent with most other majors in the College, the major was fixed at 36 credits for a B.A. degree. The program covers all the necessary courses including core courses, foundation courses, skills courses, specialization in global and regional studies and a capstone course together with an internship. The internship is an elective (See for details John Jay College Undergraduate Bulletin 2005). Students are also encouraged to participate in study abroad programs.

The required *core* of the ICJ major consists of 3 courses (9 credits): -Introduction to International Criminal Justice; Comparative Criminal Justice Systems and Global Economic Development and Crime. These courses provide the framework for understanding crime and criminal justice systems within a global context. They introduce students to the major components of the criminal justice system and to the field of international criminal justice. They provide a basic understanding of comparative approaches to criminal justice systems and of economic concepts as they relate to the international context.

The *foundation* courses consist of 9 credits that provide students with both a theoretical and practical understanding of the issues and methods involved in the study of international criminal justice. These courses come from a variety of disciplines (Sociology, Anthropology, Law and Police Science, *etc.*) and are intended to expose students to the myriad of issues regarding crime and criminal justice from an international perspective.

The *skills* courses are designed to provide students with the opportunity to develop and improve their skills in a variety of areas, including computers and their role in criminal justice operations, research and statistics, conflict resolution and a foreign language. As regards the foreign language, students are encouraged to take a language at a level beyond the College's general education foreign language requirement. This means that students will achieve some level of proficiency in a second or third language. The computer courses include crime mapping (at an introductory level) for which there is a growing demand in the criminal justice field and in research. Though students only have to take two skills courses, they are encouraged to take more of them as electives in order to fulfill their general college credits. Skills courses are generally more useful to them in their future careers.

The *specialization* courses complement the core and foundation courses by enabling students to apply what they have learned to specific criminal justice problems within the international arena and in particular developed and developing countries. The *internship,* which is elective, but highly recommended, is intended to bridge the gap between theory and practice, while the *capstone,* integrates the knowledge, learning and skills developed throughout the entire major. The overall curricular sequence is thus intended to provide both breadth and depth in this newly evolving field.

The ICJ major exposes students to gender, race and ethnicity issues worldwide. The core and foundations courses provide general theoretical understanding of these issues, but courses such as Gender Issues in International Criminal Justice and International Human Rights deal with them in more depth. The regional area courses concentrate on a variety of ethnic and racial groups around the world. For example, one course deals with Latino issues on gender, race, ethnicity and legal systems. The same applies to other courses, such as: Human Rights and the Law; Law and Justice in Africa; Drugs and Crime in Africa; Criminal Justice in European Society, 1750 to the present; The Secret Police in Western Society; Criminal Justice in Eastern Europe), Human Rights and the Law in Latin America, Comparative Perspectives of Crime in the Caribbean; Drugs, Crime and Law in Latin America; Crime and Delinquency in Asia.

Ethics and culture conflict constitute major parts of the discussions in core and foundation classes. Area study courses such as International Human Rights, Human Rights in Latin America and International Relations all make a special focus on ethical issues. Further, skills courses such as "Sociology of Conflict", "Dispute Resolution", "Security of Computers" and "Research Methods in the Behavioral Sciences" explore ethical issues at length.

The capstone course in International Criminal Justice is a synthesis course relating to key theoretical issues and problems in studying international criminal justice; ethnic and cultural concepts in international crime; interconnections among international and transnational crime, and their prevention and control; and the human rights implications of strategies designed to address international crime. Students are required to write a 20-page research paper (a "mini thesis") and make oral presentations. The research paper involves an in-depth analysis of an international criminal justice theme utilizing their knowledge. This is intended to help them think independently about a crime problem, link theory and find solutions.

Students are trained to collect and read journal articles through regular library and Internet searches, so that they are able to synthesize the relevant literature in the field. They are expected to write many papers, which provide them with practice in writing both short and long reports. Students are encouraged to make presentations using *PowerPoint*, to facilitate group discussions on international issues, and to attend seminars in and out of campuses. Apart from critical thinking, writing skills, research and analytic skills, students are expected to master some more specific skills such as conflict/dispute resolution and computer applications.

Response to Curriculum Concerns

The existing criminal justice and criminology majors include a great deal of material about other countries. This means that we need to constantly distinguish the ICJ major from the existing criminal justice major in order to avoid confusion and redundancy. The College has taken every opportunity to point out that the international criminal justice is intended to cover criminal justice issues extending beyond the national level. For example, rather than dealing mostly with conventional crime, the ICJ major focuses more on international crimes such as genocide, war crimes and crimes against humanity, including torture and terrorism, and transnational crimes such as trafficking, money laundering. And we have included several courses that focus on criminal justice systems in other parts of the world.

However, it was only possible to launch the ICJ by cross-listing relevant courses from other departments. Of the 41 courses in the major only eleven were exclusively prepared for the major and it is now time to add new courses specifically for the ICJ major. Nonetheless, the curriculum is designed to be flexible so as to accommodate new additions to the program. For example, in response to recent demands, the College is making arrangements to include Arabic language and criminal intelligence courses in the major. In addition, depending upon student interests and faculty expertise, skills and elective courses can be taught on an experimental basis. Current departmental chairs are flexible enough to substitute these courses so that the students can fulfil the requirements for the major. For example, the Government Department recently introduced a course on transnational crime, which helps in understanding terrorism and trafficking businesses. In the past two years, the Puerto Rican/Latin American Studies Department has opened up a relevant course titled "Terror and Truth in Latin America". For Spring 2004, the History Department and the Law and Police Science departments, respectively, have introduced experimental courses titled "History of Genocide" and "Landscape of Terrorism", which are timely and relevant to ICJ major students.

The departments that have faculty with expertise in international issues need to encourage them to give new, experimental courses primarily for ICJ major. There is also a need to have a foundations of scholarship course for the ICJ major which would deal with writing style, how to do proper scholarly work and how to write papers without relying on cutting and pasting from the Internet. Another gap in the course offerings is a course on Internet/cyber crimes which is highly relevant to this major.

John Jay's Faculty and Student Body

John Jay College's worldwide reputation in law enforcement education attracts faculty and students from all over the world. There are students from more than 150 nations representing regions of Asia, Latin American, the Caribbean and Europe. A number of clubs are geared to these students, as follows: Jamaican

Students Association, Latinas United for Justice, Muslim Students Association, Russian Students Club, Polish Club, Italian Club, Foreign Policy Society, Hillel Club, African Students Association, Haitian Students Association, Bangladeshi Club, United Nations Student Association, Association of Women Rights and Cultural Identities, Albanian Students Association and Asian Students Association. These clubs foster multiculturalism within John Jay and they help to integrate students from very diverse backgrounds.

According to a recent survey of 83 faculty members from a variety of departments (African American Studies; Anthropology; Art, Music & Philosophy; Doctoral Program; English; Government; History; Latin American/Puerto Rican Studies; Law & Police Science; Library; Physical Education; Psychology; Public Administration; Public Management; Science; Sociology; and Speech, Theatre & Media), it seems that faculty are involved in a wide variety of international initiatives with a focus on the following topics:

1. Criminology and Criminal Justice (General);
2. Forensic Psychology, Forensic Science and Public Health;
3. Gender Issues;
4. History, Religion, Culture, and Politics;
5. Human Rights Issues;
6. Immigration;
7. Organized Crime;
8. Policing Issues;
9. Public Administration and Economics;
10. Terrorism;
11. Arts, Language, and Literature.

The survey found that faculty has extended contacts on a regular basis with a variety of countries and members of the faculty have conducted research in Afghanistan, Bangladesh, Belgium, Brazil, Central and South America, the Czech Republic, Georgia, Germany, Greece, Indigenous Hawaii, India, Israel, Ireland, Jordan, Kazakhstan, Navajo Nation, Nigeria, Palestine Authority Territory, Poland, Puerto Rico, Russia, Sierra Leone, South Africa, Syria, Turkey, and the United Kingdom. In addition, the survey found that the following departments had some involvement in study abroad, and faculty exchange programs: Anthropology, African American Studies, Law & Police Science, Psychology, and Sociology.

Need for More Full-time Faculty

Two courses are geared solely to the ICJ major and it is important that they are taught by full-time faculty, familiar with international crime and the international criminal justice system. Many adjuncts have little knowledge of this subject. Some who teach in the program are graduate students from other countries who are trying to gain experience in teaching. The ICJ major students need more full-time professors who are experts in the field. Though John Jay College has faculty who can teach courses such as terrorism, organized crime, gender issues in ICJ, crime and delinquency in Asia, and crime and justice in Eastern Europe, it needs more full-time faculty with expertise in the above areas to take on additional sections because enrolment is increasing. Students also need to be exposed to different faculty with different expertise.

Students who register for this major are often foreign students whose first language is not English. Inevitably they struggle to communicate in classroom discussions and when writing papers. This problem becomes more severe when courses are writing intensive. This is not a problem exclusive to the ICJ major, but it is more acute for ICJ students.

Resources for the ICJ Major

The timeliness of the major was underlined by the September 11, 2001 disaster that struck just a few miles from the College. The establishment of the Terrorism Institute at John Jay may result in more resources flowing to the major. Also the Center for International Human Rights was established in 2001 with a mandate to study challenges to the promotion and protection of internationally-recognized human rights norms; analyze and assess the intersections between human rights violations and international crimes; investigate genocide historically and in the contemporary world; and devise educational programs aimed at increasing public awareness of these norms. Both institutes periodically arrange seminars by eminent people in the field on a variety of topics on human rights and terrorism. ICJ students can take advantage of the opportunities provided by these new institutes. Recently, the Puerto Rican/Latin American Studies department has instituted the Historical Memory Project, which is an ongoing project dedicated to exposing human rights abuses through scholarly publications, colloquiums, and exhibits to uncover past and present atrocities committed against indigenous peoples in Latin America. Particular areas of concern for this project include genocide, ethnocide, international human rights and the rights of indigenous peoples and women in Latin America. ICJ students have participated in this project and have learnt about the working of truth commissions.

For many years the College has encouraged visiting professors from around the world. Departments such as Law and Police Science, Government and Sociology benefit from the seminars and lectures given by these professors. Students in the ICJ major also have access to these visiting professors, which helps the students learn about criminal justice system in countries other than the United States.

John Jay College's Lloyd Sealy Library has worked consistently over the past five years to expand its holdings in international criminal justice. The library is an active member of the World Criminal Justice Library Network, which is working to provide electronic access to the world's international criminal justice information. Through the Library, students have access to databases such as NCJRS, Criminal Justice Abstracts, Psychology Abstracts and Sociology Abstracts. They also have access to other libraries such New York Public Library, Columbia University Library to read journals that we do not have at John Jay College. They can make use of Lexis-Nexus and Westlaw searches to help them in research projects. In addition, Internet facilities at John Jay College permit students to gain access to government documents such as UCR, INTERPOL and ICR.

Through the computer labs, students have access to a variety of software programs such as *PowerPoint, Excel, ACESS, ADOBE; SPSS* and *SAS*. Specialized computer labs for crime mapping are also available to use by students. The Instructional Technology Support Services maintain the general access computing labs and provide regular hands-on workshops for students in software applications and hardware maintenance.

Reading Materials

The Library holds 107 journals pertaining to international criminal justice as well as a substantial number of reports from international criminal justice institutes and agencies and documents from the United Nations and the European Institute for Crime Prevention and Control, affiliated with the United Nations. The Library is ordering more foreign criminal justice journals, but, due to budget cuts, there are still some pertinent journals not subscribed to – for example relating to human rights and genocide. Nor are there many acquisitions of videotapes in international criminal justice. New resources are needed to increase the acquisitions list for ICJ.

Apart from the journals, there is little relevant literature for the ICJ students. At the undergraduate level, especially the introductory level, reading materials in the form of textbooks are preferable, but there is no adequate textbook written on the subject of international criminal justice. Quite often reading materials are pre-packaged by the instructor and bought by the students. However, in the long run, textbooks are needed to teach courses in the major. For international criminology, there is presently only one book that meets the basic requirements (*Criminology: A Global*

Perspective by Lee Ellis and Anthony Walsh published by Pearson 2005). Chapters on comparative criminology are also included in some other criminal justice textbooks, but there is a need to develop one primarily focused on international and transnational crimes. In order to help meet this need, the author has produced a 50-chapter edited volume, *Introduction to International Criminal Justice*, which is a compilation of original work by leading experts (Natarajan 2005). It provides an introduction to the nature of international and transnational crimes and to the emerging legal frameworks for their prevention and control. Emphasis is placed on global aspects of the work of different criminal justice agencies and the international structures that have been created for crime prevention, punishment and control

Preparing for an ICJ Career

The ICJ major provides a foundation for advanced study for the more academic students, specifically in international relations, criminology, and criminal justice. The training they receive in theory and research will help them to pursue graduate degrees with confidence. The courses are geared to preparing students to develop independent thinking, to write essays and papers, and to plan and execute research projects.

Students who specialize in international law and justice, international relations and economic international public administration receive a good preparation for law school where they could specialize in immigration law or international law. Recent developments concerning ad hoc tribunals and the permanent international criminal court in Rome, together with the growing awareness of the importance of enforcing regional and global definitions of international and transnational crimes, can be especially rewarding subjects for papers and in-depth research projects.

The program also prepares students for work in a variety of law enforcement settings. These include both international agencies overseas as well as domestic governmental organizations, which are increasingly affected by international crime including terrorism. For example, issues such as assistance in the extradition of suspects from other countries, or help in building cases against offenders who cross borders, require an international perspective. Courses such as international criminal law, which emphasize police cooperation, mutual assistance and extradition, would be useful in these situations. Representatives from agencies such as INTERPOL, the United Nations, U.S. Department of Justice, Drug Enforcement Administration and Environmental Protection Agency's International Unit have indicated that they would be interested in hiring students with an international criminal justice background. The graduates are well placed to get jobs as police officers, probation officers, investigators, customs personnel, immigration specialists and federal law enforcement officers. These jobs increasingly require overseas work.

U.S. intelligence agencies failed to anticipate the World Trade Center terrorist attacks because they lacked the capacity and skills to analyze the vast amount of information collected. They also lacked the language skills and the knowledge of other cultures that would have helped them to interpret the data. The fact that the College now offers courses in Arabic should help students find jobs in the agencies.

Jobs, Internships and Study Abroad Programs

Many of the ICJ graduates find their own job openings with an international focus and wherever possible we help them obtain these jobs. However, this will become more difficult as the student body grows larger. Internships in international criminal justice need to be developed in order to:

1. Fulfill student interest: student surveys indicate that a majority of them are interested in internships;
2. Help them obtain work experience: internships help students in obtaining work experience and knowledge that could be useful in obtaining jobs after the graduation.

John Jay College has an excellent internship program involving local criminal justice organizations, and it participates in a CUNY-wide United Nations internship program. However, it does not yet have a full-fledged internship program abroad. The ICJ major would benefit from an internship program with local agencies with international divisions and internships with agencies abroad. For example, many banks with international transactions have security departments. Students could be placed as interns in these institutions to learn about the work. Such placements might help them to obtain full time jobs. The College is also interested to place students as interns in the United Nations offices. The ICJ Governance Committee is working to create an internship program and a newly-hired member of the Sociology faculty is in the process of developing an internship course by contacting a variety of institutions that deal with international matters.

John Jay College does not have its own study abroad program. Instead, the Office of Study Abroad Information (OSAI) assists students interested in enrolling in pre-existing programs run by other colleges and Universities. All the students at John Jay College should be given the opportunity to take advantage of this program, but this is particularly important for ICJ major students. ICJ students are encouraged to enrol in the study abroad program, but very few students have done this because of the lack of financial support. In spring 2005, as part of the effort to internationalize the College, President Travis sponsored 10 students accompanied by a faculty member to attend the Salzburg International Ambassador program at its facility at *Schloss Leopoldskron* in Salzburg, Austria. This is an intensive seven day program that provides students with the opportunity to explore pressing issues of global concern. This was John Jay College's first study abroad initiative.

Moving Forward

John Jay College's purpose in establishing the ICJ major was threefold:

1. To prepare undergraduate students with the knowledge, skills and perspective needed to compete for careers in the field of international criminal justice;
2. To prepare students for advanced work in graduate and professional schools;
3. To improve understanding of international crime and criminal justice through research conducted by faculty and students, ensuring that emerging global realities purposefully inform the study of crime.

September 11, 2001 brought a tremendous need to study international crime and criminal justice, not just in New York but all around the country. It is to be hoped that more universities with criminology/criminal justice departments will develop curricula to meet this need. Criminologists and criminal justice educators can no longer afford to be parochial in their outlook and the time has come to focus research attention on the increasing number of transnational crimes and human rights violations that are a serious threat to the world community (Natarajan 2002).

In April 2005, John Jay's President, Jeremy Travis, created the Committee on International Programs (CIP), which is expected to play an important advisory role in advancing the international agenda of the College. In his report (2004), he asserted that:

"two basic conditions must be met – one conceptual, one logistical – for us to engage the international criminal justice community with the rigor of a globally focused institution: First, we must widen our perception of the community itself; it should include, for example, Africa, Caribbean, Latin America, Asia, Australia, China and so forth. Second, we must provide support for our faculty and students' travel to and from our international partners and prospects. If we can satisfy these two conditions, we can pursue the following with maximum benefit."

The ICJ major and its faculty will continue to play an important part in shaping the teaching and research agenda on international crime and justice, and in promoting this agenda by preparing students for advanced study of these subjects and for employment in the international arena.

References

John Jay College Undergraduate Bulletin (2005). International Criminal Justice, Bachelor of Arts Degree Program, pp. 80-81. (can be accessed through the following website http://www.jjay.cuny.edu/catalogJohnJay/pdfCatalogJohnJay/undergraduate20052007.PDF).

Natarajan, M. (2002). International Criminal Justice Education: A Note on Curricular Resource. Journal of Criminal Justice Education, 13 (2), 479-498.

Natarajan, M. (ed.) (2005). Introduction to International Criminal Justice. New York: McGraw-Hill Publishing.

Travis, J. (2004). Looking Back / Looking Forward - Reflections on The Fall Semester 2004. New York: John Jay College of Criminal Justice Press.

IV. TRAINING EXPERIENCES IN INTERNATIONAL CRIMINAL JUSTICE ACADEMIES

Opportunities and Challenges in Delivering a Curriculum for International Police Training: the Case of the International Law Enforcement Academy (ILEA) at Roswell, New Mexico (USA)

Joseph D. Serio and Richard H. Ward[1]

Introduction

In the wake of the dramatic events of the late 1980s and early 1990s, including the razing of the Berlin Wall and the dismantling of the Soviet Union, the United States Government recognized the necessity for a training academy in Eastern Europe to enhance the skills of law enforcement officers facing a dramatically changing criminal landscape. The International Law Enforcement Academy (ILEA) concept was realized in Budapest in 1995 as a tactical-oriented training program. Before long, two other ILEAs were established, in Bangkok (Thailand), and Gaborone (Botswana). In 2001, the U.S. Department of State established the fourth ILEA, this time in Roswell, New Mexico, (USA). ILEA-Roswell was designed as a command course focusing on an academic approach to criminal justice.

International law enforcement training presents a wide range of opportunities as well as challenges. The chance to develop a network of working relationships on a global scale in law enforcement is accompanied by the difficulties of presenting material to groups that vary greatly in experience and educational backgrounds while attempting to effectively address technical considerations such as language barriers and differences in cultural norms. Some of these challenges must necessarily be considered

---

1 Joseph D. Serio was the Sam Houston State University faculty coordinator for the U.S. State Department's International Law Enforcement Academy (ILEA) in Roswell, New Mexico, from 2002 to 2005, and has delivered lectures at the Academy. He is Editor in Chief of the bi-monthly magazine, *Crime and Justice International*, and has observed criminal justice systems in operation in Russia, China, Poland, Spain, the United States, and other countries. Richard H. Ward is currently Dean of the College of Criminal Justice at Sam Houston State University. He was instrumental in establishing ILEA in Roswell and developing the curriculum. He has been involved in comparative criminal justice education for more than thirty years.

in the development stage of the curriculum, some can be addressed in the course of the program, and some are simply insurmountable.

ILEA-Roswell (ILEA-R) has made great strides since the early days of its curriculum development in providing a quality program of criminal justice education based firmly on the precepts of the rule of law and the ideals of democratic governance. Providing about seventy percent of the instructors for ILEA-R, Sam Houston State University's College of Criminal Justice has figured prominently in the development and delivery of the curriculum. This paper outlines the opportunities and challenges faced in delivering this cross cultural criminal justice program.

Problem

Law enforcement officials around the world have reported a significant increase in the range and scope of international criminal activity since the early 1990s. The level and severity of this activity and the accompanying growth in the power and influence of international criminal organizations have raised concerns among governments across the world about the threat criminals pose to governability and stability. International criminal networks have been quick to take advantage of the opportunities resulting from the revolutionary changes in world politics, business, technology, and communications.[2]

The substantial increase in global trade, movement of people, and capital flows has provided a landscape rich in targets for the criminal world. Criminals have taken advantage of transitioning economies to establish front companies and quasi-legitimate businesses that facilitate smuggling, money laundering, financial frauds, intellectual property piracy, and other illicit ventures. Multilateral economic agreements reducing trade barriers in North America, Europe, Asia, and other regions have substantially increased the volume of international trade. Criminal groups use the high volume of legitimate trade to smuggle drugs, arms, and other contraband across national boundaries.

With the breaking down of international political and economic barriers and the globalization of business, there is more freedom of movement, and international transportation of goods and services is easier. In the past, more limited travel options between countries and more stringent border checks made crossing national boundaries difficult for international criminals. Now, criminals have

---

2 This section is adapted from the Course Introduction of the ILEA-R Instructor's Guide, pp. 4-10.

a great many choices of travel routes and can arrange itineraries to minimize risk.

Modern telecommunications and information systems that underpin legitimate commercial activity in a fast-paced global market are easily used by criminal networks. Through the use of computers, international criminals have an unprecedented capability to obtain, process, and protect information and sidestep law enforcement investigations. They count on avoiding close scrutiny of their activities because of the importance to businesses and governments of facilitating commercial and financial transactions and rapid transshipment of products.

The major international organized crime groups have become more global in their operations, while many smaller and more local crime groups have expanded beyond their country's borders to become regional crime threats. Globalization has enabled organized crime groups to diversify their criminal activities. Colombian drug trafficking organizations, for example, are also involved in counterfeiting; Nigerian and Asian crime groups engage in alien smuggling; Russian and Asian crime groups traffic women for worldwide sex industries; and Russian, Asian, Nigerian, and Italian criminal syndicates engage in sophisticated, high-tech financial crimes. Many of the larger criminal organizations have established business-like structures to facilitate and provide cover for their operations, including front companies, quasi-legitimate businesses, and investments in fully legitimate firms.

Much more than in the past, criminal organizations are networking and cooperating with one another, enabling them to merge expertise and to broaden the scope of their activities. Rather than treat each other as rivals, many criminal organizations are sharing information, services, resources, and market access according to the principle of comparative advantage. By doing so, they can reduce their risks and costs and are better able to exploit illicit criminal opportunities.

The growth and spread of international crime have also fed off the many institutional shortcomings of countries around the world. Police and judicial systems in many countries are ill-prepared to combat sophisticated criminal organizations because they lack adequate resources, have limited investigative authority, or are plagued by corruption. Many countries have outdated or nonexistent laws to address corruption, money laundering, financial and high-tech crimes, intellectual property piracy, corrupt business practices, or immigration. Moreover, many governments have been slow to recognize the threat posed by criminal activities and increasingly powerful organized crime groups. Criminals use these shortcomings – and their tremendous resources to corrupt and intimidate public officials and business leaders – to find safe havens for themselves, their illicit operations, and their tainted money.

Finally, while globalization has allowed international criminals to operate virtually without regard to borders, governments and law enforcement agencies remain limited by national boundaries. National sovereignty concerns and jurisdictional restrictions are impediments to targeting criminal activities that cross international boundaries. Unlike criminals, governments and law enforcement agencies must respect other nations' sovereignty and legal statutes in law enforcement operations.

Action: Teaching or Training Program

In an effort to address the dramatic rise in transnational crime in Eastern Europe after the disappearance of the Soviet bloc and the weakening of borders through the expansion of the European Union, the Bureau for International Narcotics and Law Enforcement Affairs of the U.S. Department of State established the International Law Enforcement Academy (ILEA) in Budapest (Hungary), in 1995, operating under the auspices of the U.S. Federal Bureau of Investigation. The intention was to introduce an academy similar to the domestic FBI National Academy Program in the United States. The eight-week ILEA program focuses on leadership, personnel and financial management, human rights, ethics, the rule of law, management of the investigative process, and other contemporary law enforcement issues.

In keeping with the spirit of ILEA as a vehicle for understanding and cooperation among countries, instructors at ILEA-Budapest are law enforcement professionals from Austria, Italy, Canada, France, Germany, Hungary, Italy, Ireland, Italy, the Netherlands, Russia, Spain, Sweden, Switzerland, United Kingdom and the United States. [3]

In the wake of the successful ILEA-Budapest program, a second academy was opened, this time in Bangkok, Thailand, in March 1999, under the leadership of the U.S. Drug Enforcement Administration (DEA). Like the Budapest academy, Bangkok's ILEA focuses on training law enforcement officers from countries in the region. Training sessions address problems such as narcotics trafficking, terrorism, alien smuggling, and financial crimes, and promote the use of global crime fighting tools such as mutual legal assistance and extradition. [4]

---

3 See http://www.ilea.hu/, and http://www.state.gov/p/inl/ilea/c11279.htm.
4 See http://www.ileabangkok.com/bg/background.html and http://www.state. gov/g/ oes/rls/pg/37019.htm.

Coming on the heels of success in Budapest and Bangkok, the State Department and the Government of Botswana signed a bilateral agreement in July 2000 to establish an ILEA in Gaborone to promote international cooperation against crime in the Southern African Development Community (SADC) as well as Ethiopia, Kenya, Uganda, and other countries in the region. ILEA-Gaborone falls under the auspices of the U.S. Federal Law Enforcement Training Center (FLETC) providing courses on a wide range of law enforcement topics such as counter-terrorism, forensics, basic case management, organized crime, supervisory police training, police strategy, narcotics identification and evidence handling, customs interdiction, illegal immigration, and public corruption, among others. Specialized courses concentrate on specific methods and techniques on a variety of subjects, such as drug enforcement, financial crimes, violent crimes, border security, firearms, fraudulent documents, wildlife investigations, and others.[5]

With the three basic schools operating in Budapest, Bangkok, and Gaborone, the U.S. State Department formed a higher school, known as the Advanced Management Course, in Roswell, New Mexico, as the fourth ILEA. The idea was to provide additional coursework for officers who had already attended one of the ILEAs overseas. The program would consist entirely of an academic approach to crime and criminal justice, emphasizing the philosophy of criminal justice, the primacy of human rights, and the rule of law as the cornerstone of democratic processes.

ILEA-R, as the Roswell program is known, was created as a partnership between the U.S. State Department and New Mexico Institute of Mining and Technology. Subcontractors on that project are Sam Houston State University and Science Applications International Corporation which provide the faculty and support staff, and Eastern New Mexico University-Roswell that assists with infrastructure and logistics support.

The stated objectives of the ILEA-R program are to promote effective cooperation among law enforcement agencies worldwide; to provide an environment within law enforcement that encourages continual personal and professional development; to prepare law enforcement management officials for increased responsibilities, and to improve managerial capabilities of program participants in combating international crime.[6]

At of this writing there have been 44 sessions with a total of 1,664 participants from more than 60 countries from regions around the world including Latin America, the Caribbean, Central and Eastern Europe, sub-Saharan Africa, and Asia. While some

---

5 See http://www.ileagaborone.co.bw/ and http://www.state.gov/p/inl/ilea/c11283. htm.
6 See http://www.ilearoswell.org/ and http://www.state.gov/p/inl/ilea/ c11285.htm.

sessions are attended by English-speaking participants, many classes require simultaneous interpretation, which is provided by State Department interpreters of the highest caliber. Training has been provided in twenty-four different languages.[7] The ILEA-R instruction room is equipped with three booths for the interpreting staff.

The target audience consists primarily of, but is not limited to, experienced law enforcement middle managers (lieutenants and captains). Participants come from diverse backgrounds including criminal investigations, narcotics enforcement agencies, border patrol, customs and immigration, environmental conservation, the prosecutorial service, financial crimes units, police research institutes and others. As indicated, these managers are typically graduates of one of the other International Law Enforcement Academies located at Budapest, Botswana, or Bangkok. Because of their prior attendance at an ILEA, participants enter the Roswell academy with advanced knowledge and/or skills, which include their understanding of:

- roles and responsibilities of various U.S. law enforcement agencies (Federal Bureau of Investigation, Drug Enforcement Administration, Bureau of Alcohol, Tobacco and Firearms, *etc.*) and points of contact therein;
- basic investigative techniques for general and drug-related crimes;
- the nature of transnational crimes and the associated flows of money/contraband; the strategies for investigating those transnational crimes, and their role in these types of investigations;
- basic human rights, human dignity, and democracy in policing;
- various legal systems, and the importance of laws in identifying criminal investigation strategies.

The ILEA-R program is known as the Advanced Management Course (AMC) and focuses on academic and philosophical issues such as ethics, civility, and crime types and typologies as well as matters of administration such as records management and human resource management. Participants do not receive any tactical or weapons training.

The AMC seeks to accomplish several broad goals. Three of these goals are cognitive in nature (pertaining to learning concepts and procedures), two are affective (relating to a desired change in attitudes), and three are skill related.

---

7 Personal communication of author (Serio) with ILEA-R curriculum manager, and ILEA-R spreadsheet, "International Law Enforcement Academy – Roswell, History," covering Pilot Sessions I, II, and III, as well as Sessions 1-41.

Cognitive Goals

The course is designed to improve the technical and managerial capabilities of the participants to assist their respective law enforcement agencies in combating transnational crime; enhance the abilities of the participants to implement modern law enforcement management principles in agencies in their home country; and strengthen the participants' ability to implement strategies supporting efforts of U.S. law enforcement to intercept transnational criminal elements.

Affective Goals

The AMC is intended to instill in participants a commitment to implement law enforcement practices that reflect democratic principles, and support collaboration with international law enforcement agency efforts to intercept transnational criminal elements.

Skill Goals

The AMC offers participants the opportunity to become more proficient in the use of personal computers, in reaching individual physical and mental wellness goals, and in enhancing the participants' knowledge of law enforcement terms in English, and Basic English communication skills.

The four-week AMC consists of four academic curriculum modules: criminal justice in a global environment, modern policing strategies, key issues in policing, global trends and emerging issues in transnational crime. In addition to these four core modules there are three skill classes integrated into the program: Physical Fitness, Criminal Justice Terminology in English, and Computer Lab.

Module One – Criminal Justice in a Global Environment

In Module One, participants are introduced to the various roles that police perform in a changing, global society. Disparate challenges, such as those posed by culture, funding priorities, minorities, technology and globalization of values, which are faced by police in a modern environment are presented. Participants are provided with expectations of police conduct through the dissemination of accepted international legal and professional standards for law enforcement. In this Module, instructors present in the following areas:

- the concept of a civil society and its interactive relationship with effective policing;
- challenges of crime in a global environment and their effects on policing;
- the major crime types and typologies, and policing strategies relating to domestic abuse and trafficking in women and/or children;
- the role of criminal justice agencies in responding to crime;
- challenges facing law enforcement organizations, such as organizational culture, funding, minorities, technology, globalization of values, *etc.*;
- evolving legal and professional standards for law enforcement;
- the effects of national and international, political, economic, and legal environments on policing.

Module Two – Modern Policing Strategies

Module Two is more application-oriented than Module One. During Module Two, participants are presented with various modern manpower deployment models and their associated techniques and strategies as they pertain to patrol and criminal investigation operations. Human resource management issues such as hiring/firing, training, professional development, diversity, competency/performance evaluation, and promotion are also discussed during this module. Participants are asked to discuss the concepts of leadership and management, and then identify the differences between the two styles, and their implications. As a part of this discussion on leadership and management, participants are presented with opportunities to discuss strategies for becoming agents of change within their respective departments. Instructors provide participants with current methods for quantifying quality within the context of police management. Furthermore, instructors present existing and emerging technologies in policing to include DNA testing, Automated Fingerprint Identification System (AFIS), Geographical Information Systems (GIS), Communications/Information Systems, Records Management Systems, *etc.*, during this Module. The following is an overview of areas addressed in Module Two:

- modern deployment models for law enforcement;
- current strategies for management of patrol operations and criminal investigations;

- modern human resource strategies involving hiring/firing, training, professional development, diversity and its role in effective policing, competency, performance, promotion, *etc.*;
- the role of citizens in effective police management;
- concepts of leadership and management and the effective use of these concepts in addressing police issues;
- approaches for change management in the participant's agency, including the role of the media;
- current methods for quantifying quality in police management;
- the use of existing and emerging technologies in policing, such as DNA testing, AFIS, GIS, Information Systems, *etc.*;
- effective records management systems and plans for effective implementation in the participant's agency.

Module Three – Key Issues in Policing

In this Module, instructors address a broad spectrum of ethical and legal considerations involving issues ranging from privacy to diversity. As a part of this discussion, the United Nations standards on human rights are presented, with instructors speaking to best police practices as they relate to human and civil rights. Participants discuss corruption and its effects on effective policing. Furthermore, the course addresses specific investigative strategies for the changing dynamics of crimes such as drugs, money laundering, terrorism, cybercrime, illegal immigration, domestic abuse, trafficking in women and/or children, *etc.*, as well as strategies for addressing civil dissent. The following subject areas are discussed during this Module:

- ethical and legal considerations of key issues in policing, including privacy, fairness, equality, individual rights vs. collective needs;
- United Nations standards on human rights;
- concepts of human and civil rights and their effects on police practices (, victims, excessive force, racial profiling, policing minorities, *etc.*);
- dynamics of corruption (*i.e.*, racial profiling, bribery, favoritism, *etc*) on effective policing;
- processes for handling citizen complaints and establishing accountability within the participant's agency;
- strategies for addressing civil dissent and/or demonstrations, and the role of the police facing civil dissent and disobedience in a changing society;
- the changing dynamics for dealing with crime – specific investigative strategies for drugs, money laundering, terrorism, cybercrime, illegal immigration, *etc.*

Module Four – Global Trends and Emerging Issues in Transnational Crime

In Module Four, participants are provided the opportunity to apply techniques for conducting statistical research into crime analysis, transnational crime trends and rates, community expectations, and employee perspectives. Instructors present strategies for addressing cultural, social, legal, and political obstacles to effective policing. In this Module, the following areas are considered:

- the concept and impact of policing beyond borders;
- the concept of thinking globally and acting locally;
- challenges to and the strategies for effective police collaboration;
- evaluating sources of information and applying appropriate techniques for conducting statistical research, such as crime analysis, transnational crime trends and rates; determining community expectations and employee perspectives;
- strategies for addressing cultural, social, legal, and political obstacles to effective policing.

Participants receive a course book in their native language with each class outlined with a lesson description, instructional objectives, performance objectives, and methods of instruction (lecture, seminar, case studies, *etc.*), as well as copies of the PowerPoint presentation to be delivered.

Participants are required to complete an end-of-course critique that focuses on the value of materials in supporting the course goals and objectives and the effectiveness of instruction (instructors presented content in an understandable manner, used relevant examples, encouraged participation, and answered questions in a clear and concise manner). In addition, several months after returning to their countries, a number of participants have forwarded assessments of how the program has impacted their personal and professional lives, and offered suggestions for improving the course.

Impact and Evaluation (outcome and expected/noted returns)

Since the first pilot class on September 3, 2001, the ILEA-R program has met with great success and areas for improvement have been identified. For purposes of this paper, the authors have enumerated six interrelated areas in which numerous participants have offered positive reaction, either as inputs or outcomes.

First and foremost is an appreciation by the participants for the development of democratic institutions and creating the conditions where ILEA participants can rise through the ranks of their organizations and affect change. There is perhaps no more direct example than that of Lithuania. The return of the Lithuanian delegation from ILEA-R in 2003 coincided with the formation of a new penal code. One participant recounts how "upon our return from Roswell, we faced a tidal wave of questions from our colleagues about how law functions and how it is applied in practice in the United States. At this point we understood the importance and benefits of the ILEA training and were glad we could immediately apply the information collected in our month-long training session."[8] In this senior commander's opinion, "ILEA in Roswell made one of the biggest contributions to the Lithuanian law enforcement officers' training and preparation for working in new democratic conditions."[9]

Another important aspect of ensuring the development of democratic institutions in participant countries is the ability of participants to continue up the career ladder into policy-making roles. Two officers from Guatemala are illustrative of the opportunities the academy program created. One officer realized the value of his experience shortly after returning home. "The ILEA-R certificate is extremely important to us professionally. We get more respect and more doors are opened because of it. ILEA-R made us better equipped to do our jobs. I was promoted to 1st officer after my ILEA-R experience. My experience at ILEA-R was a factor in my promotion."[10]

His colleague experienced the same. "I have been promoted to 2nd Officer. Experience and knowledge is a must for promotion and ILEA-R helped me gain more of that."[11] Of critical importance to the development of democratic institutions is the willingness and possibility of ILEA participants to return home and share the knowledge they gained. "The lessons we learned at ILEA-R we have been able to pass along to others and now those people are moving up professionally." Not only that.... "Academically speaking we received a 'new vision.'" Referring to the Human Resources course, he continued, "We were able to implement a better system in determining the kinds of persons we wanted to work with."[12] Related to this, one of the students from the session attended by officers from Guatemala submitted a report to his superiors about the lessons learned at ILEA-R. The deputy commissioner of the

8 Augas, A. 2003, 'International Law Enforcement Academy: A Bridge to the Baltics' in Crime and Justice International, November/December, vol. 19, no. 77.
9 *Ibidem*
10 Comments offered in a meeting of four Guatemalan participants with the ILEA-R curriculum manager on July 13, 2004.
11 *Ibidem*
12 *Ibidem*

Guatemala drug school recommended that some of the ILEA-R material be incorporated into their lesson plans.

The second area that is of critical importance to the success of the program is more organizational in nature. The success or failure of a program is in large part due to the quality of front office personnel. They are the face of the program; they are the ones the participants interact with on a daily basis for a month. A participant from Slovenia indicated the importance of personnel. "I have found here something I had thought it didn't exist in the US. And that is, that people can be totally professional on one hand but on the other still can have fun while working together. That is something that I was used to in Slovenia and I am really happy that I have found the same kind of attitude now here as well. In my opinion each and every member of the ILEA staff has been performing her/his job extraordinary. And not only that, everybody carries with herself/himself that genuine human touch that makes work and life in general so beautiful and meaningful. You have made me feel like a member of your family."[13]

In February 2004, a Brazilian participant wrote "to thank you again for all the support during our stay there. In my particular case, in spite of having attending other training courses in USA, like FBI National Academy and DEA, I really liked most this one from ILEA because of the people who work there."[14]

An official from the Organized Crime Control Department of the Ministry of Interior of Croatia agreed, saying, "The organization of the course and the ILEA staff were perfect. Now I have new friends, new knowledge, and new experience."

Third, and a direct result of the high quality of personnel mentioned above, is the diplomatic success of the program and its ability to influence participants' impression of the United States. This perspective was most dramatically conveyed by the chief investigating officer in the Republic of South Africa's Asset Forfeiture Unit. After returning to South Africa, he forwarded to ILEA-R a lengthy letter saying in part, "You have a wonderful staff...I have returned to South Africa with different views of the USA I would never in my wildest dreams have thought that I could one day see myself as a friend of the people of the USA, but that is the case now. From the little I have seen of your country, I can say with certainty: You are indeed a great nation. If the development of new friendships is not one of the key success factors when evaluating the programme, then I would recommend that it be included."

---

13 E-mail communication with ILEA-R curriculum manager, date unknown.
14 E-mail communication with ILEA-R curriculum manager, February 18, 2004.

In July 2005, a similar comment came from an officer from Malawi. "I have settled back to work and already I am using some of the skills I learnt there at Roswell in my day-to-day work. I have to admit that we did learn a lot and it was an enriching experience not only professionally but also academically, socially and even psychologically. Why psychologically? Well maybe because I have now sort of changed my perception of Americans because before I perceived you Americans to be a bit pushy, bossy, stuck up and even a bit self-centered, especially when I compared you to Canadians and Europeans (not that there's really anything that is wrong with those character traits unless you overdo them which I think some Americans do), but that perception has now changed."[15]

Perhaps most the most touching accounts of the influence that the American spirit had on participants came in the wake of tragedy. In the wake of the 9/11 events, participants rolled up their sleeves and donated blood. After a Roswell police officer was wounded in the line of duty, the Hungarian delegation in Roswell at the time made the officer an honorary Hungarian police sergeant. When two women lost all of their possessions in a house fire, groups from Brazil, Bolivia, Peru and Ecuador raised several hundred dollars to assist them.[16]

One participant from Guatemala summed it up best: "I never expected to gain from ILEA what I gained when I got here. My experience was extremely valuable. Human relations are where we gained the most."[17]

Fourth, the ILEA-R program has helped to strengthen relationships among agencies in the regions of the participants. In a September 2003 e-mail to one of the authors, a senior commander from Lithuania conveyed that his country was able to develop stronger relationships with neighboring Estonia and Latvia because they went through the ILEA-R experience together and have shared ideas and impressions after returning home.[18]

The situation between Guatemala and El Salvador was similar. As one officer from Guatemala indicated, "Our minds were opened and we realized that there were effective programs to communicate and foster the ability to share information with our sister countries." This led to direct meetings between officials of the two countries. "El Salvador has come to Guatemala three different times to attend work related meetings. All the participants met at ILEA-R."[19]

---

15 E-mail communication with ILEA-R curriculum manager, July 11, 2005.
16 'ILEA students come to aid of fire victims' Roswell Daily Record, February 12, 2004.
17 Comments offered in a meeting of four Guatemalan participants with the ILEA-R curriculum manager on July 13, 2004.
18 E-mail communication with author (Serio), September 26, 2003.
19 Comments offered in a meeting of four Guatemalan participants with the ILEA-R curriculum manager on July 13, 2004.

Fifth, these relationships have led to direct cooperation in investigative matters across borders, one of the key underlying goals of the ILEA concept in general. Writing in the November/December 2003 issue of *Crime and Justice International*, the senior commander from Lithuania mentioned above recounts the success his country has had in developing active collaboration with the United States. "One of my colleagues who runs the Auto Vehicle Theft Investigation Department in the Central District Police participated in ILEA training in the summer of 2002. He was very satisfied when he was able to make direct contacts he made in ILEA and applied them in his work. For example, his team successfully investigated car theft cases from across the ocean in cooperation with his American colleagues. Nowadays, my colleague is working jointly once again with our American counterparts in investigating a company in the Chicago area that is involved in suspicious activities with companies in Lithuania." Moreover, he writes, "The October 6, 2003, arrest [in Lithuania] of an American citizen, who is suspected of being a gang leader of an organized crime group in the U.S. and involved in drug trafficking, is one more example of the successful application of knowledge and direct contact with American law enforcement officers."[20]

In Guatemala, relationships forged in New Mexico have helped to build bridges with neighboring El Salvador. "One of the most successful things to come out of ILEA-R for us was the relationship and coordination with El Salvador. There was a situation in El Salvador where a group of individuals involved in organized crime fled El Salvador and re-located in Guatemala. They were already starting to organize but we were able to apprehend them and cease their operations through communication and cooperation with El Salvador."[21]

For Guatemala, this relationship building has extended not only across the border to El Salvador but also inwardly toward its own community. "We now realize the importance of being more united with our communities. Since returning from ILEA-R, we are now involved in community meetings, something that we had never done before... We have seen substantial results in our rapport with the citizens."[22]

Sixth, to achieve these kinds of results, the training material and presentations must be clear and useful. In this way, material is not only easily digested by the participants, but can also be conveyed to colleagues back home. In a March 2005, email to the ILEA-R

20 Augas, A. 2003, 'International Law Enforcement Academy: A Bridge to the Baltics' in Crime and Justice International, November/December, vol. 19, no. 77.
21 Comments offered in a meeting of four Guatemalan participants with the ILEA-R curriculum manager on July 13, 2004.
22 *Ibidem*

General Manager, the Regional Security Officer at the U.S. Embassy in Uruguay, writes, "I wanted to thank you once again for hosting the Uruguayan Police Officers at the January Police Management Course in Roswell, New Mexico. We heard that it was by far the most organized, most interesting, most professional course that any of them had ever attended."[23]

The Lithuanian delegation had this to say about the training materials: "One important point to note is that ILEA's written training materials were understandable and useful. As a result, the trainees could obtain a lot of information about American law enforcement structures with the names of officers for further contact if necessary. If there is a need, they can always be contacted for consultation, help, or advice."[24]

While ILEA-R has enjoyed success on many levels, there are also challenges that come with a program of this nature.

First, the program consists of a series of lectures that are given from month to month to participants from countries that may vary dramatically. For example, in one month Guatemala, El Salvador, and Honduras may be represented, and in the following month participants may come from Singapore, Hong Kong, and Indonesia. These countries have drastically different economic, social, and political realities and yet will receive the same course material. Likewise, within a single session there may be two countries at very different stages of development. The presence of officers from South Africa in the same session with officers from Tanzania presents the difficulty of addressing issues that are applicable to each and taught in a way that is equally understandable to all. For example, the educational and training levels of these two countries as well as the overall knowledge base and experience may be dramatically different.

Second and related to the first is the applicability of the U.S. experience to some of the countries attending the ILEA-R course. In some cases, the instructor portrays the realities of law enforcement in the U.S. that may have little bearing on the visiting delegations. For example, in the case of the Baltic States, there are certain topics that do not apply to their realities. "Let's say we were listening about racial and religious problems, it was interesting but we were proud we didn't have them. Therefore, we couldn't imagine applying them in our line of work. Also, black riot suppression or problems with Hispanic population growth was really interesting but not relevant to the Baltic countries, as we really have neither black nor a Hispanic population."[25]

---

23 E-mail communication to the ILEA-R general manager on March 14, 2005.
24 Augas, A. 2003, 'International Law Enforcement Academy: A Bridge to the Baltics' in Crime and Justice International, November/December, vol. 19, no. 77.
25 E-mail communication with author (Serio), September 26, 2003.

A third challenge is addressing a group of officials from various criminal justice specialties. It is difficult for instructors to address a narrow topic with such an audience. While some participants will pay attention to topics unrelated to their specialty in an effort to find something applicable to their own work, many will certainly lose interest. In one session there might be officers from customs, narcotics control, the police academy, border control, human resources, and so on, making tailoring lectures all but impossible.

A fourth challenge is to provide a sufficient amount of structured and unstructured time for the participants from neighboring countries to get to know one another, brief each other on their particular criminal justice problems, and explore ways to collaborate. Given the 140 hours of classroom instruction that ILEA-R is obligated to provide, together with guest speakers, site visits, and special events, participants from a number of countries agree with the statement of their colleague from Guatemala: "We would have liked more time to share information between countries and hear from our classmates more about their own experiences, rather than the instructors and U.S. experiences. North America situations are not always relevant due to our different culture and levels."[26]

A fifth challenge is finding ways to minimize redundancy. With more than 20 different instructors, the likelihood of repetition is high, particularly regarding basic features of the U.S. criminal justice system. A high degree of coordination and communication within the group of instructors is necessary, particularly in the curriculum development phase, to avoid covering the same material numerous times. While some repetition is welcome as a learning tool, too much repetition leaves the impression that opportunities are being missed to learn new things.

Counteraction (modifications applied to address the problems)

Over the past three years of the program, ILEA-R management and instructors have examined the challenges enumerated above and have altered the approach to instruction wherever possible.

First, in an effort to reach the most participants possible, instructors began to appreciate the differences in the backgrounds, knowledge, and experience base of the participants prior to arriving in Roswell. With this awareness, instruction can be geared in such a way as to facilitate discussion among the participants during the presentations to draw out the different concerns and approaches of

---

26 Comments offered in a meeting of four Guatemalan participants with the ILEA-R curriculum manager on July 13, 2004.

each country. Establishing channels of communication among the participants is the first step in realizing the goals of the program.

Second and related to the first, instructors have built into their presentations more opportunities for each group to present information about its country, particularly information most pertinent to the subject matter of the presentation. For example, in some of the first sessions of the month, representatives from each country present are asked to give a briefing on the demographics, resources, social, political, and economic systems, as well as general contours of the criminal justice system. During specialized sessions, such as Policing Beyond Borders in which issues of transnational crime are discussed, each country is asked to prepare a more formal presentation to be delivered to the class. In this way, instructors avoid slipping into a lecture-only mode.

Third, to demonstrate a balanced perspective on the part of the instructor, examples are frequently used that involve countries other than the United States. There are lessons to be learned – positive and negative – from many countries around the world, and when addressing complex topics such as terrorism or money laundering, the presentation of experience from multiple perspectives is welcomed by the participants.

Fourth, it is not always easy to balance a presentation to participants of a single course that have widely varying knowledge bases. Over time, instructors have understood that some modification in presentations must be done to account for the specific audience. For example, a presentation to highly developed countries may not be exactly appropriate for developing countries that may have a different set of priorities and concerns. Some instructors have three different levels of presentations depending on the characteristics of the countries participating any given month. The U.S. State Department provides background materials on each participating country so that instructors may gain some appreciation for the context in which the respective countries find themselves.

Conclusion

In developing and delivering a criminal justice curriculum to an international audience several key elements must be borne in mind. First, selection of personnel to staff the program is critical. The actions and problem solving skills of the staff in a context of hospitality and diplomacy will be remembered long after the conclusion of the program and will prove to be as important as the curriculum itself in the creation of lasting impressions. Second, the curriculum must address the needs of the audience while retaining ample flexibility. Instructors must understand when and how to adjust their lectures based on the experience level of the audience. In a program like ILEA with constantly varying audiences, this requires preparation in advance of each lecture to appreciate the challenges and limitations facing each participating country as well as the relative disparities in education and training among the participants. Last, and perhaps most important, it must be recognized from day one when developing the curriculum as well as ancillary activities that, more than just imparting information, conducting a program of this nature provides an opportunity to change minds.

Human Dignity/Human Rights and the Police: Training that Manifests Rule of Law Operations

Carmen Solis[1]

Introduction

Issues of human dignity and human rights are rooted in the principles of the rule of law. In fact, in societies that are often fragile, unstable and even corrupt human dignity and rights are usually sacrificed, making it difficult to preserve the rule of law. In light of this, the goal of training in this area should be to reacquaint participants with the inherent values in the rule of law.

Many private, public and governmental institutions have developed training programs that promote peace, democratic principles, social justice and human rights education (Scanlon 2002). Internationally there are a myriad of training programs on issues related to the rule of law and human rights. Much of this training employs innovative modules and tools that speak to best practices and the development of professionalism as a means of preventing violations of human rights and sustaining peace efforts. Training in "peacekeeping, peacemaking and peace building" for example, engage models that address preventive measures towards conflict and dispute resolution through planned social change (Green 2002: 97; Iribarnegaray 2002: 8). Through a focus on strategies that promulgate peace efforts these models are inextricably intertwined in their mission to ensure grater communication and less hostility that in turn operationalize the rule of law (Iribarnegaray 2002: 8).

The Human Dignity/Human Rights and Police Course much like other training in the area seeks to build bridges of understanding

---

1 Carmen Lee Solis has been a faculty member at John Jay College of Criminal Justice, The City University of New York for 18 years. She is a social worker with extensive professional experience in community/police relationship building. In addition, she has been one of the senior trainers in the College's Human Dignity, Human Rights, and Law Enforcement course. Dr. Solis has offered the Human Dignity course for hundreds of New York City police cadets, for Bolivian and Mexican Federal Police and for United States police officers assigned as peacekeepers in Bosnia. She has also facilitated the course at the United States State Department-sponsored International Law Enforcement Academies in Bangkok, Thailand, Budapest, Hungary, and Gaborone, Botswana. She has assisted in the needs assessment and curriculum development of the International Law Enforcement Academies in Gaborone, Botswana and Latin America.

and address ways of dealing with injustice internally within any law enforcement agency as well as externally in the relationships that are developed with the community and other organizations. However, two basic tenets separate this training from others. One is the focus on dignity. The other is empowering participants to assess the issues they perceive as problems and collaborate on developing the best techniques they can use to facilitate highly participatory training sessions. In this vein, the trainers are trained to not tell the participants what to do but instead to work collaboratively, networking and paying attention to everyone's issues in order to help them determine the best approaches for their needs.

Buhler (2002), in assessing methods of participation asks us to take into consideration the struggle of the Zapatistas in Mexico who insist on achieving justice and participatory efforts by practicing human dignity. The Human Dignity/Human Rights and Police Course also emphasizes the respect for human dignity in course participation and seeks to "imbue law enforcement practice with a sharpened understanding of human dignity as an innate quality possessed by all human beings" (Curran and Rothlein 1999). By further developing this knowledge base the trainers and course participants work towards "acknowledging others [and themselves-added] as bearers of rights" (Kleinig 1999). Similarly to the Zapatistas (Buhler 2002) the focus on dignity seeks to provide an environment where respect for others and one-self is essential. The premise is not to place blame on others but to identify problems and develop solutions while at all times respecting, communicating, sharing the ideas, suggestions, thoughts and feelings of all whom are effected by the issues. Thus, the emphasis on dignity assists in providing a level of real participation which is essential in preventing "exclusionary practices" (Buhler 2002: 6).

The course facilitated an assessment of human rights, morality, personal integrity, and professional ethics (Curran and Rothlein 1999). It provided an opportunity to consider and carefully analyze our experiences and behavior in an effort to create positive institutional change by examining ethical decision-making, transitional leadership skills and creative implementation strategies via a focus on human dignity (Curran and Rothlein 1999).

The idea of a course which dealt with human dignity issues and the police was part of a collaborative initiative by faculty and administrators from John Jay College of Criminal Justice (City University of New York, New York, USA), the International Criminal Investigation Training Assistance Programme (ICITAP), and the Federal Bureau of Investigation (both U.S. Department of Justice). In keeping with the spirit of collaboration and the notion of dignity as a bridge, a team from John Jay College appointed by the College President developed the course methodology and curriculum. The methods were developed to assist participants in

162

evaluating institutionalized violations to their dignity as well as the publics. The course sought to develop self-awareness by having officers recognize how their own behavior and attitudes impacted on the public, within the organization and among peers. In groups, participants shared experiences and evaluated how negative behaviors and treatment could lead to human dignity violations that in turn result in social scars.

In all of the International Law Enforcement Academies (ILEA) the course served as a vehicle for law enforcement agencies from different countries to come together and discuss problems and solutions in approaches and methods that each organization had implemented. In country teams participants assessed policies, procedures, training and treatment that were in concert with or in violation of the rule of law practices. The groups were asked to develop a plan for implementation in their respective organizations that demonstrated how respect for human dignity, human rights and the rule of law would be strengthened and reinforced. These evaluations and the issues identified were then shared with all participants who further questioned and discussed how the commitment to human dignity and human rights was clearly reflected in the intended policies and practices presented.

Problem

Training is an essential ingredient in the preparation for any profession and is certainly significant in the professional preparation for law enforcement agencies. However, lack of training or poor training will eventually surface in issues of insensitivity during a response to any situation (Solis 2004). Thus, training for law enforcement professionals should offer greater opportunities to assess the ways law enforcement officers, as authority figures, do their jobs. It should also help them assess how they perceive themselves, their roles and their relationships to the communities they serve. According to Curran and Rothlein (1999), authority figures can do an enormous amount of good or harm in meeting their responsibilities. These authors contend that law enforcement officers "are part of a subculture prone to in-group, out group, we-they attitudes that interfere with objective analysis; that there are reasons why social outcasts are estranged from the larger society; and that given adequate self-reflection, attitudes and behaviors can change." For law enforcement officers respecting and protecting the human dignity/human rights and the rule of law, requires affirmation of the fundamental importance of these values in their day-to-day work. Thus, training in this area should not encompass lectures that prescribe what to do. Instead, training must work to reacquaint participants with the fundamental "meaning of values and ethics in their own lives" and in their daily work (Curran and

Rothlien 1999). Training in this area should also view participants as collaborative learners incorporating their experience, knowledge and analysis as an essential part of the training. In addition, the training program should train the trainer to practice and implement the skills they are learning. Yet, few training programs focus on actually training-the-trainer. Little, if any, attention is paid to providing trainers with insight into the design of a course, exploring student-centered adult learning strategies and the application of these strategies in the approaches that might be used to refine or further develop a course to fit the specific needs of the participants. In the same vein, limited consideration is given to the issue of dignity, how we respect ourselves and others (Buhler 2002), when developing and implementing training that involves participatory approaches between law enforcement personnel and the public.

The Training Approach

The human dignity course serves as a collaborative learning approach which incorporates participants' experience, knowledge and analysis. The goal of training is to reacquaint participants with human dignity and human rights which are values inherent in the Rule of Law. A variety of experimental learning approaches including: role play, simulations, case studies and structured exercises are utilized throughout the course. These non-traditional teaching and learning approaches assist law enforcement officers in examining the results of negative interactions and the power of authority figures (Curran and Rothlein 1999).

Participants and course facilitators work in a collaborative and participatory manner to define human dignity. The definition then becomes part of the process that aids in assessing how human dignity fits into their work and lives. Thus, human dignity becomes the epitome of initial discussion in the course. By reflecting on their values, work and lives, participants develop a working definition or word picture of human dignity. Initially the definition is used to demonstrate how easily one can develop words that define human dignity. Moreover, facilitators use the definition to assist participants in recognizing the difficulties in actually implementing human dignity consistently. In this way dignity is not viewed as a tool to simply define a concept. Instead, it becomes the method used to assess what they did, why they did it and how they could ensure that everyone becomes part of the process in a way that assured respect and rights (Buhler 2002: 6, Curran and Rothlien 1999). Kleinig (1999: 12-13) suggests that the focus on human dignity reinforces the "United Nations codes of conduct for law enforcement officials." The human dignity course explicitly made this connection from the very beginning via the definition exercise. This goal became implicit in the final exercise on implementation.

The implementation exercise empowered participants to assess how the values stated in the code of conduct, using the United Nations Universal Declaration of Human Rights, could be implemented in a practical way within their respective law enforcement agencies.

The historical perspectives of human dignity and rights in law enforcement were connected to the dialogue by working on an exercise that provided information about persons or events identified by participants as champions of human dignity and rights. This exercise identified the champions of human dignity and human rights who were responsible for spearheading unheard struggles in a cadre of diverse communities, cultures, racial and ethnic groups throughout the world. In most cases such champions had to make great efforts to bring their message to the top of governmental and community agendas.

Participants assessed personal dignity violations before they moved on to examine themselves as authority figures. They engaged in an exercise that began a discovery process about their own vulnerability. They were asked to examine a time prior to the age of 15 when they believed an authority figure (parent, aunt, uncle, teacher, coach, etc.) hurt, humiliated, disrespected, them in the most devastating way. Participants usually "sympathize, empathize and identify with each other" (Pitt 1999: 67) in this exercise. They learned about each others' exposure to helplessness, and gained a perspective on the power of authority and privilege (Pitt 1999: 67). Consequently, participants established trust amongst each other and with facilitators. This was the pinnacle for beginning a process of open and honest communication with all group members.

Law enforcement officers are then asked to examine the results of negative interactions with the public. They assess themselves as authority figures and learn to distinguish behaviors and attitudes and their impact on the public. They evaluate how negative behaviors and treatment could be "the results of social scars–viewing some as social outcasts, in-group/out-group subcultures and we-they attitudes" (Curran and Rothlein 1999). They critically assess police misconduct and public condemnation as well as how they are often "victimized" by their institutions (Pitt 1999: 68). Thus, the course methodology assists participants in evaluating organizational violations to their dignity as well as the public's. It also assists them in developing "practical ideas, guidelines to deal with difficult people, employers, training courses in the police academy—incorporation of human dignity" in their daily work and lives (Pitt 1999: 73-74).

The trainer's role was to facilitate real assessment of values and behaviour and to ensure that there was sincere and candid communication and identification of real native problems. The trainers role is first to create and secondly maintain an atmosphere that was free of language and behaviour "construed as violations of human dignity" (Pitt 1999: 63-64). Trainers had to maintain a respectful setting and be exemplar in the practice of human dignity. They had to be active facilitators of the learning process. Trainers needed to listen intensively to participants' presentations, acknowledge their genuine contributions and collaborative efforts. They had to provide feed back, explain the reasons behind every exercise and ensure that all group members moved to the next level. Trainers had to encourage full participation from all involved in training process.

The International Law Enforcement Academy (ILEA) in Budapest, Bangkok, and Botswana

The human dignity course was developed by John Jay College in 1992. It was initially taught throughout Central and South America, and the Caribbean. This was made possible through the sponsorship from the United States State Department via ICITAP (Curran 2001). In 1995 the course became part of the core curriculum in the leadership training program at International Law Enforcement Academy in Budapest, Hungry (Curran 2002). The success of the course at ILEA Budapest helped secure the course offering at ILEA Bangkok in 1999 and at ILEA Botswana in 2001. A senior course facilitator from John Jay College was part of the needs assessment and curriculum development conferences for ILEA Latin America opened in 2006 in El Salvador. The Human Dignity and the Police Course served as a key component in the core curriculum of federally funded international programs for thirteen years.

The U.S. Department of State and the Department of Homeland Security "conduct needs assessment conferences to determine the training needs of law enforcement agencies of countries in the regions identified for service by the International Law Enforcement Agencies" (Pate 2005). These conferences are usually held in one of the participating countries. Each of the ILEAs Budapest, Bangkok and Botswana, and Latin-America, hold needs assessment conferences for their regions prior to the establishment of ILEA in a host country. The purpose of these conferences is to "identify individual country and regional law enforcement training needs that could be addressed by specialized training courses provided by the ILEAs" (Pate 2005). The process involves networking with participating counties and gathering both qualitative and quantitative data. The data collection process is conducted by contracted services of the Police Executive Research Foundation (PERF). Representatives from the United States federal law enforcement agencies and John Jay College served as facilitators at the conferences for Latin America and Botswana. The conferences held in Budapest were facilitated by faculty from the University of Virginia with participation from the U. S. federal law enforcement agencies and John Jay College. At all the conferences the trained facilitators conduct workshops with the country teams to discuss and assess the crime problems and agency needs for each country represented. Participants are surveyed and results are tabulated by PERF representatives (Pate 2005)

Needs assessments and analysis for the ILEAs are followed through by Key Leaders Conferences. A Curriculum Development Conference is held prior to the opening of ILEA and then every year after to examine need changes in the curriculum and/or add new courses. Representatives from all of the participating countries in the region are invited to take part in all of the conferences. The United States federal law enforcement agencies have representation from The Department of Homeland Security including: Investigation and Customs Enforcement Bureau (ICE), Federal Bureau of Investigation (FBI), Drug Enforcement Administration (DEA), Alcohol Tobacco and Firearms (ATF), U.S. Marshals, International Criminal Investigative Training Assistance Program, Overseas Prosecutorial Development Assistance and Training Program (OPDAT), Department of State, the Financial Crimes Enforcement Network (FinCen) of the Department of Treasury, the Internal Revenue Service (IRS) (Pate 2005). In ILEA Budapest there were two institutions of higher education which formed part of the United States collaborative team in the conferences, the University of Virginia and John Jay College. However, John Jay College was the only institution of higher education involved in the conferences for ILEA Botswana and Latin-America.

The issue of Human Dignity/Human Rights was always identified by most participating countries. As a result of this, John Jay College has provided training in this area at all of the ILEAs. The issues of human rights are assed through the process of examining behavior as influenced by personal decisions, peers, authority figures and professional responsibility. The course assisted participants not only in evaluating their own behavior but also in focusing on the concerns of others. Participants discussed and examined comprehensive communication strategies and developed methods to enhance their services, outreach and response to the communities they service. Participants also worked on strategies to protect society's outcast, vulnerable populations, and the rights of minorities. They were encouraged to evaluate their mandate to protect all people and develop policies they deemed as necessary to protect the dignity and rights of those identified as the most vulnerable in their communities. After working on the exercises participants presented very detailed approaches to resolve issues identified in every area discussed.

The United States Embassy sponsored Human Dignity Training in the Dominican Republic

Five years ago, at the request of the of the U.S. Embassy in the Dominican Republic and in collaboration with *La Policia Nacional* and the *Universidad Iberio-Americana* a train-the-trainer program was launched in the Dominican Republic. The objective was to train participants to facilitate the Human Dignity and the Police Course. Participants first experienced the course learning about the model and the student-centered adult learning approaches. Once they had gone through that process they were then encouraged to put their new skills and techniques to practice. Participants facilitated exercises they developed to meet the specific needs of the Dominican Republic. They received feed back from class participants and the senior facilitators on how to keep the overall focus on dignity and rights and get the most participation and collaboration from their groups (Curran 2002).

The most significant part of this session was that for the first time the participants were not all from law enforcement agencies. The population of participants in this training program was comprised of people from the community and law enforcement officers. In essence we were training members of the public to work collaboratively in teams with law enforcement officers and facilitate training on issues of human dignity, human rights and the police. Another interesting factor was that the training was occurring during a time when there were serious conflicts and tensions between the police and the community in the Dominican Republic. The United States Embassy was interested in investing in resources that could assist in resolving the conflict. The current administrators of The National Police (*La Policia Nacional*) in the Dominican Republic were also interested resolving the issues they were experiencing between the community and the police. The Chief of Police and his General Council/General of the Human Dignity Institute for the National Police had actually participated in the Human Dignity/Rights and the Police Course several years earlier. As a direct result of their participation in the course when it was sponsored by the State Department via the FBI, they developed a Human Dignity Institute in the Police Department. It was at their request that the U.S. Embassy contacted John Jay College of Criminal Justice to provide this training.

The training course in the Dominican Republic exceeded all of our expectations. A primary group of facilitators were trained and the course was redesigned and tailored to address issues specific to the police and community. John Jay College senior trainers continued to work with local facilitators and moved the training into 10 different towns or provinces in the Dominican Republic. Each training session had 30 to 40 participants. All training sessions had an equal number of community and police representation. All training sessions commenced with an enormous amount of tension between both groups. As we worked and insisted on placing human dignity above all things in our discussions we achieved the respect and rights of all. Both police and community members identified and confronted common dignity violations. They gained an understanding for the power of authority and privilege. They worked intensely in subgroups identifying and resolving negative encounters with citizens, police and institutions. They were able to demonstrate and "see how very vulnerable human dignity can be in face of intense, hostile, 'in'-group/'out'-group conflict" (Pitt 1999: 71). They learned that part of the process was to initiate a cooperative relationship with others.

Police and community members discussed issues of trust, corruption, abuse and overall service. Studies on issues of trust between police and communities indicate that the public tends to view police "as part of a system that cannot be trusted" (Solis 2004: 98; Peak and Glenser 1996: 211). The community group members in the Dominican Republic initially had similar perceptions of their police force. It was only by listening, communicating and working collaboratively with each other that they gained an understanding of each other's perceptions and concerns. The focus on dignity in the collaborative participatory process enabled both the police and the community to respect each other and candidly talk about issues and gain trust in each other. Once trust was established the group was able to clearly identify problems and develop solutions. The Human Dignity/Rights Police Course in the Dominican Republic actually served as vehicle for real community policing and it supported the operation of the rule of law. Community policing was fostered in the cultivation of better communication between the police and the community which in turn promoted problem identification and resolutions and gave the community a role in the policing process (Trojanowicz, Steele and Trojanowicz 1985: 2; Solis 2004: 8). The of rule of law was applied as the ultimate goal was to create an environment where respect for human dignity and human rights was discussed, implemented and practiced at all times.

Conclusion

Despite the fact that the course fared well according to instructor evaluations in each of the ILEA academies, one of the major short falls has been the lack of follow-up program evaluation. There has only been one follow-up evaluation that dates back approximately over ten years. In 1993 there was an evaluation to study the implementation of human dignity course skills in Jamaica and Honduras. The course had received very favourable responses in class evaluations from these countries. Jamaica indicated in the implementation evaluation that they had incorporated the human dignity course into the police academy curriculum. As a result of this, they had seen both institutional and personal changes in their law enforcement personnel (Price 1999: 109). Since then, there have been no formal follow-up evaluations in any of the ILEA participating countries. Thus, there has been no official demonstration as to whether participants actually implemented the course material and training in their own institutions or academies and what success, if any they have had in implementing such a course. There have been very positive informal discussions in e-mails and courses as to the value of specific skills gained in the course. Graduates of ILEA often send e-mails or word back with current course participants about the implementation and use of skills used in the course. For example, ILEA graduates from Albania and Macedonia sent word to instructors with new ILEA participants about how a border dispute was settled between both countries. According to the information presented, those sent to settle the conflict had all participated at ILEA Budapest. They employed skills learned in the Human Dignity and The Police Course to settle the problem and there were no adverse effects. On occasion course facilitators also receive e-mail from graduates who discuss course implementation and ask further questions. While this by no means formally measures the success of the course, it does provide some insights and perhaps demonstrates a need for a more formal evaluation to be conducted.

The Dominican Republic may serve as the best example for course implementation. The Dominican Republic has actually institutionalized the program in their National Police Agency. They developed a Human Dignity Institute within the National Police after their first introduction to the course in 1993. In 2000, they reaffirmed their commitment to the Human Dignity and the Police Course through their collaborative efforts with the U. S. Embassy and *La Universidad Iberio-Americana*. Their objective was to identify and train police and community members to continue course facilitation throughout their country. To date these facilitators continue to work together to meet their goals of working with every province on issues of human dignity and human rights.

It is important to note other issues with reference to training at the ILEAs. While there was vast racial and ethnic representation between the ILEAs, women were under-represented as participants at all the academies. In comparison, ILEA Botswana usually had the highest representation of women in training courses averaging approximately 7 to 8 women per class. Participants at ILEA Botswana consistently voiced their concerns about the limited representation of women. In the Human Dignity/Human Rights and the Police Course participants from every country represented in ILEA Botswana always identified this as a problem needing resolution in their institutions.

The issue of the women's rights and dignity violations of women always surfaced at every ILEA and in the Dominican Republic. Even when there were no female participants in the course the major focus on course exercises became issues relating to women. Oftentimes, women were identified as outcasts in society and in law enforcement. Women have historically had fewer opportunities for employment and promotion in law enforcement. They have struggled with issues of sexual harassment and lack of representation (Schultz 1995). The fact that their male counterparts internationally are identifying them as more vulnerable, within and outside of the law enforcement organization, and that they demonstrate interest in protecting their rights and dignity denotes a substantial change in law enforcement practice. Thus, in the Human Dignity/Human Rights and the Police Course participants were not only assessing their relationship with the public but their relationship with their colleagues and gender issues.

Overall, the Human Dignity/Human Rights and the Police Course encouraged law enforcement officers to treat the community they service as well as each other in more humane and respectful ways. Through practical and collaborative efforts it instilled the impact of acknowledging and understanding the human dignity and rights of all persons in implementing law enforcement policies and practices. In addition, the collaborative relationship between the federal law enforcement agencies and institutions of higher education put forward a partnership that was both recognized and welcomed by international law enforcement agencies and communities. Such focused approaches can generate improved commitment from law enforcement agencies, governments and the public.

References

Buhler, U. (2002). Participation 'with Justice and Dignity': Beyond 'the New Tyranny'. Peace Conflict and Development an Interdisciplinary Journal, Archive: Issue 1, June 2002. University of Bradford UK, Department of Peace Studies.

Curran, J. T. (2002). Human Dignity & the Police: 1992-2002. A Ten- year History Brochure. New York: John Jay College of Criminal Justice.

Curran, J. T. & Rothlein, M. D. (1999). Course development and evaluation. In Lynch, G.W., Human Dignity and the Police: ethnics and integrity in police work. Springfield Illinois, USA: Charles C. Thomas Publisher, LTD.

Green, P. (2002). Contact: training a new generation of peacebuilders. Peace & Change, Vol.27, No. 1, January 2002, 97-105.

Peak, K & Glensor, R.W. (1996). Community Policing & Problem Solving. Upper Saddle River, New Jersey: Prentice Hall.

Iribarnegaray, D. (2002). Peacekeeping's new partnerships. Peace Conflict and Development an Interdisciplinary Journal, Archive: Issue 2, December 2002. University of Bradford UK, Department of Peace Studies.

Kleinig, J. (1999). Human dignity and human rights: an emerging concern in police practice. In Lynch, G.W., Human Dignity and the Police: Ethnics and Integrity in Police Work. Springfield, Illinois, USA: Charles C. Thomas Publisher, LTD.

Pate, T. (2005). Quito report. Report by Police Executive Research Foundation (PERF) presented at the International Law Enforcement Key Leaders Conference, Panama City, Panama.

Pitt, R. (1999). The Experiential Approach: The role of the trainers and its Critical Importance. In Lynch, G.W., Human Dignity and the Police: Ethnics and Integrity in Police Work. Springfield, Illinois, USA: Charles C. Thomas Publisher, LTD.

Price, B. R., (1999). Issues to be addressed in evaluating the human dignity training program. In Lynch, G.W., Human Dignity and the Police: Ethnics and Integrity in Police Work. Springfield, Illinois, USA: Charles C. Thomas Publisher, LTD.

Scanlon, C. (2002). Educating for peace: politics and human rights in Botswana

Peace Conflict and Development an Interdisciplinary Journal, Archive: Issue 1, June 2002. University of Bradford UK, Department of Peace Studies.

Schulz D.M., (1995). From Social Worker to Crime Fighter. Westport, Connecticut: Prager Publications.

Solis, C. L., (2004). The Impact of Community Policing in New York City's Puerto Rican Communities. Dissertation, ProQuest Company. UMI No.311529.

Trojanowicz, R. Steele, M & Trojanowicz, S. (1985). Community Policing A Taxpayers Perspective. Michigan: National Neighborhood Foot Patrol Center School of Criminal Justice Michigan State University.

Making Criminal Justice Transformation, Teaching and Training Work: Experiences Learned from Central Europe

Emil W. Pływaczewski[1]

Introduction

In recent years, transnational organized crime has increased in scope, intensity and sophistication. The end of the Cold War, the collapse of state authority in some countries and regions, and the process of globalization – of trade, finance, communications and information – have all provided an environment in which many criminal organizations find it profitable and preferable to operate across national borders rather than confine their activities to one country (Williams 1999, 221; Adamoli, Di Nicola, Savona and Zoffi 1998: 23-91; Lyman and Potter 2004: 316-322).

Along with the fall of socialism and the emergence of global capitalism, the gap between richer and poorer nations of the world has continued to grow. This growth can be expected to increase opportunities for organized crime, as illicit relationships develop among supply countries, transit nations, and consumer nations. In an unbalanced world economy, legal economics tends to get replaced by illegal economies (Albanese and Das 2003: 15).

The trend of criminal activities in Europe is showing a decided growth rate. An increasing number of ever more serious criminal acts is linked to organized crime (see Lesjak 2001: 61-64). For instance for the last fifteen years the Netherlands and Spain have been the leading countries in the import of cocaine from South America and its distribution to the rest of Europe (Zaitch 2003: 7-17). Besides Italian groups (*Mafia*, *N'drangheta* and *Camorra*), the main criminal groups working in Europe are the Japanese *Yakuza*,

---

1 Emil W. Pływaczewski is a Full Professor of Criminal Law and Criminology, Director of the Chair of Criminal Law, Head of Department of Substantive Penal Law and Criminology, and Vice-dean of the Faculty of Law at the University of Białystok, Poland. His literary output comprises over 260 publications (about 50 published abroad). His recent research has centered on organized crime, corruption, money laundering and criminal policy. Many times he was the guest lecturer or visiting professor at universities in Austria, Germany, Greece, India, Japan, Lithuania, the Netherlands, Italy, Republic of Korea, United States of America and Switzerland. In 1997 he won *the Distinguished International Scholar Award of the International Division American Society of Criminology*. He also lectures at the National Higher School of Police Training in Szczytno (Poland) and the Central European Police Academy (Vienna, Austria) where, since 1994, he has been representative of Poland in the International Examination Board of that Academy. Since 2005 he has been a Chief Coordinator of the Polish Platform for Homeland Security.

the Chinese Triads, Colombian Cartels, Jamaican *Posses*, Russian criminal networks, West African syndicates, Turkish Clans, Iranian elements and other ethnic groups. Among others the activities of Chinese criminal groups have caused increasing alarm among law enforcement officials in Australia, Japan, North America, Russia South Africa, Southeast Asia, and Central and Western Europe (Curtis, Elan, Hudson and Kollars 2002: 19-57; Pływaczewski 2003).

Forced by the dramatic trends of the security and crime situation, European law enforcement agencies are searching for ways and means of effective international collaboration and combating and preventing border crossing and international crime. To control organized crime, far-reaching legal and institutional reforms have been passed in all European states and *ad hoc* instruments have been adopted by all major international organizations, ranging from the European Union to the Council of Europe and the United Nations (Paoli and Fijnaut 2004: 1-17; Vermeulen and Vander Beken 2002: 201-226; Haberfeld and McDonald 2005: 286-309)

Among others, cooperation of police, founded and built on specific international agreements and contacts, can bring desired effects. They require organizational, legal and human resources. This was the basis for the initiative, originated in 1991 by representatives of the police in Vienna and Austria, which led to establishing Austro – Hungarian training for police officers.

This idea was formalized on 12 March 1992 in Budapest. The ministers of interior of both countries signed a joint declaration, which included a call for direct police cooperation of the two countries. Still in the same year, a joint Austro – Hungarian advanced training course was conducted under the aegis of the Austro – Hungarian Police Academy (AHPA). Its participants were members of the police with many years of experience, who held officer's ranks or who had university education. In order to graduate from the course the participants were required to prepare a final paper on one of pre-selected police topics and to pass an oral examination. Upon the completion of the course both parties evaluated their experiences and made appropriate preparations for future specialist training in a broader formula.

An appropriate proposal in this respect was presented in June 1992 during a meeting in the Austrian Ministry of Interior with the ambassadors of the Czech Republic, Poland, Romania, Slovakia, Slovenia and Hungary. Simultaneously, general organizational assumptions for this center were discussed. The dates of the first course and detailed organizational – programmatic assumptions of the training were approved during the next few months.

The signing of the agreement that established the Central European Police Academy (MEPA–*Mitteleuropäische*

Polizeiakademie) with the participation of the representatives of the ministries of interior from Austria, the Czech Republic, Poland, Slovakia, Slovenia and Hungary took place on 1 February 1993 in Vienna (this topic was further developed by Goettel 1995: 75-81). It is worth noticing that the first MEPA course started even before this agreement was signed, that is on 18 January, 1993, and was completed on 25 June, 1993. Among 26 participants from 6 countries, there was one representative of the Polish police. The course took the form of weekly topic blocks (11 theoretical and 10 practical blocks) which were taught in Vienna, Prague and Budapest, as well as (for two weeks) in the Federal Criminal Bureau (BKA) in Wiesbaden (Germany).

Goals and Tasks of the Academy. Criteria for Selection of Participants.

Basic goals of the joint training of representatives of leadership circles of police from various countries are:

- To deepen the knowledge and experience of participants, necessary in the process of performance of cross-border and international tasks of the police. In the face of political, social and economic changes in Europe and their impact on the growth of new forms and techniques of crime, police structures cannot work only on domestic problems, and they have to pursue trans-border and international cooperation;
- To exchange professional knowledge with respect to legal and organizational conditions, as well as the methods and forms of international cooperation of police forces from particular countries;
- To familiarize participants with socio-economic and political conditions and experiences underlying particularly dangerous forms of international crime, such as organized crime, terrorism, economic and environmental crime;
- To support personal contacts and friendships which will not only contribute to creating an atmosphere of mutual trust, but most of all will make it possible to effectively perform required actions by a quick and informal transfer of information;
- To continuously enlarge the group of police officers whose joint training and strong personal ties are particularly important for international police cooperation.

Participants in a course are selected by member states based on the following criteria:
- age between 30 and 46 years (The upper age limit, however, has been lowered to 40 years, with the possibility to allow the participation, in justified cases, of a person who is not older than 45 years);

- university graduate (police school or complemented by police school);
- at least five years of service in the police;
- knowledge of the German language on a level that enables the participant to actively participate in classes.

Since 1995, parallel to the course for police officers, a course for Border Guard officers from member states is conducted following a similar formula (Mayer 2004: 7-10).

Annual Main Courses in the Academy. Final Examinations

Because the Central European Police Academy has no permanent location, classes that constitute a part of the program of a main course are held alternately in all member states. The organization and coordination functions are performed by two MEPA offices located in Vienna and Budapest, with the first having the status of the Central Coordinating Office. The main MEPA bodies are the Board, which determines the main directions and principles of training, and the Preparatory Committee (which also plays the role of the Custodian) that is responsible for preparation and administration of a course. National Coordinating MEPA units are located in member states. The Central Coordinating Office has been given the following tasks and responsibilities:

- organization and timely coordination of training courses;
- coordination of work of national Contact Units of MEPA;
- presentation of MEPA's achievements to other institutions, organizations, government agencies, as well as domestic and international entities;
- leading the preparation and editing of publications for training and information purposes in cooperation with national MEPA Contact Units;
- leading and coordinating the works of the Editing Committee;
- preparation of meetings of the board and other working meetings, as well as
- coordination and execution of national courses and seminars.

Each MEPA member country appoints its own project manager who is responsible for furnishing the organizational, administrative and functional prerequisites of MEPA and for attending to participants on the course. During courses, the project managers keep in contact and supply the central MEPA offices all information and material required for the courses and the MEPA journals. They meet whenever required to clarify pending problems and issues.

The first Polish edition of a MEPA course took place in the Higher Police Academy in Szczytno between 25 March and 6 April,

1994. Students of the Academy were briefed among others on the following issues:

- general information about Poland and brief historical background of police services in our country;
- police bodies as bodies of special administration;
- crime prevention in Poland;
- Polish Police on the background of the international system of cooperation;
- organized crime in Poland – symptoms and conditions;
- police work in combating organized crime in Poland.

Academy students were also introduced to the main tasks of the Central Criminal Laboratory in the Main Police Headquarters in Warsaw, and visited the Regional Police Headquarters in Olsztyn and the District Police Headquarters in Szczytno. They also went through fire training using weapons used by the Polish police (Świerczewski and Merta 1994: 169–171).

The topics presented above were repeated during the consecutive Polish editions of the MEPA course, taking into account the changes and additions in both the dynamics and the structure of criminal activities in Poland, the reforms of law enforcement bodies, as well as legal changes in the acts concerning the police and in criminal law. These topics have also been a part of the courses carried out in the International Center for Specialist Police Training in Legionowo (see Flis 2003: 112). The lectures and seminars for the students are traditionally conducted by professors of the Police Academy, experts of the Main Police Headquarters and representatives of academia from civilian universities who cooperate with the Polish police.

The so-called joint Polish – German weeks, conducted initially in the Land Police School of Brandenburg in Basdorf (Germany), and then in the Higher Professional Police School in Rothenburg have become an interesting training form within MEPA. The location of the School in Rothenburg allows – besides lectures conducted by German and Polish experts – for the participants to get familiar with the work of the Polish police in Zgorzelec, the German Police in Goerlitz, the Land Criminal Office in Saxony, as well as the functioning of the German border service on the border crossing point in Ludwigsdorf – Jędrzychów (Świerczewski 1997: 120-121). For many years multiple professional seminars have been organized for the graduates of the main MEPA courses and the specialist courses of the Border Guard.

The conduct of the main courses is facilitated by the MEPA manual (two editions have been in print so far), where every country prepares its own part, while keeping intact the subject structure (Róg, Pływaczewski, Hofmański, Merta and Lagoda 2001; Lelental, Pływaczewski, Róg, Wrześniowski, Lagoda and

Urwantowicz 2003). MEPA also publishes its own newsletter and has a web site (*www.mepa.net*).

During the first years of MEPA's existence, the course participants prepared final papers on pre-selected topics. Initially they prepared them individually, and in courses taking place later – in groups of several persons from different countries. The papers were reviewed by the members of the International Examination Committee, which in Budapest administers the final examination that resembles the defense of a graduation or master's degree thesis.

Since the first final examination after the Main MEPA Course on 23 May 2002, in Budapest. its formula underwent advanced modification. A new examination formula was applied involving a "case study". All course participants have now to solve together the case in question, in the light of regulations that are in force in particular states. Generally speaking, the International Examination Committee gave a positive evaluation of this method of administering the final examination, at the same time indicating directions for its modification, also taking into account critical opinions of course participants.

The Main MEPA Course of 2004 was also of special importance because during the course Poland, Slovakia, Slovenia, Hungary and the Czech Republic became members of the European Union.

Other law enforcement training in Central Europe

In the wake of the dramatic events of the late 1980s and early 1990s, including the fall of the Berlin Wall and the dismantling of the Soviet Union, the United States Government recognized the necessity of the training academy in Central Europe to enhance the skills of law enforcement officers facing a dramatically changing criminal landscape. As already mentioned in this anthology, this Government and the Government of Hungary agreed to establish in Budapest the International Law Enforcement Academy.

The Budapest-based ILEA runs topical 1- to 2-week seminars and courses, and an 8-week core course. Its program is similar to the domestic FBI National Academy Program in the United States, but is conducted with simultaneous translation to eliminate the requirement for students to speak English. The Academy offers training opportunities for up to 130 students at one time. The ILEA program is a personal and professional development program targeted at mid-level managers in the police services of former Communist/Socialist countries.

The program is conducted for fifty students in five sessions a year, for a total of 250 students per year. Each session involves sixteen students selected from only three different countries, for a total of forty-eight students, to minimize interpreter and translation requirements. The remaining two slots are offered to Hungary, as the host country, in recognition of its support in the establishment of the ILEA Program. In addition, each country should nominate one counselor to serve as the official head of delegation during the eight-week program. The counselor should be at the appropriate rank to provide administrative and supervisory oversight to the student group. The counselors' primary duties are administrative, but each may attend classes when not otherwise occupied. Each counselor will also receive a diploma at the conclusion of the course.

Criteria for student selection have been previously furnished and are included on nomination forms which have been translated into each language and have been furnished to each embassy. Travel expenses, food, lodging, and other costs will be borne by the United States for all students and counselors.

The International Curriculum Committee (ICC) meets at the completion of each session in Budapest, to develop course content. The representative from each country should have knowledge of crime problems, training needs, and existing training programs for their particular country, and have the authority to recommend curriculum content based on these individual needs. Each representative should bring with them diagrams of their police organizational structure, and general demographic information concerning crime problems and trends in their country. This information should be submitted in English and copies will be distributed to each committee member.

The focus of the program for students is not on technical skills, but on leadership, personnel and financial management of the investigative process, and other contemporary law enforcement issues. Countries participating with the United States in providing instructors, to date, include Canada, Great Britain, Germany, Italy, Ireland, Russia, and Hungary. Other countries which are contemplating involvement in this cooperative effort include the Netherlands, Belgium, France, Spain, Austria, Sweden, and Switzerland.

It is important to emphasize that the ILEA's courses are intended to be challenging, requiring class participation, research, writing, and oral presentations. In addition, a strict code of conduct is enforced. Students not meeting these standards of performance and conduct may be dismissed from the ILEA following a thorough review of the individual by a panel of ILEA faculty and program administrators.

The ILEA creates an opportunity for interaction which facilitates close working ties and develops future international cooperation. The Budapest Office of MEPA is located in the main building of the

International Law Enforcement Academy. This is one of the factors which may improve mutual understanding and efficiency in international police cooperation and increase professional knowledge and experience as well (Caparini and Marenin 2004). Such cooperation should include more police educational institutions in Europe and beyond.

Conclusion

ILEA's and MEPA's activities lead to the conclusion that they play an important role in counteracting organized crime, especially because the requirement of international cooperation of law enforcement bodies in contemporary Europe and beyond has become a necessity. In this process of international cooperation the gained and exchanged knowledge, and the personal relations that have been established by police officers constitute a viable and constructive basis for effective fight against organized crime.

An important confirmation of this was the signing on 22 May, 2001, in Budapest, by ministers of interior of eight member countries, of the "Joint announcement in the framework of the Central European Police Academy", which constituted an unequivocal rise of the importance of the Academy to governmental level (MEPA 2001).

Currently MEPA maintains contacts with leading institutions of the European Union (EU), especially with the European Commission. It is also actively represented in the undertakings of the European Police Academy (CEPOL), AEPC (the Association of European Police Colleges - AEPC is currently conducting various training modules for the area of South Eastern Europe within the framework of the Stability Pact), in the Central Asian Project, the Organized Crime Training Network, the Police Training Seminar in Tampere, or in working groups of the EU Council in Brussels.

A majority of member states of the European Police Academy support establishing a "network of police schools", but with a better equipped Secretariat, while other countries opt for a permanent institution. In this situation, however, a unanimous decision is required, because this creates a danger – if the "network of schools" proposal is not fully accepted – of the lack of possibility for the CEPOL to obtain a legal status. The lack of legal status of the CEPOL (currently its Secretariat is in Denmark) is still causing problems. Changes in this respect are very much desired.

On the 1st of May 2004, five member states of the MEPA obtained – as was mentioned before – the status of members of the European Union, which makes it necessary to look for new solutions, also with respect to international training of police officers. However, the regional character of the Academy will also play an essential role in the future. This necessitates keeping its consistency with its own *"curriculum vitae"*. In relation to this, what is particularly important is the harmonization of law (first steps towards this goal have been made by Hungary and Slovenia).

For now, MEPA constitutes a certain model with respect to regional cooperation of police in Europe. This initiative can be a good example for other parts of the world as well for effective international collaboration as for combating transnational organized crime. Drawing on their knowledge, MEPA graduates know where to get the appropriate information and help quickly, how to use confidential information and who is allowed access to the information. Their fluency in German, knowledge of the police terminology and personal contacts provide the prerequisites for simple and effective border-crossing co-operation, therefore cutting through the red tape. Such improved communication will help to counteract the disadvantages arising from the widespread international networking of organized crime. Trust and quick collaboration between MEPA graduates from the various countries has already achieved success in numerous cases of international organized crime that would have been difficult if not impossible to attain without such cooperation. The academy should follow the rules that have been set so far and strengthen its position, which makes it necessary to intensify training and assume new directions for its activity.

References

Adamoli S., Di Nicola A., Savona E.U. and Zoffi P. (1998). Organised Crime around the World, Helsinki: European Institute for Crime Prevention and Control (HEUNI), 23-91.

Caparini M. and Marenin O. (eds.) (2004). Transforming Police in Central and Eastern Europe. Process and Progress. Geneva Centre for the Democratic Control of Armed Forces, Muenster: LIT Verlag.

Curtis G.E., Elan S.L., Hudson R.A. and Kollars N.A. (2002). Transnational Activities of Chinese Crime Organisations. A Report Prepared under an Interagency Agreement by the Federal Research Division, Library of Congress, Trends in Organized Crime, Vol. 7, Number 3.

Fijnaut C. and Paoli L. (2004). General Introduction. In Fijnaut C. and Paoli L. (eds.) Organised Crime in Europe. Concepts, Patterns and Control Policies in the European Union and Beyond, Dordrecht: Springer, 1-7.

Flis M. (2003). Rola Międzynarodowego Centrum Szkoleń Specjalistycznych Policji we współpracy szkoleniowej polskiej Policji z Unią Europejską (The role of the International Center for Specialist Police Training in training cooperation of the Polish Police with the European Union). In: Pływaczewski, W. Kędzierska, G. and Bogdalski

P. (eds.)) Unia Europejska – wyzwanie dla polskiej Policji (European Union – challenge for the Polish Police), Wydawnictwo Wyższej Szkoły Policji, Szczytno: (Editing House of the Police Academy), 112 et seq.

Goettel M. (1995). Środkowoeuropejska Akademia Policyjna (The Central European Police Academy), Przegląd Policyjny (Police Review), no. 1–2, 75-81.

Haberfeld M. and McDonald W.H. (2005). International Cooperation in Policing. In Philip Reichel (ed.), Handbook of Transnational Crime & Justice, London - New Delhi: Sage Publications, Thousand Oaks, 286 et seq.

Lelental S., Pływaczewski E., Róg M. Wrześniowski W., Lagoda K. and Urwantowicz J. (2003). Landesteil: Republik Polen in: Zentrales Koordinationsbüro der Mitteleuropäischen Polizeiakademie Wien (Hrsg.), Wien: Das MEPA-Handbuch.

Lesjak K. (2001). Organisierte Kriminalität – eine Herausforderung für Europa. In Aktuelle/Neue Erscheinungsformen der Organisierten Kriminalität. Redaktion Weiss B., Wien: Zentrales Koordinationsbüro der Mitteleuropäischen Polizeiakademie, 61-64.

Lyman M.D. and Potter G.W. (2004). Organized Crime, Upper Saddle River and New Jersey: Pearson Prentice Hall, 316-322.

Mayer F. (2004). Die MEPA–Grenzausbildung. Entstehung und grundlegende Bedeutung für die Sicherheit in einem gemeinsamen Europa, MEPA report, no. 2, September, 7-10.

MEPA (2001). Gemeinsame Erklärung zur Zusammenarbeit im Rahmen der Mitteleuropäischen Akademie, MEPA–Report, no. 2, June

Pływaczewski E. (2004). Chinese Organized Crime in Western and Central Europe. In Broadhurst R.G. (ed.), Crime and its Control in the People's Republic of China: proceedings of the Annual Symposia 2000-2002, Hong Kong: Centre for Criminology, The University of Hong Kong.

Róg M., Pływaczewski E., Hofmański P., Merta M. and Lagoda K. (2001). Landesteil: Republik Polen, in: Zentrales Koordinationsbüro der Mitteleuropäischen Polizeiakademie Wien (Hrsg.), MEPA-Handbuch, 1. Ergänzungslieferung, Stuttgart-München-Hannover-Berlin-Weimar-Dresden, Richard Boorberg Verlag; and Landesteil: Republik Polen (co-authors: Lelental S., Pływaczewski E., Róg M. Wrześniowski W., Lagoda K., Urwantowicz J.). In Zentrales Koordinationsbüro der Mitteleuropäischen Polizeiakademie Wien (Hrsg.), Wien: Das MEPA-Handbuch, 2003.

Świerczewski J. and Merta M. (1994). Polska edycja kursu Środkowoeuropejskiej Akademii Policyjnej (Polish edition of the Central European Police Academy course), Przegląd Policyjny (Police Review), no. 2-3,169–171.

Świerczewski J. (1997). Polska i polsko-niemiecka edycja Środkowoeuropejskiej Akademii Policyjnej (Polish and Polish – German edition of the Central European Police Academy), Przegląd Policyjny (Police Rewiew), no. 3,12-121.

Ward R. H. and Serio J. D. (2005). Opportunities and Challenges in Delivering a Syllabus for International Police Training. The Case of the International Law Enforcement Academy (ILEA) at Roswell, New Mexico (paper presented at the 57th Annual Meeting of the American Society of Criminology, Toronto, Ontario, November 16-19).

Vermeulen G. and vander Beken T. (2002). International/Regional framework for combating organized crime. In De Ruyver B. Vermeulen G. and vander Beken, T (eds.), Strategies of the EU and the US in Combating Transnational Organized Crime, Antwerp – Apeldoorn: Maklu, 221-226.

Williams P. (1999). Emerging Issues: Transnational crime and its control. In Newman G. (ed.), Global Report on Crime and Justice, published for the United Nations Office for Drug Control and Crime Prevention, New York and Oxford: Oxford University Press, 221.

Zaitch D. (2003). Recent trends in cocaine trafficking in the Netherlands and Spain. In (eds.) Siegel D. van de Bunt H. and Zaitch D., Global Organized Crime Trends and Developments, Dordrecht, Boston and London: Kluwer Academic Publishers, 7-17.

Education and Training in Four Countries: Getting Rule of Law Messages Across

Andrew Millie and Dilip Das[1]

Introduction

For policing in democratic nations there is an assumed tension between "crime control" and "due process", effectively between getting things done, and getting things done properly. For public policing to be effective, the public needs to have confidence in policing decisions; that these decisions have legitimacy in that they are carried out in the public's interest and follow rule of law principles. In the contemporary climate of globalization, in terms of criminal behaviour and international and trans-national enforcement arrangements, developed nations should lead by 'rule of law' example. In this chapter our focus is on policing in four developed nations: Germany, Japan, Switzerland and France. We take the view that, without educating the police at home, such nations are less equipped to implement the rule of law.

This chapter considers the education and training of the public police from a rule of law perspective, in terms of trainee selection, the background philosophy of training, general organization and curriculum. The chapter draws largely from a series of interviews, observations and conversations conducted by one of the authors between 1998 and 2001 in each of the four countries. This has been supplemented by evidence from the research literature.

To summarize the findings, all four countries have an increasing emphasis on community in their training. In terms of recruitment, it is important to have recruits that agree with rule of law messages. This may be possible via psychological testing (Switzerland) or greater academic emphasis (France and Japan). A better understanding of minority issues and rule of law application may be possible simply by recruiting more from minority groups (Germany). Across the four countries there appears to be three distinct training

---

1 Andrew Millie, Midlands Centre for Criminology and Criminal Justice, Department of Social Sciences, Loughborough University, Leicestershire, LE11 3TU, UK; Dilip Das, International Police Executive Symposium, 6030 Nott Road, Guilderland, New York 12084. Dr Andrew Millie is a Lecturer in criminology and social policy, and Senior Research Fellow at the Midlands Centre for Criminology and Criminal Justice, Loughborough University, UK. Dr Dilip Das is Editor in Chief of Police Practice and Research: An International Journal and of the World Police Encyclopedia. Dr. Das is President of the International Police Executive Symposium (www.ipes.info), and human rights consultant to the United Nations.

philosophies: the law and democracy (Germany); community and citizen involvement (Japan and Switzerland); and human rights and multi-culturalism (France). There are not necessarily any right or wrong ways of doing things and rule of law messages are apparent in all three approaches; however, it may be sensible to tackle the issue from all angles possible. There are also lessons apparent in the training curricula of the four countries. For instance, the Swiss police training has a focus on "emotion, sensibility and understanding"; Baden-Württemberg in Germany offers conflict resolution training; and Japan's training program includes cultural and personal development - which may make recruits more aware of wider societal norms and values.

However, none of the four systems are perfect and there have been concerns over police brutality and poor community relations in some of the nations. Where the four countries appear to be heading in the right direction is in their increased professionalism and work to make the police more representative. In order to improve, or maintain, public confidence it is important that policing is professional, has legitimacy in terms of representation and adheres to rule of law principles. We believe the quality of training and education that officers receive is central to this.

Problem

The very idea of policing is in many ways fundamentally problematic for democracy and the rule of law. Controlling the police has always been seen as one of the most difficult aspects of statecraft, as the Roman writer Juvenal's famous question *'quis custodiet ipsos custodes*?' - 'who guards the guards?' indicated two millennia ago (Reiner 2002: 21).

In order to achieve criminal justice in a democratic society it is often assumed there is a choice between a crime control model and a due process model (Packer 1969). On the one hand there is the pressure to gain enough evidence for a conviction (crime control) while on the other hand there is the need to protect the rights of the suspect (due process). How far to the left or the right we travel is a factor in the type of society in which we want to live; that the more crime control we have, the less due process, and the more due process, the less crime control (see also Skolnick 1966). In simple terms it is a balancing act between the pressure to get things done, and the pressure to get things done correctly. Of course it is not a simple dichotomous choice with many other pressures including those of culture, system, politics, public and media. Due process is intrinsically linked to the concept of "rule of law"; essentially characterized by neutrality, equality and universality. And central to 'rule of law' is the question of how much power is given to the public police, and whether this power is used appropriately.

Rule of law as a concept certainly has a lot of political capital. As Carothers (1998) has observed: "The concept is suddenly everywhere - a venerable part of Western political philosophy enjoying a new run as a rising imperative of the era of globalization". Internationally it is often assumed that democratic countries are more likely to adhere to rule of law principles alongside strict adherence to criminal justice and human rights; and it is the job of developed nations to teach these principles to those less developed. This view is somewhat misplaced, particularly post-9/11 with terror suspects having been held without charge in both the US and UK (certainly a "crime control" rather than "rule of law" emphasis). Following the United Nations Millennium Summit in 2000, the United Nations Secretary-General has reported:

> "I strongly believe that every nation that proclaims the rule of law at home must respect it abroad and that every nation that insists on it abroad must enforce it at home. Indeed, the Millennium Declaration reaffirmed the commitment of all nations to the rule of law as the all-important framework for advancing human security and prosperity" (UN Report of the Secretary-General 2005: 35 (para.133)).

Some of these broader discussions are beyond the scope of this chapter. However, the declaration that "every nation that insists on [the rule of law – emphasis added] abroad must enforce it at home" is pertinent. Here we consider police education and training from a rule of law perspective in four developed nations. We take the view that, without educating the police at home, such nations are less equipped to lead by example. This is particularly true in the contemporary climate of globalization in terms of criminal behaviour and international and transnational enforcement arrangements. There is always difficulty in comparing different policing systems as each system has its own history, culture and problems (*e.g.*, Mawby 1990). However, there is value in comparative study; the differences between the systems mean that ways of working can be identified that may not have been considered before.

Methodology

This chapter draws largely from a series of interviews, observations and conversations conducted by one of the authors between 1998 and 2001 (see also Das and Pino 2007) in Germany, Japan, Switzerland and France. The four countries represent a range of police systems and approaches to police training and, as such, a variety of lessons can be learnt. Evidence was gathered from police leaders, lower-level police officers, and academy instructors about their training programs. Various levels of police training programs were visited: recruit training schools; training for intermediate level officers; and academies for the training of higher ranking officers. At each level program directors, teachers, and students were interviewed. Interviews were unstructured and all records were anonymized. The data collected was analyzed for key themes, with reference to the literature. The research was conducted within the major cities and centers of police activity in each of the four countries. While the training and education of senior officers is considered, the main emphasis of the chapter is on the training and education of police recruits[2].

Policing Systems

In order to understand better the emphasis placed on rule of law in police training and education within different countries, it is important to recognise the diversity of police systems and cultures. To consider the European[3] examples first, there is no uniform system of policing across continental Europe; however, according to Mawby (2003), the traditional European model is centralized. Three main systems can be identified:

- Structurally centralized and militaristic;
- Functional emphasis on political and administrative tasks; and
- Closely tied to government and therefore less accountable to the public or law (see also Mawby 1990; 1992)

The model of public policing followed in France closely follows that of "structurally centralized and militaristic", although some elements have become more localized (see Journes, 1993). France has two public forces, in theory allowing no one institution to carry too much power. The State Police (*Police Nationale*) come under the Ministry of the Interior, whereas the *Gendarmerie Nationale* has a militaristic emphasis, coming under the control of the Ministry of Defence. The French *Gendarmerie* now also contribute to a smaller European Gendarmerie Force (EGF), formed in collaboration with Italy, Spain, Portugal and the Netherlands - and inaugurated in January 2006 (see www.eurogendfor.org) - to be used in international post-conflict peacekeeping.

---

2 This was part of a larger project on police structure, leadership, functions, police-community relations and training which is being published as 'Cross-Cultural Profiles of Policing' by Dilip Das. It was recognized by the author that police training and education was one of the most important elements for professionalism of the police.

3 The Interpol website has a useful summary of criminal justice in many European countries; see http://www.interpol.int/Public/Region/Europe/ pjsystems/ Default. asp.

Germany's public police are divided by federal states (or Länder). In terms of education and training, each state has its own state police school (*Landespolizeischule*). The unique history of Germany, leading to reunification in 1990, has added extra pressure to police training and education as the West German police took responsibility for the former East Germany. As Harlan (1997) has documented, the East German police system followed a completely centralized model. It may be assumed that rule of law issues were more prominent in the former socialist East; however, things were not clear-cut. Harlan observed that complaints against the police certainly occurred in Western Germany. And even though members of the public in East Germany were "obliged" to forward information to the *Stasi*, according to Wolfe (1992: 97), "it appears that with infrequent exceptions police did adhere to the principles of rule of law". Of course the two nations may have had different understandings of what constitutes rule of law.

Switzerland has a distinctive area-based structure to its public police based on Cantons, and supplemented by various city police and border guard corps. There is slight variation in structure across Switzerland; to put things simply, German-speaking cantons are divided into criminal, security and traffic police, and French-speaking cantons have criminal police (*Sûreté*) and security police (*Gendarmerie*)[4]. Switzerland is often thought of as having low crime. Research by Eisner and Killias (2004) indicates that the Swiss may have a crime rate below the European average, but that this is not especially low. As with many countries, the crime rate rose over recent decades. Police training and education is based within each canton, although where regional differences were observed, these were not substantial. Some further training is now centralized at the Central Swiss Police School (*Zentralschweizerische Polizeischule*). Training was traditionally militaristic, however, the current curriculum at the Central Swiss Police School includes community policing, human rights and professional ethics.

That said, the United Nations has expressed concern about deviation from rule of law principles in some elements of the Swiss police:

The Committee is deeply concerned at reported instances of police brutality towards persons being apprehended and detainees, noting that such persons are frequently aliens. It is also concerned that many cantons do not have independent mechanisms for investigation of complaints regarding violence and other forms of misconduct by the police. The possibility of resort to court action

---

4 The Ticino (Italian-speaking) canton has its own geographical system with forces divided by sectors - see http://internet.bap.admin.ch/e/portrait/pol_ struktur/i_index.htm.

cannot serve as a substitute for such mechanisms (UN Human Rights Committee 2001).

The supposed unique selling point of the public police in Japan (and the country's low crime rate – although this is rising) is its emphasis on community-oriented styles of policing (*e.g.*, Bayley 1976; 1991; Ebbe 1996); that the West has much to learn from the police's involvement in counselling, advise, mediation and collective responsibility – that the police work with the community. However, according to Aldous and Leishman (1997) and Chwialkowski (1998) this style of policing owes much to post-war reconstruction. Before the Second World War Japan's public police was largely centralized, under direct control of the national government. After the war paramilitary police organizations were disbanded, the constitution rewritten along US lines, and the public police decentralized; "If power could be returned to the local communities, it was theorized, then the powers of democracy would be strengthened in Japan" (Chwialkowski 1998: 724). There have been changes; however, the local emphasis remains. The public police in Japan is divided into three tiers of operation. Firstly there is overall control by the National Police Agency (NPA) – answerable to the National Public Safety Commission of the Cabinet Office. Secondly, there is the regionally divided prefectural forces. And thirdly, public policing is delivered locally via community-centred stations, known as police boxes or koban.

As for the importance of rule of law within the Japanese police, there is no real consensus among scholars. According to Bayley (1991: 4), "the incidence of misconduct is slight and the faults trivial by American standards". However, according to Johnson (2003: 32):

> [A] recent wave of police scandals raises doubts about officers' normative commitment to integrity and about previous claims that Japanese police behaviour is "astonishingly good".

The four nations included in this study have policing systems that have evolved in different ways due to various cultural, historical and political reasons. Nonetheless, all should have a common focus on the rule of law; as the United Nations Secretary General has observed, 'the rule of law [is] the all-important framework for advancing human security and prosperity'. (2005: 35 (para.133)). An understanding - and practical implementation - of rule of law, professional ethics and human rights (*e.g.*, Das and Palmiotto 2002; Kleinig 1996; Neyroud and Beckley 2001) is essential for public confidence in policing, and for maintaining legitimacy for policing decisions. However, various policing scandals or reported misconducts have distracted from this, at least in some of the four nations. This chapter focuses on the role of police training and education in getting rule of law messages across. The focus is on the public police in each country. There has been much research into non-public forms of policing/security - or plural policing (*e.g.,*Shearing 1992; Loader 2000; Jones and Newburn 2005; Zedner 2006). Such developments have occurred within the four countries considered here. Whilst the need for rule of law training for these 'plural' agencies is essential, this falls outside the scope of this chapter.

Police Education and Training

The education and training of the public police within France, Germany, Switzerland and Japan is considered in terms of four key themes: trainee selection; the background philosophy of training; general organization; and curriculum.

Trainee Selection

One way to have police officers with greater regard for rule of law principles is to more carefully select raw police recruits. The four countries included in this research were somewhat different in their requirements for new trainees. The requirements varied mostly in the kinds of education needed for eligibility (they also varied by the type and number of examinations that needed to be successfully completed).

To start with Switzerland, in order to attract recruits for the *Kantons Polizei* in Zürich, the school advertises in newspapers and on the radio. There are usually 40-50 applications every month, and an approximate 20 per cent acceptance rate. There is no need for any specific level of schooling, but recruits are required to have had another profession before joining the police and are tested on:

- Knowledge of German and French;
- Arithmetics and geography;
- Political knowledge of Switzerland; and
- Sports and psychological tests.

The sports component is seen as very important. Interviews are held with the chief, the personnel chief, the police psychologists, and others. The requirements for males and females are the same. For the gendarmerie in Geneva there are height requirements, but not for the *inspecteurs* (police detectives in the *Sûreté*).

In Japan greater emphasis is placed on school or university education. For instance, high school graduates receive 21 months training whereas this is reduced to 15 months for university graduates. At the International Research and Training Institute for

Criminal Investigation, recruits need to be college graduates. Thirty percent of the total police personnel have university degrees, and about 50 per cent of the new constables, the lowest ranking uniformed police officers (*Junsa*), have degrees.

In Germany most recruits join the police as *Wachtmeister-anwärter* (trainee constable) after the *Mittlere Reife* (school examination at age 16) – although the situation has changed in many states with the abolition of lower ranks and hiring starting at *Kommissar* level (see Das and Palmiotto 2004). In one area visited, Baden-Württemberg, the following avenues were available for entering the police:

- Those with high school final examination (Hauptschulabschluss) up to the age of 15, plus 3 years in a profession which includes the Vocational School Certificate (Berufsschule) – 15 per cent entered through this avenue, although this has since discontinued;
- Persons with Mittlere Reife certificates at age 16 - this accounted for 55 per cent of the students; and
- Those who had completed education in a Gymnasium (at age 19), and had achieved university entrance qualifications - 30 per cent of all police entered through this avenue.

Black and minority ethnic groups are under-represented within the German police (Murck and Werdes 1996). According to recent media reports (*e.g.*, Phalniker, in *Deutsche Welle* 2006) the police in Berlin are trying to address this issue. Non-German recruits have been accepted by the police since the early 1990s; however, the entrance exam is thought to be a barrier to immigrants (with its demand for good high school education and fitness), along with other cultural or psychological issues of acceptance.

In France, the candidates for the 'Guardians of Peace' positions must pass a National Entrance Examination. There are additional age, health, and educational requirements. Candidates must have studied up to Baccalaureate level (although they may not have completed) and hiring takes place on an order of merit based on the results of the entrance examination. Inspectors and Officers of Peace (commissioned uniformed officers) also have to fulfil special requirements in regard to height, weight and other physical characteristics (and Inspectors have to have passed the Baccalaureate examination). *Commissaires* must have completed three to four years of university education and there is a National Examination for this position.

The four countries all have their own style and criteria for police recruitment. How effective each system of recruitment is for gaining candidates in sympathy with rule of law principles is unknown. The psychological testing and the need for some level of knowledge of the political system in Switzerland might filter out some "undesirable" candidates – depending of course on the type of testing used. That said, this expectation might also filter out certain social or ethnic groups, leading to poor representation. The efforts in Germany to recruit more people from Black and minority ethnic groups is commendable and may eventually lead to a force that better understands minority issues – perhaps improving rule of law application? Japan and France have a strong emphasis on academic education. This may produce candidates that are better equipped to understand rule of law training and this is certainly an area where more research is needed.

Background Philosophy of Training

If candidates are successful, the training they receive in France, Germany, Switzerland and Japan appears to have an increasing emphasis on community – be it via a focus on community-styles of policing, or broader public-relations awareness training.

However, this was not always the case. In Switzerland, for example, police training has historically been militaristic. That said, the current emphasis is on developing integration of a number of competences:

- Appreciating and understanding emotions;
- Developing sensibility;
- Developing a comprehension of all types of situations that police are likely to become involved in during the course of their work; and
- An equal emphasis on technique and psychological and value-oriented comprehension.

Police training currently emphasizes the use of psychology, citizen involvement, and developing good public relationships. Through this 'softer' focus, the community's, the victims' and the defendants' situation is hopefully understood and this in turn leads hopefully to fewer breaches of rule of law principles.

Current police training and education in Japan focuses on community-policing alongside ethics and cultural training. In terms of 'rule of law', the ethics training that recruits receive is especially influential. Ethics courses focus on:

- The correction of negative attitudes;
- Warm-heartedness and common sense; and
- A sense of justice, responsibility, and service.

The Hyogo Prefecture Academy and the Tokyo Academy are run in a militaristic and formal manner, with cadets staying in dormitories during the week. However, on weekends the cadets can go home and are now not asked to wear suits and ties (this used to be a requirement). This particular policy is supposed to allow cadets to identify with the rest of their community, especially their own age group. While there is not a specific course covering public relations, it is emphasized through all aspects of training. The staff of the academies are aware that there has been a negative police sub-culture in Japan, and they try to control it.

Police training in post-war Germany had a particular focus on how democracy works and the separation of the powers of the various branches of the government. According to Fairchild (1988), police reform movements tried to include demilitarization, communalization, democratization, and improved community relations and public accountability. More recent reforms have involved community-oriented policing, communication, conflict resolution, and modern management skills and techniques (Feltes 2002).

There used to be a strong emphasis on militaristic discipline within German police training. This has diminished and current training is concerned primarily with education on police laws (university law degrees have a greater focus on general laws). Law is the main focus in the training of lower ranks, and only about 10 per cent of training of higher ranks involves working with people. The police laws tend to be taught within the context of rule of law and democracy; that the State must be built on the rule of law (*Rechtsstaat*) and that democracy (*demokratischer staat*) must co-exist with it.

In France the training of the State Police (*Police Nationale*) has 'generalization' as a guiding philosophy; that the police should be generalists. The objective is to produce officers who can perform all of the required tasks associated with police work (see Souchon 1981). Police officers are given also a general level of criminological understanding. In terms of rule of law principles they are also trained to be:

- Aware of the pluralistic facets of the community; and
- Sensitive to human rights issues.

As the *Gendarmerie Nationale* is in effect a military organization, the training very much reflects this with recruits living in barracks.

The training philosophies of these different countries appear to include rule of law messages, but from different perspectives. Germany, for example, emphasizes the law and the interplay between rule of law and democracy. Japan has more militaristic training structures but emphasizes, for example, positive attitudes, warm-heartedness and a sense of justice. Although Switzerland had historically a militaristic training emphasis, the police currently receive training in psychology, citizen involvement, and developing good public relationships. And finally, the French National Police are made aware of rule of law issues through training in human rights and multi-culturalism. All four countries have in common an increasing emphasis on community-oriented policing philosophies that focus on working with the public to solve problems.

General Organization of Training

Each country has different categories of training, and there is variation in duration of basic and on-the-job training. Much of the variation in requirements is related to the preparation for the different specialized tasks, level of previous education, and the general organizational structure of the public police in each country.

In Switzerland there are different forms of training for the criminal police (*Sûreté*) and the Gendarmerie, on-the-job training from lateral appointees, and an emphasis on continuing education. There is also a great emphasis on the role of sports in training. As noted, the public police in Switzerland is based on area Cantons; so too is police training. In the Zürich canton, for instance, recruits train for five months and then take an examination in order to become the lowest ranking police official. They then have to do two and a half years of training with the Emergency Police (*Bereitschaftspolizei*). After that they come back to school for professional police courses (*Polizeifachkurs*) for five additional months. After completing this training, they are given the choice of going to traffic police, or to the prosecutor's office (*Bezirkanwaltschaften*) where they serve as secretary of the examining magistrates (*Untersuchungsrichter*). After four to five years of service, they can choose to work for the *Sûreté*, traffic police or police district (*Bezirk*). In other cantons the training program may vary. For instance, in Lausanne, the *Sûreté* and the Gendarmerie are trained together. Cadets are trained for one year with 90 per cent training in common and 10 per cent devoted to specialization. In Geneva the Training Academy has two parts - one for the *Sûreté* and one for the *Gendarmerie*. After seven months of theoretical training, a cadet remains for three more years as a trainee working alongside a more experienced officer. On average, basic training lasts one year throughout Switzerland, but it can range from five months to two years, depending on the police role and the canton.

At the Hyogo Prefecture Police Academy in Japan, the Personnel Division of the Hyogo Prefectural Police selects trainees. Dormitory accommodation is provided for up to 600 trainees. Across Japan, high school graduates receive 21 months training

194

(10 months pre-service training, 8 months on-the-job training and 3 months for a pre-service comprehensive course). University graduates have 15 months training (6 months pre-service training, 7 months on-the-job training and a 2 month pre-service comprehensive course) (see NPA 2005). Japanese police officers are divided into uniform police and detectives, with detectives engaging in criminal investigations. After Prefectural Police School, officers can move onto a Regional Police School for Sergeant or Inspector training, and then the National Police Academy for Inspector or administrative training.

Police training in Germany is very much practice-oriented. As noted, Germany's public police is divided across its federal states (or *Länder*). Taking the state of Bavaria as an example, here there are seven police schools, all under the Emergency Police Department. In some other states where lower ranks have been abolished (Hessen, for example) basic police training is given by the Police Technical College (*Polizeifachhochschule*) (after one years training they receive a certificate). Other training can be provided by the common police school (more of a theoretical school). An alternative practice-oriented model first assigns candidates to a police station where they take leave from police work to attend police school for training. Regular training is undertaken in the Police Technical College (*Fachhochschule*) where training lasts for 3 years. If officers do not have University Entrance Qualifications, they must have the Police Technical College certificate. After finishing the Technical College, the pupils go to work with the Emergency Police; however, they are sent to police stations to work when there are no emergency situations.

Training in France has become more professional, has been redesigned to reflect social priorities and is no longer confined to the narrow goals of the police organization. Key areas of concern include having a dynamic approach, awareness of diversity issues and psychological aspects to policing. Police recruits go to a police training school for one year and go through practical training for another year. More emphasis has been placed on continuing education for the officers. French police leaders in supervisory positions and at executive rank are all university graduates. Although university education is not required at the lower levels, more university-educated people are joining the police.

Again, the four countries have their own approaches to training in terms of organization and structure, and there is also some variation within countries. If rule of law messages are to get across to recruits, it is important to appreciate these different contexts. While the variation in the total length of time required to train as an officer may not be too important (beyond the simple observation that the longer the time, the more the opportunity), the different availability of basic, theoretical and on-the-job training will be important. Similarly, the type of organization, be it the practice-oriented German system, or the wider professional approach of the French system, will make a difference.

Police Training and Education Curriculum

Differences in training curriculum among the four countries center on how much training is in class versus on-the-job. There are different emphases on techniques, law, psychological exams, public relations, and length in school.

In Switzerland, the curriculum is concerned primarily with the appreciation of emotion, sensibility, and understanding of situations the trainees might find themselves in. There is less emphasis on policing techniques. Along with psychological training, these 'softer' qualities are considered essential for a professional police officer. However, despite the encouragement of a professional approach some police officers are, as noted above, still said to be repressive (*e.g.,* UN Human Rights Committee 2001).

Taking the Geneva canton as an example, those training for the *Sûreté* and the *Gendarmerie* share courses in self-defense and sports, first aid and anatomy. For the *Gendarmerie* a range of competences are emphasized including: computer training, weapons training, physical training, psychology and public relations. Sports instructors have an important role as physical well-being is stressed. Martial arts training is also available.

The training curriculum in Japan has changed little over the past 30 years (Parker 2001) and was very similar at the Hyogo Prefecture Academy, the International Research and Training Institute for Criminal Investigation, and the Tokyo Police Academy. Trainees at the Hyogo Prefecture Academy are given courses in general academic subjects, such as Japanese, geography, and economics. They also take a law class focusing on the constitution, police administration law, criminal and civil laws, criminal procedure, and the law in general. Professional on-the-job training includes patrol, investigation, traffic regulation, crime prevention, and guarding duties. Physical training includes classes on arrest techniques, physical exercise and, where force is required for arrest, the students are taught numerous forms of martial arts, including karate, judo, and kendo along with boxing. There are also shooting classes and riot drill training. About thirty specialist courses are run every year, and last from ten days to three weeks. These courses include traffic, investigation, English language and computing. Of particular relevance to this chapter, ethics classes are also taught, along with community-oriented policing. As noted, the Academy has a very strict militaristic schedule for each day. This discipline extends to the students' personal development. For instance, each Wednesday, an hour-long class is devoted to personal refinement, including activities such as the tea ceremony, flower arrangement, calligraphy, painting, Japanese chess, folklore, music and poetry.

In the Bavarian *Land* in Germany all stages of training are completed with the Emergency Police. The curriculum is comprehensive and includes the following:

- English (communication);
- Psychological training (how to treat people in everyday situations);
- Information and communication (including computer handling);
- The law (traffic laws, criminal law, police laws and procedures);
- Police work (police duties, rights, filling in forms);
- Criminalistics (interrogation, protection of the crime scene, and collection of evidence);
- Special police laws (environmental laws, asylum law, *etc.*);
- Self-defence and sport;
- Special training (driving, first aid, guard duty, *etc.*);
- Weapons training,
- Group strategy and operations;
- World affairs and elections; and
- Study time (all police trainees live in the academy, although local students can stay at home).

In Baden-Württemberg the police training is less structured, although subjects can include German, natural sciences, communication and typing, psychology and how to work with the public. While some instruction is given in police-community working - including conflict resolution - it is expected that trainees will learn more "on the job". There are also refresher and vocational courses on offer. The present form of training allows a lot of freedom. The downside of this is that trainees may still need to learn a lot of practical work when they arrive at their first station. In Lahr (Baden-Württemberg) an emphasis is placed on policing techniques (*Polizeidienstkunde*) - for instance, filling out the forms, making arrests, how to stop a car, do a search, testify, and other similar actions. Also covered are emergency techniques (how to handle demonstrations, events or disasters). Other areas covered include operational work, working with mentally ill persons and self-defence.

In France there tends to be a dynamic and pragmatic approach to training with courses frequently changing - recent additions being psychology and computing. As noted, officers in the *Police Nationale* are trained to be generalists. In terms of rule of law principles they are also trained to be aware of the pluralistic facets of the community and to be sensitive to human rights issues. In the *Gendarmerie Nationale* there are courses on surveillance, drug addiction, techniques of investigation, evidence gathering, financial crimes, portrait drawing and detecting the use of false documents. Inspector trainees in the *Gendarmerie* take courses in law, penal procedures, police procedure, "criminalistics", civil law, police intelligence, legal commentary, sports, self-defence, typing, police techniques, weapons and emergency rescues.

Lessons can be learnt from each of the four countries in terms of their training curriculum. The emphasis that the Swiss police training has on "emotion, sensibility and understanding" ought to be positive for rule of law understanding. From a practical perspective, the coverage of police laws and procedures by the German trainers in Bavaria should give trainees an understanding of what they can and cannot do. If this is taught alongside the conflict resolution covered in Baden-Württemberg then breaches of "rule of law" ought to be less frequent. This of course is an ideal, and this chapter does not indicate the quality of training that is on offer; however, the basic principles remain. Japan leads the way in cultural training and personal development and the Police Nationale in France has training in human rights and multi-culturalism. However, as the riots of 2005 in Paris demonstrated, police-community relations in France are strained in some areas. When and where such tensions occur, it is imperative that the police have a real understanding of rule of law.

Conclusion

The training of police officers in all four countries includes elements that ought to make rule of law messages more apparent. However, the countries are clearly marked by diversity in how these messages are delivered. As the police in each country is professionally trained, there are some similarities in training curricula, the amount of education needed and other factors. Differences are due to a combination of historical, cultural, political, and other pressures. They are also a result of the different policing structures.

In terms of recruitment, it is important to have recruits that are amenable to rule of law messages. The psychological testing used for Swiss recruits and the strong emphasis on academic education by France and Japan may produce 'better' or more able students, although more research would be needed here. The efforts in Germany to recruit more people from Black and minority ethnic groups may lead to a force that better understands minority issues - perhaps improving rule of law application. The German police could look towards England and Wales where all new police recruits are meant to take part in a two-day "attitudinal" course", "aimed at ensuring they have a healthy attitude towards people from different

198

backgrounds"[5]. England and Wales has also been actively recruiting from Black and minority ethnic groups.

While all four countries included in this study have an increasing emphasis on community, there appears to be three distinct training philosophies. Firstly, in Germany the emphasis is on the law and the interplay between rule of law and democracy (see also Das 1998). It may be important for students to understand what they can and cannot do under the law; however, there is a risk that this is at the expense of training centred on police-community relations. The conflict resolution training provided in Baden-Württemberg goes some way to address this issue. Both Japan and Switzerland have a more militaristic tradition. Despite this, training in both countries focuses on community, including such things as positive attitudes, a sense of justice, good public relations and citizen involvement. The third approach is provided by the French, with rule of law issues presented through training in human rights and multi-culturalism. There are not necessarily any right or wrong ways of doing things and rule of law messages are apparent in all three training philosophies; however, it appears sensible to tackle the issue from all angles possible.

The four countries have their own approaches to training in terms of organization and structure, and there is also some variation within countries. If rule of law messages are to get across to recruits, it is important to appreciate such local contexts, especially in terms of the availability of basic, theoretical and on-the-job training. Similarly, the type of training organization is important, be it, for example, the practice-oriented German system, or the wider professional approach of the French system.

Lessons can be learned also from the training curricula of each country. For instance, the emphasis that the Swiss police training has on "emotion, sensibility and understanding" ought to be positive for rule of law understanding. The conflict resolution on offer in Baden-Württemberg is an important development, of course depending on the quality of that provision. Japan's inclusion of cultural training and personal development may make recruits more aware of wider societal norms and values (*e.g.* Sellin 1938). And the training in human rights and multi-culturalism provided for the *Police Nationale* in France may similarly help to make rule of law breaches less frequent.

However, none of the four systems are perfect and they really ought to be described as "works in progress". As noted above, in Switzerland there have been concerns over police brutality. This has been a concern also in Japan, along with corruption and nepotism (Johnson 2002: 2003). The riots in Paris and other major cities in France during 2005 have shown that - despite all the

---

5 See www.homeoffice.gov.uk.

training in multi-culturalism - police-community relations can still be strained. In Germany, there has been the added pressure of policing a reunified country and inheriting police organizations with very different histories, cultures and, perhaps, understandings of rule of law.

There are pressures on the public police through increases in the privatization of security. There are also many external pressures due to the globalization of crime and law enforcement. Numerous countries are facing rapid change and challenges to accepted rule of law principles; police organization and training must be aware of these realities and the renewed tension between rule of law/due process and crime control. That said, the United Nations has produced a set of standards and norms for crime prevention and criminal justice (UNCJIN 1999), and rule of law is very much part of these standards.

Where the four countries appear to be heading in the right direction is in their increased professionalism (and improvements to police training are central to this) and in work to make the police more representative, particularly in Germany. In order to improve, or maintain, public confidence in the public police it is important that the service the public receives is professional, has legitimacy in terms of representation and, finally, adheres to rule of law principles.

References

Aldous, C. and Leishman, F. (1997). 'Policing in post-war Japan: reform, reversion and reinvention'. International Journal of the Sociology of Law 25(2), 135-154.

Bayley, D.H. (1976). Forces of order: policing modern Japan. Berkeley CA: University of California Press.

Bayley, D.H. (1991). Forces of order: policing modern Japan, Revised Edition. Berkeley CA: University of California Press.

Bayley, D.H. (2005). Changing the guard: developing democratic police abroad. New York NY: Oxford University Press.

Carothers, T. (1998). 'The rule of law revival'. Foreign Affairs 77(2), 95-106.

Chwialkowski, P. (1998). 'Japanese policing - an American invention'. Policing: An International Journal of Police Strategies and Management 21(4), 720-731.

Das, D.K. (1998). 'Working with people: a comparative analysis of police capacity'. Police Forum, 8(2) 1-8.

Das, D.K. and Palmiotto, M. (2002). International human rights standards: guidelines for the world's police officers. Police Quarterly 5(2), 206-221

Das, D.K. and Palmiotto, M. (2004). German police: marching ahead on the road to elitism. International Journal of Comparative and Applied Criminal Justice 28(2), 189-199.

Das, D.K. and Pino, NW (2007). A comparative account of police training in four countries. In Das, Dilip and Nathan W. Pino, in: Kratcoski, Peter and Dilip Das (Eds.), Police Education and Training in A Global Society. Lanham, Maryland: Lexington Books.

Ebbe, E.O.N. (ed.) (1996). Comparative and international justice systems. Boston MA: Butterworth-Heinemann .

Eisner, M. and Killias, M. (2004). 'Switzerland', European Journal of Criminology 1(2), 257-293.

Fairchild, E.S. (1988). German police: ideals and reality in the post-war years. Springfield IL: Charles C. Thomas Publishers

Feltes, T. (2002). Community-oriented policing in Germany: training and education. Policing: An International Journal of Police Strategies and Management 25(1), 48-59.

Harlan, J.P. (1997). The German police: issues in the unification process. Policing: an international journal of police strategies and management 20(3), 532-554.

Johnson, D. (2002). The Japanese way of justice: prosecuting crime in Japan. New York NY: Oxford University Press

Johnson, D. (2003). Above the law? Police integrity in Japan. Social Science Japan Journal 6(1), 19-37.

Jones, T. and Newburn, T. (2005). Plural policing: a comparative perspective. Abingdon UK: Routledge.

Journes, C. (1993). The structure of the French police system: is the French police a national force? International Journal of the Sociology of Law 21(3), 281-287.

Kleinig, J. (1996). The ethics of policing. Cambridge: Cambridge University Press.

Loader, I. (2000). Plural policing and democratic governance. Social and Legal Studies 9(3), 323-345.

Mawby, R.I. (1990). Comparative policing issues: The British and American experience in international perspective. London: Unwin Hyman.

Mawby, R.I. (1992). Comparative police systems: searching for a continental model. In K. Bottomley, T. Fowles and R. Reiner (eds.): Criminal justice: theory and practice. London: British Society of Criminology.

Mawby, R.I. (2003). Models of policing. In T. Newburn (ed.): Handbook of policing. Cullompton UK: Willan.

Murck, M. and Werdes, B. (1996). Veränderungen in der Personal Struktur der Polizei: Altersaufbau, Frauenanteil, ethnische Minderheiten. In M. Kniesel, E. Kube and M. Murck (eds.), Handbuch für Führungskräfte der Polizei. Lübeck: Schmidt-Römhild

Neyroud, P. and Beckley, A. (2001). Policing, ethics and human rights, Cullompton UK: Willan.

NPA (2005). Overview of Japanese police. National Police Agency, Japan http://www.npa.go.jp/english/kokusai/index.htm [accessed March 2006].

Packer, H. (1969). The limits of the criminal sanction. Stanford CA: Stanford University Press.

Parker, L.C. (2001). The Japanese police system today: a comparative study. New York NY: East Gate.

Phalniker, S. (2006). Wanted: ethnic minority cops for Germany. In Deutsche Welle, 02 March 2006 http://www.dw-world.de/dw/article/ 0,2144,1920604,00.html [Accessed March 2006].

Reiner, R. (2002). The organization and accountability of the police. In M. McConville and G. Wilson (eds.), The Handbook of the Criminal Justice Process. Oxford: Oxford University Press.

Sellin, T. (1938). Culture, conflict and crime. New York NY: Social Science Research Council.

Shearing, C.D. (1992). The relation between public and private policing. In M. Tonry and N. Morris (eds.), Modern Policing, Crime and Justice: A Review of Research Vol. 15. Chicago IL: University of Chicago Press.

Skolnick, J.H. (1966/1994). Justice without trial: law enforcement in democratic society. New York NY: Macmillan.

UNCJIN (1999). Compendium of United Nations Standards and Norms in crime Prevention and Criminal Justice. Vienna: United Nations Crime and Justice Information Network http://www.uncjin.org/Standards/ compendium.pdf[Accessed March 2006].

UN Human Rights Committee (2001). Concluding observations of the Human Rights Committee: Switzerland 12/11/2001, CCPR/CO/73/CH. (Concluding Observations/Comments) http://www.unhchr.ch/tbs/ doc.nsf/0/d87e8c5469b66856c1256afb 00318a7b?Opendocument [Accessed March 2006].

UN Report of the General Secretary (2005). In Larger Freedom: Towards development, security and human rights for all. United Nations General Assembly, 59th session, agenda items 45 and 55, 21 March 2005. http://www.un.org/largerfreedom [Accessed March 2006].

Wolfe, N.T. (1992). Policing a socialist society: the German Democratic Republic. New York NY: Greenwood Press.

Zedner, L. (2006). Policing before and after the police: the historical antecedents of contemporary crime control. British Journal of Criminology 46(1), 78-96.

V. INTERNATIONAL CRIMINAL JUSTICE TEACHING AND TRAINING AGENDA

Culture of Lawfulness Training for Police[1]

James O. Finckenauer[2]

Introduction

Too often, in too many places, the police – although charged with upholding and enforcing the law – instead engage in practices that are outside legal boundaries; that are in many instances indeed criminal. For any of a variety of reasons, *e.g.*, because they are outmanned and outgunned, because they are poorly trained and poorly supervised, because they are unprofessional and unaccountable, and/or because they are simply brutal and corrupt, the police operate in lawless fashion. As country after country today strives to become or maintain itself as a rule-of-law state, these countries find that this already ambitious and challenging goal becomes impossible to achieve if their principal law enforcement entity – the police – do not themselves accept and adhere to the rule-of-law.

So what then is specifically meant by the rule-of-law? What part do the police play in a society that embodies the rule-of-law? And, can anything be done to improve police performance in playing their part? In particular, can education and training assist in accomplishing this? After briefly addressing each of these questions, I will then focus upon the last one. My specific consideration will be ideas for a so-called *culture of lawfulness* curriculum for the police. I will offer an outline of such a curriculum,

---

1 The education and training approach described here has been developed over the past decade by the National Strategy Information Center in Washington, DC. Its driving force is Roy Godson, the president of the NSIC, and a professor of government at Georgetown University. The author has been a consultant for the project on and off for most of its duration, and in particular worked with both the Colombian and Mexican police curriculum developmental effort.

2 James O. Finckenauer is a Professor II (Distinguished) at the Rutgers University School of Criminal Justice, Newark, New Jersey, USA. Between 1998 and 2002, while on leave from Rutgers, he was Director of the International Center at the National Institute of Justice, Washington, DC. His research and publications have focused most recently on organized crime, transnational crime, comparative criminal justice issues, legal socialization, and criminal justice education. Dr. Finckenauer has been active with the Culture of Lawfulness project since 1997.

in this case for the Colombian National Police, as an illustrative case example.

Society and the Rule of Law

The rule-of-law is an eighteenth century Enlightenment idea. The rule-of-law principle is derived from the idea that the state – the government – exists to serve and protect the people. The people's lives, liberty and property are to be protected against arbitrary government actions as well as from lawless fellow citizens.

The rule-of-law in practice means that the laws apply equally to everyone, including the police, judges and other government officials; that there are means and methods for people to participate in the making and changing of laws; that laws protect and preserve the rights of each individual; and, that there are formal means for enforcing the law and for sanctioning violators. Most importantly for this discussion, the rule-of-law means that the police cannot and must not act outside of the law – must not engage in criminal actions – in carrying out their duties. Their police shield is not a shield for abuse of authority and criminal behavior.

The rule-of-law is the very basis for the legitimacy of the police. We know from the research literature that citizen's compliance with the law emanates in major part from their perception that legal authorities and procedures are fair (See, *e.g.*, Tyler 1990). As I have written elsewhere, the rule-of-law "is a concept intricately tied up with public perceptions of legitimacy, with acceptance of the necessity of law, and with compliance" (Finckenauer 1995: 14). If the police do not support and adhere to the rule-of-law, they not only betray the citizens they are supposed to serve, but they also sow the seeds of chaos in the very society they are expected to protect. Citizens cannot be expected to be law-abiding when the police are not. As the philosopher John Rawls pointed out: "not only must the authorities [*e.g.*, the police] act in good faith, but their good faith must be recognized by those subject to...laws and commands" (Rawls 1971: 235-43).

A Culture of Lawfulness

We should recognize that in reality the rule-of-law is largely an abstract concept. It is an ideal. This ideal must be translated into a set of policies and practices – it must be operationalized – in order to exist in actuality. Before subjects can be expected to abide by the law, they must first know what the law is. Beyond that, however, they must hold attitudes that are favorable to law-abidingness. A means for shaping such attitudes, and for translating the rule-of-law into practice, is to augment or create what has become generally known as a *culture of lawfulness* (COL) The ideas and practices encompassed in trying to build a culture of lawfulness have themselves evolved over nearly a decade (See, *e.g.*, Godson and Kenney 1999; and Godson 2000). These ideas are derived from a combination of historical experience (especially in Hong Kong and Sicily), from some of the principles of civics education, and from legal socialization theory and practice (See Finckenauer 1998).

What is a culture of lawfulness? COL describes a culture in which the great majority of citizens and the civil institutions of society (religious, educational, business, labor, cultural and social organizations) support the rule-of-law; and, where the average person believes that the laws and the system for creating, changing and enforcing laws are fundamentally fair, and that the laws and the legal system operate in their best interest as well as in the best interests of the society. Building this support and belief in societies where such ideas have been suppressed, or perhaps never really existed in the first place, requires active intervention. It requires interventions of the kind first practiced in, for example, Sicily and Hong Kong. In the case of Sicily, beginning in the early 1980s, Sicilian children were introduced to what was called "educating for legality." Arising as part of an anti-mafia crusade, this new pedagogy constituted "a profound change in the way that crime and mafia [were] represented – at school, in the media, and in public life...." (Schneider 1998: 12). In Hong Kong, where the problem was pervasive corruption, the Independent Commission Against Corruption (established in 1974) produced a wide spectrum of moral education packages that emphasized activity and life exposure in a "whole-school" approach (Lo 1998: 29). The ICAC effort included workshops for teachers and the provision of teaching aids and manuals as part of the "systematic teaching of moral education." Although neither of these examples was a total success, they each provide a good foundation and good source of lessons learned for any new COL initiatives.

Creating a culture of lawfulness requires engaging the major institutions of society in pursuit of the rule-of-law goal. As indicated above, these institutions include religious institutions and other centers of moral authority, and the media – newspapers, television, and so on. But importantly, and perhaps most amenable to intervention, are the institutions of education and training. This is why the first efforts in this direction have been concentrated upon schools.

It is not, and not surprisingly, only school children and high school students who need this instruction. A key assumption underlying a culture of lawfulness is that citizen support for the police, as well as a strong civil society, are critical to a society that is to be law-abiding. Civil society operates (or unfortunately does not as the case may be) pretty much independently of the police. But citizen support for the police in particular is very much determined by their perception that the police are legitimate and deserving of respect and compliance. Just as the rule-of-law is a necessary governor on the actions of the police, so too is police recognition that they must be part of a culture of lawfulness.

As Godson has pointed out, a culture of lawfulness needs enforcement, but at the same time the enforcers (especially the police) very much need that culture (Godson 2000). The latter is true for several reasons. For example, new police recruits come out of the dominant culture of their society, and as such come imbued with the attitudes and beliefs of that culture. To the extent that they bring with them negative attitudes of distrust, disrespect and disdain for the police, this constitutes a significant challenge for orientation and training. Why might persons holding such ideas want to become police officers in the first place? Perhaps because the job is secure and pays relatively well, or perhaps because it gives them a position of power and a license to steal and collect bribes? In any event, any ideas of the latter kind obviously must be confronted and rejected during police training, and any police recruits continuing to hold on to those sorts of beliefs must be dismissed.

The police need also to understand – and this is key – that their being part of the culture of lawfulness is vital to their success and effectiveness. In such a culture, lawbreakers will find themselves targeted not only by law enforcement, but also by other sectors of the society. Community cooperation and collaboration with the police is in fact a prime component of the universal move to community policing as the dominant policing style. Policing in accordance with rule-of-law and culture of lawfulness principles is not only more humane and consistent with democratic values, but is also far easier, safer and more effective – an unbeatable combination!

A Culture of Lawfulness Curriculum

Building upon the foundations mentioned previously, the first experimental offering of what was specifically a culture of lawfulness curriculum was in secondary or middle schools in Mexico (and to a very limited degree in the United States) in 1999. From a 30+ hour pilot, the curriculum was expanded to 60 hours, and has since been offered in *secundaria* (secondary) schools throughout Baja California, Mexico. It has also been offered in schools elsewhere in Mexico, in the Republic of Georgia, in Colombia, El Salvador, and Peru, and now (in adapted form) in Lebanon. There has recently been added a companion high school curriculum that builds upon the lower school program, and is also being offered in Mexico.

The Baja secundaria COL curriculum focuses upon first, the connection between personal and societal values and decision-making, and the consequences of individual decisions. The goal is for students (and now police trainees) to understand that although many factors influence their behavioral choices, ultimately they have control over the choices they make and must be prepared to accept the consequences of those choices. A second focus is on the similarities and differences among customs, rules and laws; what is the rule-of-law (ROL) and how it differs from "rule *by* law"; what is the culture of lawfulness and how do ROL and COL relate; and, what happens when laws and values conflict. The third area deals with crime and corruption, including their different forms and their threats to the community, and the "ripple effect" from seemingly minor forms of crime and deviance outward upon the community and the larger society. Finally, the fourth focus is upon how societies can resist crime and corruption, the implications of individual choices, exercises in problem-solving, and the use of role playing. The book *Lord of the Flies*, and the film *Goodfellas* have been used to illustrate and drive home the points of emphasis in the lessons. In addition, field exercises and guest speakers are also relied upon to make the material covered real and practical.

An evaluation of the initial effort in Baja and U.S. schools produced mixed results in terms of its effects upon knowledge, attitudes, and legal reasoning (Godson & Kenney 1999). One conclusion from that study was that increased social competency skills could be an important outcome from the COL educational program. Thus, it was recommended that the problem-solving component be strengthened – engaging students in problem identification, analysis, and response formation. Specifically, it was recommended that the program should stress practicing these skills interactively. The proposed COL curriculum for police incorporates this element into the offering.

A subsequent study of over 10,000 Mexican youth who participated in the COL program for *secundaria* schools also produced very mixed results (Grant 2004). As in the pilot study, teacher competency, creativity and mastery of the material were quite variable. There was also considerable variability in the actual completion of the 60 lesson curriculum, with many teachers unfortunately falling short. Nevertheless, Grant (2004: 81) found that students demonstrated positive changes in such areas as locus of control, social responsibility and fatalism in the pre-post test evaluation. He concluded that interactive curricula that offer increased chances to participate in governance, rule creation, self-reflection, and problem-solving might best enhance these sorts of changes.

Not surprisingly, weak and poorly trained teachers who get through only a portion of the lessons do not provide a valid foundation and test of the worth of the COL curriculum. Obviously, any move to build COL subject matter into police training must make every effort to insure that the instructors are carefully chosen, fully qualified, and well-trained; that sufficient time is allotted to permit full and complete coverage of the material; and, that there is clear organizational support and commitment. Consistent monitoring must occur to insure that these requirements are being met.

In general, assessments of the school-based program in Mexico (and to some degree in Georgia as well) suggest that affective learning methods (active, interactive, hands-on) are the preferred method for presenting this curriculum. And to reiterate, these assessments also demonstrate the critical importance of having creative, committed and innovative teachers and instructors. Rote learning methods do not work; and, instructors who are simply going through the motions and do not evince a real commitment to rule-of-law and COL principles are not effective. The latter observation will become especially important in choosing instructors for the police training program.

As authorities, and particularly police leaders, in Mexico and Colombia have become aware over the past several years of what was happening in the schools, they became intrigued by the possibilities for the development of a COL training curriculum geared specifically for the police. We (NSIC and its consultants) were aware at the outset that developing such a curriculum would present some additional challenges – mainly arising from the critical differences between being a student and being a police trainee. One difference comes from the fact that the trainees are generally older, and thus more experienced and worldly-wise. In addition, given that in these cases they have grown up in Colombia or Mexico, they might be expected to be especially cynical and skeptical about such ideals as the rule-of-law. We thus decided at the outset that the COL police training must be focused upon showing how the rule-of-law and a culture of lawfulness actually contribute to more effective and professional policing. It is therefore not, or at least not only, idealistic, but also quite pragmatic.

A second important difference between the civilian and police students is the fact that for the former the COL curriculum is primarily an educational experience. It is intended to convey knowledge, understanding, and an appreciation of the importance of the principles of law and justice toward the end of challenging negative stereotypes and instilling more positive attitudes. For the police, on the other hand, this is "training." As such, it is intended to not only impact knowledge and attitudes, but also to provide specific tools and techniques for application on the job. It is intended to directly influence behavior and performance. For police officers and police supervisors, the purpose of the COL training is to spell out what specific actions and behaviors they must engage in – and avoid – in order to uphold the rule-of-law and to build and maintain a culture of lawfulness.

A Case Example: Colombia

The following describes a preliminary effort to develop, in conjunction with the Colombian National Police National Police School, a COL curriculum that is to be incorporated into the existing training regimen. Although not yet operational, the proposed curriculum is illustrative of how rule-of-law and COL principles and ideas might become part of law enforcement training. There is certainly every reason to think that this same sort of curriculum could be adopted and adapted for widespread application. To set the stage and provide an appropriate context, let me begin with a few words about policing and police training in Colombia more generally.

Plagued by guerrilla warfare, paramilitary groups, drug cartels, and violence, Colombia has long been one of the most troubled countries in Latin America. Its justice system – and specifically the police – has consistently been cited over the years by, for example, Amnesty International and the United Nations for human rights violations in responding to its multitude of crime problems. Corruption has also infected nearly every institution of the society, including most especially the police. In a recent report, the Special Mission of the Colombian National Police (Final Report 2004) concluded that a culture of laxity and permissiveness existed. When corruption occurs, according to the report, the police focus on preserving their image and covering up any wrongdoing from public view.

A jointly funded U.S./Colombian initiative, known as Plan Colombia, was introduced in 2000 in an attempt to address that country's crisis situation. A $7 billion initiative, Plan Colombia is aimed at reducing and preventing guerrilla/paramilitary violence, interdicting and eradicating illegal drugs, and introducing human rights reform through fostering a culture of lawfulness in Colombia. Some of the key reforms – including training – are centered on the Colombian National Police (CNP).

With respect to training, the *Special Mission of the Colombian National Police* listed a number of criticisms of the CNP training programs. There was, they reported, an excessive emphasis on acquiring diplomas; and, the training was not oriented toward police professionalism, and the personal, social and ethical areas. This report has been a stimulus to seeking to incorporate COL training into the National Police School training. In her analysis of police reform in Colombia, Maria Llorente (2004) describes a reform effort known as the "cultural transformation," begun in 1995. This transformation was specifically focused upon improving relations between the police and the civil society, being more responsive to public demands, and promoting police-community partnerships. The desire for COL training is also related to this.

The Colombian National Police (CNP) is a force of some 99,000 sworn and uniformed officers. Roughly 80 percent are considered "professionals," meaning they have graduated from the police training schools. The remainder are the *auxiliaries de policia* (police assistants) doing their mandatory military service with the CNP. There are also about 6,000 civilian employees (Llorente 2004). The Police Administration or Cadet School accepts both high school (roughly 75 percent of total) and college (25 percent of total) graduates, with between 150 and 200 cadets in each class. The former attend for three years, with an additional one year field training requirement. The latter attend the school for one year, and then also have a one year field training requirement. All become sub-lieutenants – the entry-level officer rank – upon graduation. The existing curriculum is a combination of requirements and electives. It is in this context that a COL curriculum was requested and proposed for the training of the officer cadets for the CNP.

The goals of the proposed COL course are as follows:

1. To enhance understanding of and support for the rule-of-law and a COL;
2. To demonstrate how support for the rule-of-law and a COL contributes to effective and professional policing;
3. To provide cadet trainees with concrete tools and skills that will enable them to promote a similar understanding and appreciation among their subordinates and in the communities they serve.

To achieve these goals, a course requiring 60 hours of classroom instruction and additional fieldwork outside of the classroom has been designed. The latter is particularly intended to provide the kind of hands-on opportunity to apply skills referred to earlier. It is proposed that this instruction come towards the end of the training period in order to maximize the potential for post-training application. The following is the structural outline of the course.

TOWARD A CULTURE OF LAWFULNESS

PROPOSED CURRICULUM FOR OFFICER CADETS OF THE COLOMBIAN NATIONAL POLICE

1. The Rule of Law and a Culture of Lawfulness

Purpose: Connect the goals of policing, community support and police effectiveness to ROL and COL

a. What is ROL? What are the roles/responsibilities of police under the ROL?

b. What is COL? What are the roles/responsibilities of police in fostering COL?

c. Why adhere to ROL when nobody else does? What if all the police are corrupt?

2. Goals of the Police: Defining and Measuring Effective Policing

Purpose: Increase knowledge/understanding of goals of the police and of police effectiveness

a. Why are police needed?

b. Goals: fight crime and seek justice

c. What is "effective" policing and how to measure effectiveness?

3. Fostering a Culture of Lawfulness within the Police

Purpose: Teach cadet/trainees how to foster COL among the police they will supervise. Gain perspectives of patrol officers on the roles of police and community in fostering support for ROL and COL

4. Obstacles to Community Support: Identifying Problems and Possible Responses

Purpose: To recognize differences within/among communities affecting efforts to mobilize citizens

a. Challenges to community support, *e.g.*, community lacks confidence in police effectiveness

b. How do differences in communities affect police work?

5. Keys to Effective Policing: Community Support and Engagement

Purpose: Demonstrate how police effectiveness is linked to community engagement

a. Challenges to effective policing

b. How to increase police effectiveness (involve the community)

c. Challenges to community mobilization (police crime and corruption)

6. Fostering a Culture of Lawfulness in the Community

Purpose: Teach cadet/trainees how, as individuals, to foster COL in the community. Gain perspectives of the community on the roles of the police and the community in fostering support for ROL and COL

a. Creating and using a "beat profile"

7. Developing an Officers' Guide for Culture of Lawfulness in the Field

Purpose: Create an action plan to guide behaviour as individual officers, and as supervisors of other police, in the field. Create understanding of situational leadership

The following are some specific examples of suggested content and teaching approaches for Sections 6 and 7 of the proposed curriculum.

Section 6: Fostering a Culture of Lawfulness in the Community

Among the core elements here is the development of a "beat profile." This is a detailed picture of a neighborhood or community, including geography, transportation features, business and commerce, crime and delinquency problems including drugs, and most importantly, citizen views on neighborhood problems and possible solutions. The police trainees are instructed in interview techniques and question development and are then sent into the field to actually collect all this information. They are subsequently then to work in small groups (5 or 6 trainees) to develop a profile of each neighborhood from the information they have collected. These profiles must address a number of specific points, and it is recommended that a community member or activist (*e.g.*, from a non-governmental organization) be brought in to assist and advise in this process. Once the profile is complete, the groups are asked to consider and address the obstacles they perceive in their respective neighborhoods to the creation of a culture of lawfulness. The focus is upon what individual officers might do to promote a culture of lawfulness through their interactions with citizens and community leaders.

Section 7: Developing an Officer's Guide for Culture of Lawfulness in the Field

In this final part of the course, the trainees assess their previously gathered information (from both community and police interviews) in terms of what this means for effective policing. Working in groups, they then develop a guide that will help them work within the different situations they are expected to face. This guide is to be a plan of action for how the trainees will act as individuals, as supervisors, and as active promoters of a culture of lawfulness. Each group must present their plan to their classmates and instructors, and (preferably) to an in-house board of senior police officers as well. An even more ambitious goal is to have these plans also presented to the affected communities. Once finalized, the intent is that the guides become an obligatory document binding not only the individual officers to their goals, but also gaining the commitment of the police organization and the community as well. Plans may still be revised and improved based upon actual experience during the immediate post-training period (the CNP Police Administration Program contains both a block of instruction called "applied research in service," and another called "practical level"). These would be appropriate times to test the plans in action.

Conclusion

Much of what is proposed here is radically different from the traditional and fairly universal police training curricula. It obviously builds upon ideas derived from the experience with community policing. It also effectively combines idealism and utilitarianism. As such, the COL police training curriculum echoes the arguments of such policing experts as David Bayley about broadening the teaching of law and ethics to police recruits by introducing utilitarian arguments into the lessons, along with instruction on due process and the value of the rule-of-law in democratic societies (Bayley 2002). Further, Bayley's recommendation that it is most important that senior police executives be the focus of this kind of instruction is pertinent here as well. Although the Colombian police cadets are new entrants to the force, they are coming in as officers and thus will be well-positioned to influence both their subordinates and the organization as a whole.

In sum, the kind of *culture of lawfulness* training outlined here can move us in the direction of what a number of police experts have recommended, namely convincing the police (and especially the police leadership) that, in Bayley's words, "it is in the interests of the police, both individually and collectively, to adhere to the rule-of-law... [because] defending human rights enhances police effectiveness [rather than] hampers it. [And because] illegality in policing is a risky and generally unproductive strategy" (Bayley 2002: 146).

References

Bayley, D. (2002). "Law Enforcement and the Rule of Law: Is there a Tradeoff?" Criminology & Public Policy, Volume 2, Number 1.

Final Report: Special Mission of the Colombian National Police, Bogota, Colombia, March 2004.

Finckenauer, J. (1995). Russian Youth: Law, Deviance and the Pursuit of Freedom. New Brunswick, NJ: Transaction Publishers.

Finckenauer, J. (1998). Legal Socialization: Concepts and Practices. Trends in Organized Crime, Volume 4, Number 2.

Godson, R. and Kenney, D. (1999). School-Based Education to Counter Crime and Corruption: Evaluation of the Initial Pilot Curriculum. Washington, DC: National Strategy Information Center.

Godson, R. (2000). Guide to Developing a Culture of Lawfulness. Washington, DC: National Strategy Information Center.

Grant, H. (2004). Fostering a Culture of Lawfulness: Examining the Relationship between Perceptions of Law Enforcement Legitimacy, Legal Reasoning, and Behavior. Doctoral Dissertation, New York, NY: City University of New York.

Llorente, M. V. (2004). Demilitarization in Times of War? Police Reform in Colombia. Unpublished paper.

Lo, T. Wing (1998). Pioneer of Moral Education: Independent Commission Against Corruption (ICAC). Trends in Organized Crime, Volume 4, Number 2.

Rawls, J. (1971). A Theory of Justice. Cambridge, MA: Harvard University Press.

Schneider, J. (1998). Educating against the Mafia: A report from Sicily. Trends in Organized Crime, Volume 4, Number 2.

Tyler, T. (1990). Why People Obey the Law. New Haven, CT: Yale University Press.

214

A Content Analysis of Comparative and International Issues in Popular Introductory Criminal Justice Texts

Sheryl L. Van Horne[1]

Introduction

While the focus of introductory textbooks in criminal justice is on the purposes and process of the American criminal justice system, crime has become increasingly international and transnational. This study investigates the amount of space allocated to international issues in five of the bestselling criminal justice introductory textbooks. It was hypothesized that very little space will be devoted to international issues in the primary introductory texts. Since this particular research has not been attempted in the past, the types and topics of international information in the main text were also examined. The results indicate that a relatively small percent of space discusses international issues or international comparisons, though the results do vary by the text and subject matter, which is broken down as crime, police, courts, corrections and juvenile justice.

The Problem

Criminal justice programs have crept up across the country, and are still on the rise, with many new undergraduate and graduate programs being created. Colleges that have had criminal justice in their curriculum are expanding their course offerings. Typically, the criminal justice major is one of the most popular majors on American college campuses. Usually students who major in criminal justice are required to take some form of introductory class, which is often taught as a lecture-based class with a basic introduction text and covers the key components of the criminal justice system (police, courts, and corrections), and include discussions of crime trends and theories of criminality. Shichor (1982) suggests that introductory textbooks socialize the students of a particular discipline. They set the stage and framework for students who choose to take additional courses in that discipline. It is therefore important to know and understand the content that

---

1 Sheryl Van Horne is currently an instructor at Penn State University, working on her dissertation at the School of Criminal Justice at Rutgers University. She has published on comparative drug policy, structural correlates of violent crime, and terrorism in the media. Her primary research interests are comparative in nature.

students are exposed to, as well as material that they are not learning.

While each introduction to criminal justice course content is to some extent instructor-driven, the material in the textbooks plays a key role in the material that is covered in classes. Certainly, American faculty enjoy their academic freedom and may choose not to use a text or to not use a traditional introductory text, the majority of criminal justice faculty still teach using a traditional introductory text. Instructors have a wealth of textbooks for introductory criminal justice courses. According to Withrow, Weible, and Bonnett (2004) finding the right text can be a daunting task. Thus, it is important to understand what material is covered in introductory texts, and how that material is presented. The way in which material is presented can have an impact on students' perceptions to this new material, as most college students have not had prior academic exposure to the criminal justice system and its processes (Meier 1980).

To date there have been no published studies examining the space devoted to international and comparative issues in introduction to criminal justice texts. There have, however, been content analyses conducted on textbooks for a variety of other purposes. Some studies have focused on introduction to criminal justice or criminology texts, examining specific types of content, including research methods and ethics (Rhineberger 2006), career criminals (Wright 1994), and white collar crime (Wright and Friedrichs 1991). One study examined the space devoted to critical theory, finding that critical theory in introductory texts was rarer than in introduction to criminology texts (Wright and Schreck 2000). Some studies examine particular topics to determine whether they are covered and the extent of their coverage of that particular topic. For example Wright (2000) examined the coverage of critical theory in introduction to criminology texts published between 1990 and 1999 and examines the average number of pages and the number of inches devoted to critical criminology. Other analyses of criminology texts have found coverage of biocriminality lacking (Wright and Miller 1998) or a minimal focus on female criminologists (Miller, Wright and Smith 2000). Another study examined the extent of coverage of jails in criminology and criminal justice introductory texts (Burns 2002). Thus, there have been a number of research studies examining criminology and criminal justice introductory textbook content, but nothing regarding the international or comparative content.

Content analyses of textbooks have been performed in other disciplines as well. Lynch and Bogen (1997) conducted a content analysis of introductory sociology textbooks to determine the sociological core curriculum and whether or not specific themes were addressed in the texts, specifically how the texts examined the sociology of scientific knowledge. In a similar study of introductory psychology texts, Nairn *et.al.* (2003) looked at the important concepts in six best-selling introductory psychology texts to determine which core concepts seem to be the most important in the psychological curriculum. Another study examined how boys and girls were portrayed in educational psychology texts by examining 15 texts and how they described male and female characters within the texts (Yanowitz and Weathers 2004).

Many students move on to the field as police officers, attorneys, or correctional officers with little or no understand of or sensitivity to international issues. With the increased concern about terrorism, especially international terrorism, it is becoming more important that individuals have an understanding of the global concerns and agreements. Of course, terrorism is not the only crime that crosses national borders. In fact, if criminal justice students are made aware of other crimes that they may have to deal with in their career they may be better able to deal with them. Additionally, a better understanding of international norms and rules would benefit students in their careers in criminal justice, since it may enable them to be more critical in their thinking about the treatment of others in the criminal justice system.

Methods

This research examined five of the bestselling introduction to criminal justice textbooks, as ascertained by searching the Barnes and Noble website for "criminal justice" and ordering them by best-selling books. Then, only primary introductory texts were considered as the sampling frame. That is, texts that are written by one author, containing chapters that would be covered in typical Introductory Criminal Justice Courses across the country. Anthologies, texts that were not for an introductory criminal justice course, and supplementary materials were excluded. Five of the six best-selling texts that would be used in an introductory course were chosen based on the ranking of their sales. The fifth ranking text by Frank Schmalleger was excluded since Schmalleger had another text ranked number one. Since the texts would most likely contain similar coverage of the criminal justice system and related issues, the exclusion makes sense. In the end, the following texts were examined (in order of their best-selling ranking from first to sixth):

Criminal Justice: A Brief Introduction by Frank Schmalleger
Criminal Justice in America by George Cole and Christopher Smith
Introduction to Criminal Justice by Siegel and Senna
Introduction to Criminal Justice by Bohm and Haley
Criminal Justice by Inciardi

Incidentally, the same search was performed on Amazon.com, another popular internet location for students to obtain their textbooks, and yielded 4 overlaps (Schmalleger, Cole and Smith, Siegel and Senna and Bohm and Haley), further validating the choices. The second most popular text at the time the search was performed on Amazon.com was Adler, Mueller and Laufer's *Criminal Justice: The Core*.

While Introduction-to-Criminology texts could have been utilized in such a research venture, introductory criminal justice texts were chosen for two reasons. First of all, there is a significant difference between the two. Criminology texts focus primarily, if not exclusively, on theory, while criminal justice texts focus on the main components of the criminal justice system, including laws, policing, courts, corrections, and sometimes on juvenile justice.

The primary purpose of this research was to ascertain the extent of international and comparative content that students in Introductory Criminal Justice courses read in their primary text. Once the sample was selected, each text was read in its entirety and each line of main text was measured. Many researchers have analyzed textbooks by examining the topics in the index; however, there are significant problems with this method. First of all, different publishers and authors may have different methods for what should be placed in an index. Additionally, many topics may not be indexed at all. Other content analyses involved counting the inches of text; however, centimeters is a more accurate measure of text, so centimeters were measured instead, rounded to the nearest half-centimeter. Thus, the number of centimeters was the unit of analysis.

This analysis only examined the number of centimeters of the primary text. Although many international comparisons will be found in textboxes, they were not coded for two main reasons – one practical and the other conceptual. Most textbooks that use textboxes use a different size font, which complicates the coding. For example, ten centimeters of text in 16 point font would be less text than the same length in 12 point font. Additionally, the majority of students may not read textboxes and ancillary material, presuming it is less important. So, it made sense to focus on the main text. Additionally, added importance is placed on material in the main content of the text. Any coverage in textboxes implies that there is something fundamentally different about such information, suggesting to students perhaps that it is separate information that does not quite fit with the main text.

International issues were defined as issues that the text described as affecting any country other than (or in addition to) the United States. Thus, content that mentioned another country, an important figure who lived in another country, statistics from other countries, and any event that had global significance was counted as international. It was hypothesized that relatively little of the material would discuss international issues, concepts or comparisons. It is important to note, too, that if a theorist was mentioned who happened to be from another country, but that his country of origin was not mentioned, this was not coded as comparative. The reason for this exclusion is that introductory students would only know the individual's origin if their professor happens to mention it and the students make significant note of it. In other words, if the text did not indicate that the individual's origin was another country it is unlikely that students would know this, so it would have little impact on the student's perceptions of the importance of learning about international events.

Since this is the first analysis of criminal justice introductory textbooks that systematically investigates the percentage of text devoted to international and comparative issues, it was exploratory in nature. After examining the international content, three types of content emerged. The first was comparative content that was historical in nature and explained the American criminal justice system's European roots. Another type of international content was comparisons of current information. This includes similarities and differences in the rates of offending and recent crime problems discussed in other countries. The final type of international content was the material that focused on international issues. That is, discussions of crimes which are transnational by nature or crimes that were referred to in an international context, such as international terrorism. All of the content that either discussed issues that were of international import or any material that referred to another country or an international organization in some way was coded, then categorized as fitting into one of the above three categories.

Results

Many of the international and comparative issues pertained to historical beginnings of current U.S. criminal justice practices, especially the beginnings of law enforcement. Some of the text devoted international issues to the history of punishment in chapters dealing with corrections. Other comparative issues related to theories posited by non-American scholars. Though such information is not truly an international issue per se, it is important in that it lets students know that the American understanding of crime was and is influenced by thinkers from other countries.

Table 1: Percent of Different Types of Comparative and International Content by Text

	Comparative Historical	Current Comparison	International Issue	Total Percent
Inciardi	3.09	0.03	0.26	3.94
Schmalleger	0.42	0.28	2.47	3.16
Cole and Smith	1.59	0.33	1.89	3.67
Siegel and Senna	2.46	0.41	0.13	3.11
Bohm and Haley	2.48	0.35	4.40	6.89
Mean	2.01	0.28	1.83	4.15
Standard deviation	1.04	0.15	1.76	1.57

The text that clearly contained more international content than any other in the sample was Bohm and Haley's. The Bohm and Haley (2005) text had a greater percentage of main text devoted to international and comparative issues mainly because of its greater coverage of international issues, specifically its focus on terrorism and the American response to the events of September 11, 2001. While terrorism is certainly an international issue, the majority of the space devoted to it focused primarily on that one event and other policy implications of terrorism for the United States. Inciardi (2005) also had a significant amount of text devoted to historical comparisons, but offered very little text that examined international issues or compared other country's current experiences with crime and the criminal justice system. Generally, the texts did not devote much space to current comparisons, although percentagewise, Siegel and Senna (2005) did a slightly better job than the others at recent international comparisons. Overall, Inciardi (2005) had the second greatest percent of main text devoted to international or comparative issues, while Siegel and Senna (2005) had the smallest percentages overall.

Table 2: Percent of International and Comparative Coverage by Topic for Each Text Examined

	Crime	Police	Courts	Corrections	Juvenile Justice
Inciardi	3.56	4.14	1.91	5.41	1.11
Schmalleger	8.55	2.76	1.15	0.00	N/A
Cole and Smith	6.43	5.90	0.06	2.66	2.57
Siegel and Senna	3.56	2.46	2.66	3.26	3.43
Bohm and Haley	10.86	12.09	1.25	4.02	0.00
Mean	6.59	5.47	1.41	3.07	1.78
Standard deviation	3.18	3.94	0.97	2.00	1.52

Table 2 examines the types of chapters and the percent of text devoted to international issues and comparisons by type of chapters in each of the texts. The first category of crime includes chapters on crime statistics, victimization chapters, chapters on criminal law, and theories of crime. The categories of police, courts, and corrections are relatively self-explanatory, but it is important to note that juvenile justice was just one chapter when it existed. Schmalleger's text did not include a chapter on juvenile justice. The percent indicated in each cell is the percent of centimeters of main text of chapters that fell into that particular category that contained some type of international or comparative information. Chapters on courts and juvenile justice have the least amount of space devoted to international issues or comparisons. It is also quite clear from the table that the majority of international material in Bohm and Haley's text is in chapters devoted to either crime or the police. This is true of most of the texts, although Siegel and Senna (2005) spread their international content out more equally among each type of chapters. Inciardi (2005) has the largest percentage of international material in his corrections chapters largely because he committed a great deal of space to penal reformers like Cesare Beccaria, Jeremy Bentham, and Alexander Maconochie. Inciardi (2005) also devotes a great deal of space discussing the origins of American jails and their English roots.

The sections with the greatest percent of material extending beyond a purely American focus are "crime" and "police". This makes sense since many sections on criminal law examine the English roots of the American common law tradition as well as the English roots of the police today. Sections on types of crimes in each of the textbooks devote at least some space to a discussion of terrorism. Both Schmalleger (2006) and Bohm and Haley (2005) are above the average of percent of space devoted to international areas relating to crime. Both Bohm and Haley (2005) and Cole and Smith's texts are above average on international content with respect to chapters discussing policing issues. Siegel and Senna (2005) and Inciardi (2005) are above average on the courts chapters, while Bohm and Haley (2005) and Siegel and Senna (2005) are above average with respect to the percent of space devoted to international content on corrections chapters. Siegel and Senna (2005) and Cole and Smith on average have a greater percent of international coverage in the chapter on juvenile justice.

Table 3: Percent of Different Types of Comparative and International Issues in Chapters by Topic

	Historical Comparison	Current Comparisons	International Issues	Total Space in Chapters (cm)
Crime	3.0	0.4	3.7	220837
Police	2.1	0.2	3.0	206165
Courts	0.8	0.3	0.2	209121
Corrections	2.6	2.9	0.0	186173.5
Juvenile Justice	1.4	0.0	0.0	38263.5
Mean	2.0	0.8	1.4	
Standard deviation	0.91	1.22	1.82	

Table 3 shows how the international and comparative material can be broken down by types of chapters. The primary international issue was terrorism, although some texts devoted a significant amount of space to organized crime or drug trafficking. Since a great deal of centimeters of space devoted to international issues focused on terrorism, it makes sense that the chapters dealing with crime and the police had the greatest percent of space devoted to international issues. Generally, terrorism is framed as a crime problem for the police to deal with. The types of chapters that had the greatest percent of historical comparisons were chapters dealing with crime and chapters about corrections. Most of the historical material about crime had to do with early notions of justice, the Code of Hammurabi and the history of common law. Much of the historical international comparisons in chapters about corrections dealt with early notions of punishment. Nearly all of the material of current comparisons in corrections chapters dealt with uses of the death penalty, or more specifically, a reduction in the use of the death penalty in other countries.

International and supranational organizations are one outcome of an increasing global village. The United Nations has significant importance in the international arena. In the sample of five texts the United Nations is mentioned in only three. In one sentence of Bohm and Haley's text the U.N. is mentioned in the context of the death penalty. Specifically, the United Nations Commission on Human Rights is cited as condemning the death penalty in the United States. The United Nations is mentioned in passing in Siegel and Senna's text which specifically refers to the United Nations Convention on the Rights of the Child and its prohibition of the death penalty for individuals under 18 years of age. In Inciardi's text the United Nations is mentioned on two pages. The first briefly discusses the United Nations' role in seeking to prevent the trafficking of women and girls in Eastern Europe. The second mention of the U.N. is more in-depth and discusses the World Court as the "principal judicial organ of the United Nations" (Inciardi 2005: 325), mentioning the United Nations four times on the same page and discussing the role of the International Court of Justice as well as the International Criminal Tribunal. It should be noted, too, that in all but the one sentence in Bohm and Haley's text the material about the United Nations was in a text box, and not part of the percentages listed above.

Thus, overall very little space was devoted to comparative or international issues. Most of the coverage of international issues focused on terrorism, which is a problem because it may suggest to students that terrorism is the only international issue worth concerning themselves with. Additionally, the context of the material focusing on terrorism was largely about what the United States can do to prevent future attacks, not on how America can learn from other countries that have had greater experiences with terrorism, or of any lengthy discourse on whether the way we are going about "fighting" terrorism is the best method possible. Moreover, most texts focus on the threat of international terrorism, belying the fact that the United States has had more instances of domestic terrorism over the past decade or so.

Discussion

In many respects, it makes sense that introductory texts cover the basic material about the American criminal justice system. That is, it is expected that such texts teach first year college students how the American criminal justice system functions and what the jargon means. At the same time, a better approach to criminal justice learning would be to examine how other systems function and to what extent the American system is similar or dissimilar to other criminal justice systems. If introductory textbooks contained more international or supranational information students would learn that what occurs in other countries or in other supranational bodies is important and may reduce the ethnocentrism of many first year criminal justice students. Clearly, the amount of information devoted to international issues in introductory texts is insufficient.

It would not be difficult to tie in important criminal justice information of crime and criminal justice processing in other countries. This would achieve multiple goals. The first benefit of such international comparisons would be a broadening of students' understanding of crime and criminal justice. Americans are stereotyped as lacking in their understanding of international politics and issues more than students in European countries, for example. Such lack of knowledge may lead to the erroneous belief that one's own country's way of processing criminals, for example, is the same everywhere. So, the expansion of coverage would also help reduce ethnocentrism and narrow-minded thinking. To that end, additional international coverage would enhance students' abilities to apply critical thinking skills and foster the growth of such skills. When students know of the many different ways in which criminals are processed they are more likely to question what happens in America, and would therefore be better prepared to approach various problems differently. Since many criminal justice students graduate to work in the criminal justice field in some capacity, additional awareness of international issues and concerns as well as being well informed of various criminal justice applications in other countries will benefit them greatly, increasing the likelihood that they focus on fixing problems in intelligent and informed ways.

Since the world is living in an increasingly global community, international issues are of significant concern. If students were more aware of the fact that policies in one country can have a significant impact on other countries, they may have a greater concern for what takes place in other countries, causing students to want to learn more about other countries. Faculty can always supplement traditional introductory texts with additional information about international issues and comparative statistics.

Conclusion

Additional research needs to be conducted on the content, benefit, and perceptions of a more global focus of criminal justice material. It would be interesting to view the results of a systematic study of other kinds of criminal justice textbooks, like courts texts and corrections texts. From my own perceptions and experiences with assigning such texts in criminal justice courses that I teach I would hypothesize even less international coverage on upper level criminal justice texts (with the exception of comparative courses, naturally). Of course, one course cannot cover all relevant information, but a more international approach would be beneficial in so many different respects. It is very important to realize that texts and course content help shape students' understanding of criminal justice and students' ethnocentricities should be countered by providing them with a more well rounded view of the criminal justice process.

References

Burns, R. (2002). Assessing Jail Coverage in Introductory Criminal Justice Textbooks. Journal of Criminal Justice Education 13, 87-100.

Lynch, M. and Bogen, D. (1997). Sociology's associological core: an examination of textbook sociology in light of the sociology of scientific knowledge. American Sociological Review 62 (3), 481-493.

Meier, R.F. (1980). Different Criminologies: A survey of recent introductory criminology textbooks. Contemporary Sociology 9, 626-631.

Miller, J.M., Wright, R.A., and Smith, M.M. (2000). Mostly male and American: The reporting of women and crime scholarship in introductory criminology textbooks. The Justice Professional 13, 233-245.

Nairn, S., Ellard, J., Scialfa, C., and Miller, C. (2003). At the core of introductory psychology: A content analysis. Canadian Psychology 44 (2), 93-99.

Rhineberger, G. (2006). Research Methods and Research Ethics Coverage in Criminal Justice and Criminology Textbooks. Journal of Criminal Justice Education 17 (2), 279-296.

Shichor, D. (1982). An Analysis of Citations in Introductory Criminology Textbooks: A Research Note. Journal of Criminal Justice 10 (3), 231-37.

Withrow, B.L., Weible, K., Bonnett, J. (2004). Aren't They All the Same? A Comparative Analysis of Introductory Criminal Justice Textbooks. Journal of Criminal Justice Education 15, 1-18.

Wright, R.A. (1994). Stopped for Questioning, but Not Booked: The Coverage of Career Criminals in Criminology Journals and Textbooks, 1983-1992. Journal of Criminal Justice Education 5, 251-256.

Wright, R. A. (1990). Ten recent criminology textbooks: Diversity without currency or quality. Teaching Sociology 18, 550-561.

Wright, R. A. (2000). Left out? The coverage of critical perspectives in introductory criminology textbooks, 1990-1999. Critical Criminology 9 (1/2), 101-122.

Wright, R.A., and Friedrichs, D.O. (1991). White-Collar Crime in the Criminal Justice Curriculum. Journal of Criminal Justice Education 2, 95-121.

Wright R.A. and Miller, J.M. (1998). Taboo until today? The coverage of biological criminology in textbooks. Journal of Criminal Justice 26 (1), 1-19.

Wright, R. and Scheck, C. (2000). Red-penciled: the neglect of critical perspectives in introductory criminal justice textbooks. Journal of Crime and Justice 23 (2), 45-67.

Yanowitz, K. and Weathers, K. (2004). Do boys and girls act differently in the classroom? A content analysis of student characters in educational psychology textbooks. Sex Roles 51 (1/2), 101-107.

Appendix:

Full references of textbooks examined

Bohm, R. and Haley, K. (2005). Introduction to Criminal Justice, fourth edition. Boston, London, Toronto: McGraw-Hill.

Cole, G. and Smith, C. (2005). Criminal Justice in America, fourth edition Belmont CA, Sinapore, Southbank, Australia, Toronto, London, Colonia Polanco, Mexico, Madrid: Thompson Learning, Inc.

Inciardi, J. (2005). Criminal Justice, seventh edition. Boston, London, Toronto: McGraw-Hill.

Schmalleger, F. (2006). Criminal Justice: A Brief Introduction, sixth edition. Upper Saddle River, NJ: Prentice Hall.

Siegel, L. and Senna J. (2005). Introduction to Criminal Justice, tenth edition. Singapore, Southbank, Australia, Toronto, London:
Thompson Learning, Inc.

Developing an Agenda for International Criminal Justice Teaching and Training

Jay S. Albanese[1]

Introduction

Emerging democracies, rampant corruption, the threat of terrorism, police abuses, and official misconduct by government officials, combine with economic disparity, cultural traditions, and history of an underground economy to create a need for planning and professionalism in responding to these problems and issues. Many social and economic problems result in crime problems, and corruption is criminal in its nature by exploiting public office for private gain. Therefore, the need for an organized response is manifest.

These issues are not limited to developing countries, although they suffer from multiple threats (economic, political, social), and therefore are in the greatest need. On the other hand, many developing nations continue to experience corruption, terrorism, and other forms of criminality, placing them in need of assistance to confront these problems effectively.

What Is Being Done?

The need for an improved response to crime, its causative conditions, corruption, and related matters has provoked a small industry in which "experts" travel around the world and offer training and technical assistance of various kinds. Some of this assistance is competent and helpful, and some is not.

Some technical assistance, education, and training is carried out by non-governmental organizations (NGOs) , the United Nations and other international bodies, other countries, and private

1 Jay S. Albanese received the Ph.D. from Rutgers University. He is Professor of Government & Public Policy at Virginia Commonwealth University. In 2002-2006 he served as the Chief of the International Center at the National Institute of Justice (NIJ). NIJ is the research and evaluation arm of the U.S. Department of Justice. The views expressed are those of the author and do not necessarily reflect the position or policies of the U.S. Department of Justice. He is Executive Director of the International Association for the Study of Organized Crime (www.iasoc.net).

consultants paid by one of groups. Often the assistance is provided only when funds are forthcoming from donor countries to support the work needed or requested. The result is a hodge-podge of uneven assistance, not always provided to the places most in need, in the form most useful, or by the best available providers.

Can We Improve?

There are four ways in which a better effort can be made to provide useful education, training, and technical assistance in the most appropriate way. These include: cataloging providers, organizing curriculum, documenting experience, capturing and disseminating best practices.

Catalog providers

It is crucial to develop a catalog of who is doing what kind of education, training, technical assistance, and in what locations. Such a catalog, and interviews with providers, would help "map" the universe of these services, the source of the demands for training, education, and technical assistance, and the materials used.

Organize curriculum

The curriculum currently being used must be documented and catalogued to develop a clear understanding of the types of education and training that is available, in what locations, to what types of clients, in what languages. The relationship between available curriculum and requests for assistance should also be documented to assess gaps between demand and supply.

Documenting experience

Much work in criminal justice is characterized by the failure to document activity, outcomes, or long-range impacts. There has to be a great deal of activity in recent years in providing criminal justice education and training. What has been the impact of this training? What is its cost-benefit? What are the circumstances under which it was provided? Do some kinds of curriculum, delivery method, instructors, work better than others? What appear to be the reasons for observed differences?

Capturing and disseminating best practices

A better effort is needed to document the reasons for success or failure of various crime and justice interventions. Such documentation helps insure that "best" practices are being documented and finding their way into teaching and training curricula. Systematic effort to create and disseminate good teaching and training materials also helps to insure the best teaching practices are preserved and imitated.

An Agenda for International Teaching and Training

The agenda for international teaching and training should be based on a rational approach for selecting subjects of greatest need—and linking them to good curriculum and instructors, and assessing the impact of this work in reaching its objectives. In developing an agenda for the future, seven elements must be addressed:

1. Institutional base – university, government, NGO, private organization?
2. Sources – proactive, reactive, specific?
3. Educational basis – Degree/certificate v. training programs?
4. Curriculum – source, how developed, goal?
5. Instructors – who are they – backgrounds?
6. Delivery method – types, comparative effectiveness?
7. Impact – retention, cost-benefit, professionalism measures?

If the answers to these seven questions were systematically gathered and organized, a clearinghouse of criminal justice teaching and training curriculum would exist. Once instructional materials from around the world were gathered and organized, experts could review it and add to it, revising it into "state-of-the-art" teaching and training material.

This work should be coordinated insuring that recent findings, cases, and best practices became incorporated into teaching and training efforts. Meaningful distinctions between on-line and in-person options for instruction could be made and recommended, as well as overcoming language barriers. Experimentation with the documentation required to assess various combinations of in-person and distance teaching and training and the results that they produce (in terms of retention, student satisfaction, cost, and professionalism).

The result would be a database which agencies, potential instructors, students, and agencies could query to determine availability of who is doing training, the types of materials being used, and the delivery methods being used.

In this way, existing broken connections among instruction, curriculum, and student/agency needs would be addressed in a systematic way, producing a cohesive linkage among training needs, available content, and instruction. Such a systematic approach offers a rational approach to developing an international agenda for criminal justice teaching and training.

Table 1: Examples of training and education for criminal justice agencies

Agency	Type of service	Substantive areas	Clients
International law enforcement training academies	Supervisory police training	Police in Eastern Europe, Africa, Asia	Mid-level police managers from around world
Science Application International Corporation (private) for the Department of Justice	Investigative training	Drug enforcement, anti-terrorism, community policing	U.S. states and non-U.S. police
International Criminal Investigation Training Assistance Programme	Investigative training	Democratic anti-corruption, terrorism, organized crime, police professionalism	17 developing countries
United Nations Office of Drugs and Crime	Field-based technical cooperation projects to improve capacity of Member States to counteract illicit drugs, crime and terrorism	Services by request, based on funding from governments	All government personnel
World Bank	Programs on anti-corruption, money laundering, capacity-building	Services by request	Mostly government personnel
Sam Houston State University	In-service training for police and corrections personnel	Management, supervision, command, community policing	Police and corrections officers

North Carolina Justice Academy	In-service training for police officers	Management, Investigation and Traffic, Legal, and Tactical	Police officers in southeastern U.S.
Virginia Commonwealth University Public Safety Institute	In-service police training	Public Safety and Your Anti-terrorism, leadership management, legal aspects, research, planning, budgeting	Mid-level police managers

Table 1 presents the results of a Google search using the terms "international criminal justice training." These agencies turned up in the first 100 hits. (When the term "education" was added, a very large number of university programs in criminal justice entered the search.) It should be noted that there is a mix of government, private, NGO, and university-based organizations providing criminal justice training. It is also clear that the vast majority of this training is directed toward police. This emphasis on police is probably due to the fact that there are more police than any other kind of criminal justice professional, but it begs the question whether the training needs of others in the field are being served adequately. A more comprehensive survey is needed to assess that possibility.

From what could be gleaned from web sites, it appears that most international criminal justice training is paid for by donor governments (primarily to enhance the capacity of developing nations), and by criminal justice agencies themselves (by paying for the training of individual officers or by contract with a service provider).

The evaluation of web sites indicated that instructors were primarily contractors who developed their own curriculum, or used curriculum that had been developed by a government agency or other sponsor. Instructors most often were those with practitioner experience on the subject they taught, or were academics.

It was difficult to get a sense of the delivery method of the curriculum through Internet accounts, although most appeared to use face-to-face instruction, supplemented by web-based materials and correspondence between instructors and students. No information was found that offered data about impact, cost-benefit, retention, or professionalism. Such information is crucial to determine which type of curriculum and delivery methods produced the best results. Follow-up would be required to generate this kind of data, and it is unlikely that much emphasis has been placed on the importance of this information in training efforts thus far. As training needs and providers become more numerous, however, it is likely that some indicators of impact will be needed to distinguish the highest quality instruction.

A final note related to the source of the training. It appears that nearly all training arises from perceived needs based on new crime, legislation or dramatic negative incidents (*e.g.*, riots, corruption, use of force against citizens). It is difficult to document without conducting a series of interviews with those in the field the rational connection among these incidents, perceived and actual training needs, curriculum design and delivery in practice to those in greatest need. The training is later assessed to evaluate its impact in practice. Figure 1 diagrams this connection.

Figure 1: The connection among incidents, training needs, and delivery in practice

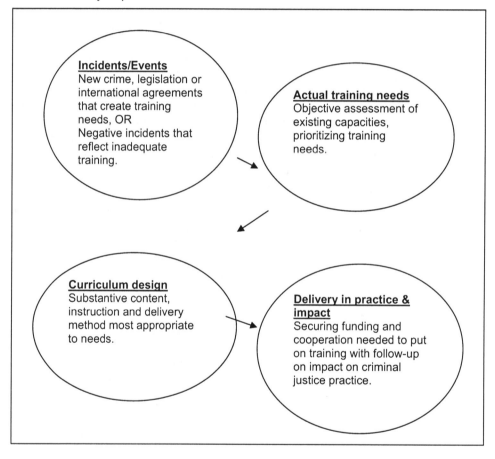

Conclusion

There is a great need for increased professionalism in criminal justice agencies. Emerging democracies, new crimes, negative incidents in all countries, and new legislation and international agreements have created the need for criminal justice training, education, and technical assistance on a broad scale.

The response to this need has been largely unplanned thus far with a plethora of trainers, curricula, and instruction delivery methods that have not been assessed to determine their success in improving the capacity and professionalism of criminal justice agencies. The rationale steps outlined here should be carefully followed to insure that the resources devoted to improving criminal justice practice are not wasted and produce the results desired by all.

VI. TEACHING AND TRAINING EXPERIENCES IN INTERNATIONAL CRIME PREVENTION

Criminal Justice Training in Korea – Korean Institute of Criminal Justice Policy and the Development of Training Program for Asian Developing Countries

Joon Oh Jang[1]

Introduction

The Republic of Korea has a long tradition of rule of law. This idea has been realized according to political and social situations[2]. Korean people see the modern idea of rule of law, or *Rechtsstaat*, as a standard of justice and human rights in a society. They also understand well that teaching and training of legal principle and laws is essential in realizing the idea. Criminal justice education and training is thus top priority of criminal justice policies of the Korean Government. Several government agencies such as the Ministry of Justice, Public Prosecutors' Office, National Police Agency, and National Intelligence Service provide various training programs to carry out the rule of law in the field of crime prevention and criminal justice.

Among diverse criminal justice education and training programs, those related to cybercrime are prominent. The number of Internet users in Korea has dramatically increased since the 1990s. The rate of cybercrime has also skyrocketed from 121 to 77,099 in 1997

---

1 Ph.D., Korean Institute of Criminal Justice Policy (KICJP), Seoul, Republic of Korea. He is concurrently director of International Cooperation Center of the KICJP. He is an adjunct professor of the Graduate School of International Studies at Yonsei University in Seoul. As an advisor, Dr. Jang is also involved with the Korean Financial Intelligence of the Ministry of Finance and Economy and with the Korea Independent Commission Against Corruption. He is a vice-president of the Korean Society of Criminology. His recent researches have been on "Crime Victim Survey on North Korean Defectors" (2006), "Establishment of the Crime Control Unit for Security in North-East Asia" (2006), "Illegal Entry from China into Korea (2005)", "Establishment of Systematic Border Control in North-East Asia" (2005), "Crime in Korea" (2004), "Juvenile Delinquency in Cyber Space (2003)", "Illegal Foreign Workers in Korea (2002)", "Political Corruption in Collusion with Business in Korea (2001)", "International Crime Victimization Survey 2000" (2000), and "Money Laundering in the 1990s: International Tendency and Korean Situation" (1999).
2 Chongko Choi, 'Historical foundation of Rule of Law in Korea'. In Dokyun Kim *et al* (eds.), *The Foundation of Rule of Law*, Seoul National University, 2005.

and 2004 respectively.[3] To combat cybercrimes, such government agencies as those mentioned above have built cybercrime-specialized centers and training programs from the mid 1990s.

The Korean Institute of Criminal Justice Policy (hereinafter KICJP), a government financed research institution, joined the initiative of the United Nations Office on Drugs and Crime in criminal justice education and training. As a member of the United Nations Crime Prevention and Criminal Justice Programme Network of Institutes (PNI), in cooperation with the Korean Ministry of Justice, KICJP is developing the Virtual Forum against Cybercrime. One of the main objectives of the Virtual Forum is to provide on-line training program in cybercrime control and prevention for law enforcement personnel in Asian developing countries.

Law Enforcement Training Program of the National Police Agency

The Korean National Police Agency (NPA) has classified cybercrime into "cyber-terror type crime" and "general cybercrime". Cyber-terror type crime includes crimes such as hacking, denial of service (*dos*)[4] and virus distribution that require high level of technology and attack the information and communication network.[5] Denial of service is an attempt to make a computer resource unavailable to its intended users. Hacking covers a "simple intrusion[6], user id theft and spam mail.[7] Virus distribution means a distribution of malicious codes, ranging from Trojan horse, Internet worm to spyware. General cybercrime is illegal behavior using the Internet, such as fraud, violation of copyrights, illegal and harmful sites, cyber defamation, intrusion of privacy, and cyberstalking.[8]

---

3 Website of Cyber Terror Response Center, http://ctrc.go.kr.
4 *Dos* means all types of activities that cause interruption of the service by sending massive amount of data to the network or causing system overload, originated from Website of Cyber Terror Response Center, http://ctrc.go.kr
5 Website of Cyber Terror Response Center, http://ctrc.go.kr.
6 Simple intrusion means invasion into information and communication network without proper authority or in excess of allowed authority, originated from Website of Cyber Terror Response Center, http://ctrc.go.kr.
7 Website of Cyber Terror Response Center, http://ctrc.go.kr.
8 Website of Cyber Terror Response Center http://ctrc.go.kr. These criminal activities are covered by the following acts: Act on Promotion of Information and Communications Network Utilization and Information Protection, *etc.(Amended in 2006 Act No.8031, Hacking, Infringement of Personal Data, Harmful Internet Site, Cyber Defamation, Sexual Crime, Spam mail)*, Act on the Protection of Information and Communications Infrastructure *(Amended in 2005 Act No.7428, Hacking, Virus Distribution)*, Criminal Act *(First enacted in 1953, Internet Fraud, Infringement of Personal Data, Harmful Internet Site)*, Act on the Punishment of Sexual Crimes and Protection of Victims Thereof *(Amended in 2005 Presidential*

In 2006, the Cyber Terror Response Center of the National Police Agency established "Internal Training Course" for domestic cybercrime police officials and "International Cybercrime Investigation Education" for foreign cybercrime investigators.[9]

The Internal Training Course includes a basic program for cybercirme investigation, an intermediate program, and an advanced program. Through these courses, participants acquire Internet skills, knowledge in digital evidence, and cybercrime investigation and related laws.

Internationally, the Center has also participated in several international cybercrime investigation training courses and overseas training programs to broaden cybercrime response skills and investigation techniques.

Law Enforcement Training Program of the Supreme Prosecutor's Office

The Supreme Prosecutors' Office put the current High-Tech Crime Investigation Division in place in 2000. It has developed effective investigative methods and systems to ensure swift and effective responses to high-tech crimes by training and personnel management, operating the digital forensic center, and managing cybercrime information and database.

The High-Tech Crime Investigation Division has established a cooperative network system with relevant private, business and government sectors. Internationally, it plays a role as contact point of the Republic of Korea in "the International Cooperation System for High Tech Crime Investigation" on a 24 hours/7 days basis.

The Seoul Central District Prosecutors' Office (hereinafter SPO) has also recently launched a Digital Investigation Team[10] affiliated with Internet Crime Investigation Center of the High-Tech Crime Investigation Division in April 2007. The team has ensured digital forensic equipment and digital forensic expert investigators.[11]

Decree No.18873, Sexual Crimes), Protection of Communications Secrets Act *(Amended in 2005, Presidential Decree No.19011, Infringement of Personal Data)*, Copyright Act *(Amended in 2006, Act No.8101, Violation of copyright)*, Computer Programs Protection Act *(Amended in 2001, Act No.6357, Violation of copyright)*, Resident Registration Act *(Amended in 2006 Act No.7900, Infringement of Personal Data)*.

9 Presentation Paper of the National Police Agency, introduced in: *Expert Group Meeting on the Development of Virtual Forum against Cybercrime Report*, published June 28-30, 2006, Seoul, Republic of Korea.

10 Digital Investigation Team has responsibility for ensuring information, which is saved in digital devices such as computer, to go to court as evidence (Report Paper of Prosecutors' Office, 2 April, 2007).

11 The Digital Forensic Expert Group is composed of 1 Director and 6 Investigators (Report Paper of Prosecutors' Office, April 2, 2007).

The SPO led an initiative to establish the "National Computer Crime Research Institute" in 2001 to conduct joint research on cybercrime with prosecutors and law professors. In 2005, the SPO launched a one year-long academy course, titled "Experts Program for High-Tech Crime Investigation," covering accounting auditing, asset investigation, computer-related crime investigation, technology outflow and intellectual property related crime investigation as well as interrogation techniques. The program is specified by course levels and personal grades to secure experts in cybercrime.[12]

In the same year, the SPO also hosted "the third APEC Cybercrime Legislation and Enforcement Capacity Building Conference of Experts"[13] to develop effective response measures to cybercrime. In addition, in 2007 the SPO has established the "Advisory Committee on Digital Crime Investigation" to provide technical and academic advice and develop its specialty in the cybercrime.[14]

Law Enforcement Training Program of the National Cyber Security Center of the National Intelligence Service

The National Cyber Security Center (hereinafter NCSC) of The National Intelligence Service (NIS) has six major operations. The NCSC coordinates efforts in national cyber security policy, and conducts cyber security proactive actions. It also takes the roles of collecting, analyzing and disseminating information on cyber threats. Its tasks include ensuring the safety of information technology security products, responding and analyzing incident, providing recovery supports, and sharing cyber threat information with domestic and international relevant organizations[15] to crack down cybercrime.

The NCSC co-hosted "ASEAN Regional Forum (ARF) International Seminar on Cyber Terrorism" with the Korean Ministry of Foreign Affairs and Trade in 2004. Since then, the NCSC has held a nation-wide "Cyber Security awareness tour" every year for officials responsible for information security in governmental

---

12 Report Paper of Prosecutors' Office June 13, 2005.
13 "APEC Cybercrime Legislation and Enforcement Capacity Building Conference of Experts" was co-hosted with KICJP and U.S. Department of Justice in June 22-24, Seoul, Korea (Report Paper of Prosecutors' Office June 21, 2005).
14 The Advisory Committee on Digital Crime Investigation is co-established with the Electronics and Telecommunications Research Institute (ETRI) and Korea Information Security Agency (KISA), originated from the Established Rule of SPO, published in May 23, 2007.
15 A guideline published by NIS and Website of NCSC, http://www.ncsc.go.kr.

organizations and 16 local governments. The NCSC has developed "Cyber Incident Handling Courses" as a curriculum of the NIS graduate school and retained over 100 cyber security experts annually.[16]

In addition, based on a "Basic plan for *Eulji* drill"[17] from the Emergency Planning Commission under the Office of The Prime Minister, the NCSC carries out security mock drills in coordination with the private, public and military sectors in order to enhance nation-wide response capabilities against cyber attacks.[18]

The NCSC has established the "Korea National CERT Council" to respond to various forms of cyber attacks coming from overseas and establish information sharing systems with foreign countries in 2006.[19]

KICJP and International Cooperation in Criminal Justice Training

The Korean Institute of Criminal Justice Policy organized the meeting "United Nations Crime and Justice Information Network: Providing Information to and from Developing Countries" held in Seoul in 1996, in collaboration with the Korean Ministry of Justice. Since then, KICJP has been actively involved in international efforts against cybercrime.

In 2004, KICJP has become the fifteenth member of the PNI. In 2005, the declaration adopted by the Eleventh United Nations Congress on Crime Prevention and Criminal Justice noted that:

"In the current period of globalization information technology and the rapid development of new telecommunication and computer network systems have been accompanied by the abuse of those technologies for criminal purposes. We therefore welcome efforts to enhance and supplement existing cooperation to prevent, investigate and prosecute high-technology and computer-related crime, including by developing partnerships with the private sector. We recognize the important contribution of the United Nations to regional and other international forums in the fight against cybercrime and invite the Commission on Crime Prevention and Criminal Justice, taking into account that experience, to examine the feasibility of providing further assistance in that area under

---

16 A guideline published by NIS and Website of NCSC, http://www.ncsc.go.kr.
17 South Korea-U.S. joint military drill known as *Eulji Focus Lens*.
18 A guideline published by the NIS and Website of the NCSC, http://www.ncsc.go.kr.
19 Cyber Security, a Monthly Magazine of the NCSC, published in January 2006.

the aegis of the United Nations in partnership with other similarly focused organizations".[20]

At the same Congress, KICJP organized the workshop on "Measures to Combat Computer-Related Crime." Many experts made presentations on cybercrime, including recent trends in cybercrime, the universality of the problem and the need for international responses to cybercrime, legal harmonization in cybercrime control in substantive criminal law and procedural law, international cooperation to prevent and combat cybercrime, international cooperation in cybercrime research, technical assistance in investigating computer-related crime, training legislators and criminal justice professionals, and a public-private strategy in the digital environment.

At the Workshop it was Noted that:

"Considerations should be given to the establishment of a virtual forum or online research network to encourage communication among experts throughout the world on the issue of computer-related crime[21]; Technical assistance and training should be provided by UNODC to States in order to address the lack of capacity and expertise to deal with the problems of computer-related crime. International cooperation should be developed in the areas of information exchange, research and analysis concerning computer-related crime."[22]

KICJP produced the outcome of the Workshop at the fourteenth session of the United Nations Commission on Crime Prevention and Criminal Justice in 2005. The Crime Commission noted in its reports that:

"The observer for the Korean Institute of Criminology made a presentation on the Workshop on Measures to Combat Computer-Related Crime. The outcome of Workshop could be practically translated into a proposed technical assistance project on the prevention and control of cybercrime, the scope of which would be the development of a model training course for law enforcement personnel from developing countries with a rolling curriculum that included control and prevention. An expert group meeting will be held in Seoul in 2006, with the Criminal Justice programme network and the private sector, to develop the

---

20 In the declaration adopted by the Congress and endorsed by the United Nations General Assembly (A/RES/60/177).
21 A/CONF.203/18para. 340 (a)
22 A/CONF.203/18para. 340 (b)

project to produce the model training course. The project would include a virtual expert forum under the auspices of UNODC to facilitate the exchange of information on new trends and approaches in the fight against cybercrime"[23]

As a result of the Workshop, the Virtual Forum against Cybercrime has been adopted to be implemented for strengthening international cooperation in cybercrime prevention and control.

Development of the Virtual Forum against Cybercrime

Since the workshop on "Measures to Combat Computer-Related Crime" in the eleventh United Nations Congress on Crime Prevention and Criminal Justice in 2005, KICJP and UNODC took efforts to establish the Virtual Forum against Cybercrime.

The main goal of the Virtual Forum against Cybercrime is to provide a training program for law-enforcement personnel to combat cybercrime and disseminate practical information on cybercrime for researchers and the public at large.

The Virtual Forum has four objectives: first, to deliver technical assistance; second, to provide training and education; third, to build a network of cybercrime research; and fourth, to act as a clearinghouse in the field of cybercrime control. Its cybercrime training program is for law enforcement and other relevant government officials engaged in the prevention and control of cyber crime of developing countries.

So far, KICJP in conjunction with the UNODC has organized three Expert Group[24] meetings in Korea: a preparatory meeting in June 2006, a steering committee[25] in November 2006, and International Consultant Group Meeting[26] in May 2007. Through those meetings, decisions were made on the organizational structure including the secretariat, roles and functions of three ICGs, development plans for the training program and infrastructure of the pilot project.

The first Expert Group Meeting was held in Seoul, Korea from 28th to 30th June in 2006. A total of 45 participants from 11 countries attended the meeting to discuss the development of the Virtual Forum against Cybercrime. The objectives of the first meeting were to assess the steps for developing the virtual forum and the modalities for developing the research and training

---

23 A/CONF.203/18para. 52.
24 Expert Group Meeting (official title is the 1st Expert Group Meeting).
25 Steering Committee Meeting (official title is the 2nd Expert Group Meeting).
26 International Consultant Group Meeting (official title is the 3rd Expert Group Meeting).

components of the forum by discussing some of the key challenges posed by computer-related crime.

As to the recommendations and action plans of the meeting, KICJP has taken the lead role in partnership with other relevant institutions including the recipient country and decided to establish the platform in Korea for developing the pilot project.

As a follow-up of the first meeting, the second Expert Group Meeting was convened in Gyeongju, Korea on 8th - 9th November, 2006. The second Expert Group Meeting was organized as the steering committee meeting with 11 participants from 4 countries to assess the practical steps and needs for developing the Virtual Forum against Cybercrime.

The steering committee decided to set up 3 working groups called International Consultant Group (ICG): Infrastructure ICG, Training ICG and Research Network ICG, and the secretariat of the Virtual Forum. The steering committee also discussed the needs of the pilot project and has chosen the pilot project recipient country as Vietnam and the People's Police of Vietnam as the partners in the recipient country.

The Third Expert Group Meeting was organized as the ICG meetings in Seoul, Korea on 14th - 15th May in 2007. A total of 19 participants from 6 countries attended. The objectives of this meeting were to define the role of each working group; to discuss the pilot project with implementation plan in detail and the training program guidelines; to establish follow-up schedules.

Three International Consultant Groups have been set up as proposed at the steering committee meeting, with the detailed role of each ICG and the chair for each ICG and the secretary general for the secretariat have been appointed. The preliminary action plan for the pilot project, a training curriculum and the development of a cybercrime research network were discussed in this meeting as well.

Training Program of the Virtual Forum against Cybercrime

The training program of the Virtual Forum consists of introductory course for officials in the criminal justice system, and introductory and advanced courses for specialists. The Introductory Course covers the issues of understanding emerging trends in ICT and cybercrimes in the information age, structure of the Internet, digital divide, vulnerabilities of ICT, forms of ICT and network security, forms of intrusion and hacking, E-commerce and forms of electronic payment.

For understanding cyberspace laws, the course includes the topics of definitions of cybercrime, cyber-violence, anti-social contents in cyberspace, cyber-property crimes, cyber-terrorism, jurisdiction and the roles of national and cross national law enforcement, international developments in the control of cybercrimes, compatibility of international conventions on cybercrime with domestic laws, mutual legal assistance, procedures and practices for online cooperation for law enforcement agencies, and digital evidence, preservation and presentation of evidence for non-forensic specialists.

In the introductory and advanced courses for specialists, the following topics will be covered : Computer investigation techniques of PCs and Networks, investigation system and procedure of advanced countries, understanding the rules of digital evidence, *modus operandi* of cybercrimes and countermeasures, including computer viruses, hacking and botnet, cyber stalking and electronic vandalism, computer fraud and phishing and computer terrorism, and digital evidence, preservation and presentation of evidence, cybercrime monitoring and automated systems, network security, criminal threats against e-commerce and banking, incident response teams: priorities and team building, and case studies of investigative best practices.

The topics of the digital forensic course are to understand and apply the rules of digital evidence, to acquire forensic images and preservation of computer evidence, computer forensics tools testing, analytical procedures and investigation techniques, including program analysis, network analysis, database analysis and digital evidence analysis, e-mail investigation, keyword analysis, Internet activity analysis, encryption and stenography, and computer security risks and remedies, including e-commerce security and e-mail security.

The advanced course consists of special online-seminars with issues on Privacy and data protection, Obscenity and offensive/racist materials, Online gambling, Assessment of potential threat from wireless technology, Biomatrix/bioinformation applications in cyberspace, Intellectual property, and Cyber-terrorism: forms, functions and *modus operandi*.

Pilot Project of Cybercrime Training Program

A Pilot project must be implemented to determine the contents of virtual forum training program and identify technical requirements. KICJP and UNODC had considered Vietnam as the first recipient country, and eventually expand the project to other developing countries in Asia.

The pilot training program for Vietnam consists of 7 modules and 10 lessons (60 minutes for 1 lesson) as the introductory course for officials in the CJS. The course title is "Understanding Information & Communication Technology" and consists of lessons: Understanding emerging trends in IC & cybercrimes in the information age, Structure of the Internet & digital divide, Vulnerabilities of ICT, ICT & network security, Forms of intrusion & hacking, E-commerce & form of electronic payment, and Digital evidence & digital forensics.

To develop and launch the pilot training program in Vietnam, the KICJP has had constant consultation with the People's Police of Vietnam. The expert visit[27] to Vietnam took place between 3rd - 8th July, 2007 with a fact-finding mission to verify the feasibility of the pilot program with Vietnamese authorities. Currently, the KICJP is working on the infrastructure of the forum and the course outline.

According to the action plan of developing the pilot project, the fourth Expert Group Meeting will be held soon to finalize the training program and infrastructure issues. After reviewing the details of the pilot program, the KICJP plans to sign the Memorandum of Understanding with the People's Police of Vietnam and implement the pilot training program. By the first quarter of 2008, training ICGs and Infrastructure will perform thorough evaluation on the pilot program.

Conclusion

As modern society has rapidly shifted into the age of information and communication technology, a new type of crime, cybercrime, has emerged. Cybercrime spreads quickly without borders and poses threats to personal freedom and the security of society. This demands the rule of law in cyberspace. Proper training programs for law enforcement should be provided to control crimes, and thus to protect people in cyberspace. In this respect, the Government of the Republic of Korea has since 1996 been actively involved in such efforts to promote teaching and training programs in cybercrime control.

As efforts to create a global system of cyber-security have become a major policy initiative around the world, the KICJP is now organizing a Virtual Forum against Cybercrime, in cooperation with the UNODC. This will deliver a comprehensive understanding of cybercrime to law enforcement as well as the public, and will support Asian developing countries to build effective criminal justice systems against cybercrime. The Virtual Forum will promote international cooperation in developing criminal justice training

---

27 The expert visit is the visit to Vietnam to have consultation with Vietnamese authorities.

programs, which will contribute to raise the quality of the rule of law.

References

Broadhurst,R. and P. Grabosky (2005). Cyber-Crime – The Challenges in Asia.

Chongko Choi (2005) Historical foundation of Rule of Law in Korea (in:) Dokyun Kim et al (Eds.), The Foundation of Rule of Law, Seoul National University.

Presentation of the National Police Agency (2006). Expert Group Meeting on the Development of Virtual Forum against Cybercrime Report, published 28-30 June, 2006, Seoul, Korea.

Supreme Prosecutors' Office, Report Paper of Prosecutors' Office, 13th June, 2005.

Supreme Prosecutors' Office, Report Paper of Prosecutors' Office, 21st June, 2005.

Supreme Prosecutors' Office, Report Paper of Prosecutors' Office, 2nd April, 2007.

Supreme Prosecutors' Office, The Established Rule of SPO, 23rd May, 2007.

National Intelligence Service (2006). Cyber Security, Monthly Magazine of the NCSC, January.

National Intelligence Service (2007). A guideline on cybersecurity.

KICJP, The 1st Preparatory Meeting on the Workshop 'Measures to Computer-related Crime' for the 11th UN Congress on Crime Prevention and Criminal Justice, 2004.

KICJP, The 2nd Preparatory Meeting on the Workshop 'Measures to Computer-related Crime' for the 11th UN Congress on Crime Prevention and Criminal Justice, 2005.

KICJP, The Expert Group Meeting on the Development of Virtual Forum Against Cybercrime Final Report, 2006.

KICJP, The 2nd Expert Group Meeting on the Development of Virtual Forum Against Cybercrime Final Report, 2006.

KICJP, The 3rd Expert Group Meeting on the Development of Virtual Forum Against Cybercrime Final Report, 2007.

Teaching Cybercrime Prevention: Lessons Learned from Academia[1]

R.G. Broadhurst[2]

Introduction

The rapid uptake of information communication technologies (ICT) and its convergence with the Internet has required law enforcement agencies to prepare investigators for the demanding roles required of collecting evidence about cybercrime. The demands for training in computer literacy, investigations and forensic applications are now ubiquitous and a focus on training a few experts no longer suffices: both generic and specialist training with common standards are now demanded. The complexity of this task in the context of the transnational nature of much of cybercrime is also a challenge and the provision of training and technical assistance to less capable jurisdictions is essential.

The UNODC and KICJP initiative to establish a "Virtual Forum on Cybercrime" arose from the deliberations of the Eleventh United Nations Congress on Crime Prevention and Criminal Justice (2005) workshop on "Measures to combat computer related crime", and is an example of how active e-ready states and international agencies may set out to meet this challenge. The key to the success of such a global project is the stress upon developing partnerships between industry, academia and law enforcement. The role of meshing the results of research (including the significant contributions of industry and the universities) with the practical needs of investigators is a fundamental task of the academy. Research and training about cyber-crime will increasingly focus on the problems of crime prevention in 'cyberspace'. Evaluative research will attach greater importance to evidence-based methods and theoretical developments in information communication technology (ICT) and criminology about deviant behaviour in "cyberspace" will merge. Educational qualification and industry training will become more

---

1 This papers draws on the author's earlier papers: Broadhurst 2005; and Broadhurst and Chantler 2006.
2 Professor and Head of School of Justice, Queensland University of Technology. He is also Associate Fellow, Australian Institute of Criminology, and Honorary Professor University of Hong Kong (People's Republic of China). He is editor of the Asian Journal of Criminology and with Peter Grabosky co-editor of "Cybercrime: the challenge in Asia" published by the University of Hong Kong Press in 2005. Research interests include organised crime, cybercrime, homicide and violence, and policing in transitional states.

tailored for various groups, including law enforcement and information security specialists.

Universities will also become increasingly involved in accreditation, continuing professional education and the research that underpins these activities and those of practitioners. A greater emphasis will also need to be placed on general public education and computer user awareness. The work undertaken for AGIS[3] in developing standards and guidelines for the training of various levels of law enforcement from first responder to forensic specialist marks a significant start in developing common standards and raising the quality of forensic and other specialist education.

Crime involving technology is now part of everyday policing and has an effect on all types of crime. "A comprehensive training program that reaches the widest audience is therefore essential... Any crime scene could be an electronic crime scene and the correct handling of this type of evidence can positively affect an investigation. However, detections, disruptions, prosecutions and crime reduction/prevention can only be achieved with properly trained personnel who are appropriately equipped to investigate the various aspects of computer-enabled criminality that they encounter in their daily duties" (Jones 2005: 1).

The diversity of the forms of teaching and research in the academy about the "information age" engages many disciplines and crucially, novel cross-disciplinary approaches. Multi-disciplinary collaborations have begun to be fostered within the academy to address the complex problems arising in cyberspace and are more successful when partnerships with police and the ICT industry occur. Given the cross-border character of many crimes experienced on the Internet, mobile telephones and other networked environments, a strong comparative (law and criminology) element will also be obligatory in any training program. As we learn more about the dynamic phenomena of cyber-crime, and especially the response of governments, industry and private actors, the dissemination of what is known will be a vital element in crime prevention. In addition there will be the need to constantly update the training of non-specialists and continuing education will be mandatory for them.

The rapid progress made in some jurisdictions provides models for others. For Example in 2003, the United Kingdom (UK) National Police Training (Centrex) began to develop a high-tech crime training program for all UK police and this is now a key component of the National Specialist Law Enforcement Centre (NSLEC). With this background the UK made a bid for funding under AGIS—an EU

---

3 AGIS is the European Union integrated crime and justice assistance programme for member states and through the funding provided the EU Cybercrime Training programme has recently been developed. Agis was one of the dual kings of classic Sparta.

246

funding program—to provide an accredited, modular European training program to enable law enforcement agencies to combat cyber-crime[4]. There were several objectives of the AGIS project also applicable to the broader aims of a *Virtual Forum* in Asia:

- Develop, deliver and evaluate a collaborative cyber-crime training program for law enforcement and harmonize training across international borders;
- Identify and liaise with countries able to contribute to the program and deliver training in the future;
- Provide a sustainable framework for delivering and developing cyber-crime training;
- Make available the training materials *free of charge* to encourage sharing and ensure consistency of standardized training;
- Realize significant cost savings by avoiding the need for everyone to devise their own training material;
- Involve academia to establish accreditation and to support the development of advanced level training (Jones 2005).

With AGIS a regional program developed for Europe some of the challenges for the East Asian based Virtual Forum are less daunting but the diversity of Asia presents unique problems of implementation.

The Global Context: the Problem of Combating Cybercrime

The emergence of trans-national networks of Computer Emergency Response Teams (CERTs), G8 24/7 law enforcement contact points,[5] Internet Crime Reporting Centres, On-line Child Safety Networks[6] and other public/user interest groups (*.e.g.,* cyber-patrol, cyber angels) shows the intrinsic importance of crime prevention. However, the development of equivalent research and training responses has been less intensive and spontaneous. Crime prevention and the common training of specialist investigators, regardless of background or region, become essential when communities perceive that they indeed 'share the same fate'

---

4 Courses for sixty police commenced in 2004, with trainers from the U.K., Germany, Denmark, Ireland, Greece and Hong Kong. See also the related EU Cyber Tools On-Line Search for Evidence (CTOSE) program designed to enable faster mutual legal assistance (MLA).
5 Co-ordinated by US Department of Justice Computer Crime and Intellectual Property Section, involving some 40 countries in mutual legal assistance: http://www.cert.org.
6 A number of US sites illustrate: CyberSpacers.org, Cyber-Hood-Watch.org, and StaySafeonline.info: an example is the animated program created by Microsoft and Boys and Girls of America to help children make safe use of the Internet, chat rooms and e-mail.

regardless of how distant or different they may be. The pressing need for international cooperation may be most readily realised by sharing training and educational opportunities.[7] Nevertheless, why should a global research and training website focus on Asia in its initial phase?

The risks of cyber-crime are not uniform and will reflect the diversity of criminal opportunity, the capacity of policing agencies (public and private) and the scope of the digital divide (in terms of e-commerce activity and the extent of technology uptake) both within and across nations. Risk of cyber-crime and the capacity to respond varies dramatically across nations but nearly half of Interpol's member countries lack the infrastructure for online communication (Noble 2003).[8] Thus the response to cyber-crime (as with trans-national crimes in general) can be no stronger than the "weakest link" applies and compels the more able to assist the less able. A key priority is keeping abreast of legislative and enforcement capability across nations given differential risks arising from the relative development of ICT. A number of multi-lateral organizations (*e.g.,* Council of Europe (CoE), Asia Pacific Economic Forum, Organization of American States, European Union, Organisation for Economic and Cooperative Development) have already undertaken initiatives to monitor legislative developments[9] and undertake training but without co-ordination there is a real risk of duplication. Thus initiatives such as the *Virtual Forum on Cybercrime* provide a vehicle for minimizing the risk of duplication and offering model international programs of training and research dissemination.

---

7 For example, the Scientific Working Group on Digital Evidence (SWGDE) standardizes the exchange of computer forensics information among law enforcement agencies and guides the judicial system about the admissibility of digital evidence and the qualifications of experts.
8 Interpol has stressed financial and high-technology crime along with drugs, terrorism, people smuggling and organised crime as the top five priorities. Note that mobile telephone technologies may reduce these disparities rapidly.
9 Macro-risk or global assessment protocols have not been developed although strategies for harmonising legal definitions and procedures have been suggested (Kaspersen 2004).

Table 1: WORLD INTERNET USAGE AND POPULATION STATISTICS

World Regions	Population % of World	% Population (Penetration)	Usage % of World	Usage Growth 2000-2005
Africa	14.1 %	2.6 %	2.3 %	423.9 %
Asia	56.4 %	9.9 %	35.6 %	218.7 %
Europe	12.4 %	36.1 %	28.5 %	177.5 %
Middle East	2.9 %	9.6 %	1.8 %	454.2 %
North America	5.1 %	68.6 %	22.2 %	110.3 %
Latin America/Caribbean	8.5 %	14.4 %	7.8 %	342.5 %
Oceania / Australia	0.5 %	52.6 %	1.7 %	134.6 %
WORLD TOTAL	100.0 %	15.7 %	100.0 %	183.4 %

NOTES: (1) Internet Usage and World Population Statistics were updated for March 31, 2006. (2) Demographic (Population) numbers are based on data contained in the world-gazetteer website. (3) Internet usage information comes from data published by Nielsen//NetRatings, the International Telecommunications Union, local NICs, and other reliable sources. Source: Miniwatts Marketing Group www.Internetworldstats.com.

The general variations in access to the Internet around the globe are shown in Table 1 and this also shows growth rates are now slowing in those countries where access has been well established and growth elsewhere is still moving at a rapid 'catch-up' rate – a growth for Africa is estimated at 400% plus but from a very low base. Asia's growth rate remains higher than the rest of the world at around 219% in the past 5 years compared to the average of 185%. The digital divide thus remains extreme across the regions of the globe and in respect to Asia remain extreme and within countries themselves. A consequence of this is the variation in the uptake of e-commerce. On line sales as market share has been estimated to account for over 13% of transactions in the USA, 16% of transactions in Korea and Australia, about 9% for Japan and the Netherlands, and 7% for the UK. Forrester Research also noted that while the "...United States and North America currently preside over the majority of online transactions, that will shift in the coming years as Asia and European nations become more active."[10]

The economic consequences of these digital divides are significant as many countries are unable to benefit from the

---

10 North America had the lion share of the e-commerce market with 51% (47% in the US), Asia's share about 24% (Japan 13%), Europe 23% (Germany 5.7%) and Latin America 1.2%; see Forrester Research Inc, accessed June 18, 2006, http://glreach.com/eng/ed/art/2004.ecommerce.php3.

efficiencies and opportunities provided by e-commerce. In addition the social capital associated with access to both markets, networks and educational resources should not be underestimated.[11] Nor should the potential role of serious cyber-crime on unprotected sites or the exploitation of ill-prepared states to prevent there ICT services being used as launching pads for attacks in other states. The *Virtual Forum* in East Asia therefore responds to the region likely to develop e-commerce rapidly.[12] A number of Asian and Central Asian states are likely to be the focus of the pilot development of on-line training modules adapted from AGIS and the Korean National Police.[13] These existing programmes offer a starting point but are not offered on-line.

Because of the digital divide, only a small number of jurisdictions will have the capacity to provide for comprehensive training and research capabilities. In the advanced ICT countries governments and relevant corporations have taken the initiative to support training; however, the focus has largely been on ensuring criminalization and intellectual property issues with child pornography catching most attention as a public safety problem.

While Internet and ICT connectivity continues to grow exponentially, how ready are the key players in the academy, private sector and government to undertake a global program of training research and dissemination? What should such a training program look like and how can it be done? This paper describes the educational agenda through the prism of (cross-disciplinary) criminology rather than the systems engineering or information security perspective. Such a perspective sees cyber-crime as a social rather than as a technical problem and, although it recognizes that the criminal behaviour is said to be taking place in 'cyberspace' or a 'virtual world,' the actors involved and their intentions are not, as sometimes supposed, literally in another dimension. Thus any research and training agenda must begin by finding a common language to identify the training priorities. For example addressing "social engineering" (referring to the human element in identity theft) requires sound knowledge about offender and victim interactions and so a clear picture of the various forms of cybercrime is crucial.

---

11 Forrester Research, a US market analyst, predicted that online commerce would reach $7 trillion for both online business-to-business and business-to-consumer transactions – about 8.6% of worldwide commerce in 2004. Based on an estimated $657 billion sales in 2000 e-commerce sales had grown tenfold to $6,790 billion by 2004 a rate that represented an approximate doubling of sales volume every year. If indeed these rates continue to grow the value and market share of this form of trading will be increasingly crucial to economic wealth.
12 The web portal will be based on servers and systems developed by KICJP and NHN Corporation of Korea.
13 Training programmes offered by the US Department of Justice, Australian Federal Police and the Hong Kong Police.

Cybercrime Offences

A crucial challenge to developing training from first responder to specialist is to be clear about the scope of activity to be included. One problem is that in many jurisdictions any crime might involve computers but only some are substantively computer related. Although there is no definitive list of what constitutes cybercrime or computer related crime a consensus has emerged about what falls within the scope of the offences that occur in cyberspace. These are as follows:

- Telecommunications theft;
- Illegal interception of telecommunications;
- Piracy copyright theft;
- Cyber stalking;
- Electronic money laundering and tax evasion;
- Electronic vandalism, Cyber-terrorism, denial of service, extortion;
- Sales and investment fraud, forgery;
- Electronic funds transfer fraud and counterfeiting (carding);
- Identity theft and misrepresentation;
- Content crime - offensive materials;
- Espionage;
- Resource theft - illegal use of PC.

Hence as we can see from the above list cybercrime ranges across a wide spectrum of activities and behaviours. At one end are crimes that involve fundamental breaches of personal or corporate privacy, such as assaults on the integrity of information held in digital depositories and the use of illegally obtained digital information to blackmail a firm or individual. Also at this end of the spectrum is the growing crime of identity theft. Midway along the spectrum are transaction-based crimes such as fraud, trafficking in child pornography, digital piracy, money laundering, and counterfeiting. These are specific crimes with specific victims, but the criminal hides in the relative anonymity provided by the Internet.

Another aspect of this type of crime involves individuals within corporations or government bureaucracies who deliberately alter data for either profit, personal or political objectives. At the other end of the spectrum are those crimes that involve attempts to disrupt the actual workings of the Internet. These range from spamming, hacking, and denial of service attacks against specific sites to acts of cyber-terrorism—that is, the use of the Internet to cause public disorder or disturbances and even death. Cyber-terrorism focuses upon the use of the Internet by non-state actors to affect a nation's economic and technological infrastructure. Since the September 11 attacks of 2001, public awareness of the threat of cyber-terrorism has grown dramatically.[14] Training programs need to address this diversity and provide for some understanding of the vectors of attack. Some of the most worrying forms of attack involve what has become known as 'malicious code' and among these 'botnets' that target networks are among the most serious.

Malware or Malicious Code

Malware is software designed to infiltrate or damage a computer system, without the owner's consent. The term is a portmanteau of "mal-" (or perhaps "malicious") and "software", and describes the intent of the creator, rather than any particular features. Malware is commonly taken to include (often in combination):

- Computer viruses;
- Worms;
- Trojan horses;
- Spyware; and, in some cases adware;
- Botnets;
- Rootkits.

In law, malware is sometimes known as a computer contaminant. Malware should not be confused with defective software, that is, software which has a legitimate purpose but contains errors or bugs.[15] A large part of any general and forensic training programme in computer-related crime will focus on the role these different forms of malware operate to effect crime.

Although we don't have comprehensive information about the prevalence of cybercrime in Asia a survey series in Hong Kong (HK) shows that the risks are high in e-ready jurisdictions. Questions about the extent of cyber crime were included in the household omnibus *UN International Crime Victim Survey* (UNICVS) implemented in HK early 2006[16] and also in the *UN Crimes against Business Survey* (UNCABS). Amongst the 1192 HK UNCABS business respondents connected to the Internet in this survey (total n=1817) 61% experienced some form of cybercrime but they also shared the general pattern found with individual users who responded to the UNICVS, However, the differences between household and businesses experience of cyber crime are shown in table 2 below – the principal difference was that business were more often specifically targeted for monetary gain.

---

14 Cybercrime 2006, Retrieved June 15, 2006, from Encyclopædia Britannica Premium Service: http://www.britannica.com/eb/article-235699.
15 See http://en.wikipedia.org/wiki/Malware.
16 Results for the 2291 HK UNICVS respondents to a telephone protocol found that 58.3%[16] had access to computer and 98% of these computer users had access to the Internet (n=1332).

Table 2: Types of cyber crime victims in Hong Kong in 2005[17]

Have you experienced any of the following computer-related incidents in the last 12 months?

	% ICVS	% CABS
Fraud in purchasing something over the Internet?	1.6	1.0
Threats of harm or physical attack made while online or through E-mail?	2.5	2.1
Unrequested lewd or obscene messages, communications, or images while online or through E-mail?	41.5	4.7
Software copyright violation in a home business?	1.6*	4.0
Something else that you consider a computer-related crime?	7.6	5.6
Any attack on your computer from a source such as a virus, spyware, hacker, malware, etc.?	49.0	45.0

Notes: % not adjusted for don't know or refusals and estimates based on weighted samples for the UNICVS sample only; * % based on number of home businesses – raw estimate 0.3%.

Of the household respondents with access to a computer 67% experienced at least one form of cyber crime in the past year, somewhat more than the 61% of businesses. Nearly 12% either did no have a firewall or anti-virus software installed (4.7%) or did not know if they did (7%). Among business respondents 8.3% reported not having a firewall or anti-virus programme and 5.4% did not know. The main types of cyber crime reported by household and business respondents were obscene content and 'malware'.[18]

Action: Training and Research Networks

Growing concern about law enforcement capability in cybercrime has quickened the pace of development as shown in the gathering

---

17 I am grateful to my colleagues Dr. Kent Lee and Dr. John Bacon-shone for providing me with the preliminary findings of the HK UNICVS. Results are provisional.
18 About 13% of household respondents claimed that the cybercrime event incurred monetary loss and of these approximately 26% estimated the loss to be greater than $HKD1001. Among businesses the losses were significantly higher with 14.5% reporting monetary losses and of these 40% had losses greater than $HKD1001 and 12.5% losses exceeding $HKD10 001.

of law officers, academia and the private sector[19] at the Interpol General Secretariat for the *1st International Cybercrime Investigation Conference*, 19-20th September 2005 hosted by the Interpol Financial and High-Tech Crime Sub-Directorate.[20] Further regional conferences on training for cybercrime investigators (per those organised in the recent past for Child Safety on the Internet) are planned. Among the topics was an outline of the Interpol Training and Operational Standards Initiative for High-Tech Crime (TOPSI) and the introduction of Interpol's high-tech crime training web server. With such a dedicated web server a peer-to-peer undercover investigation training and forensic consultation and training service was mooted.[21] As part of this conference the potential role of external accreditation was also raised with the example of the University College Dublin, (Ireland) proposed Master of Science degree programme in cybercrime investigation (see also Ciardhuan, Patel and Gillen 2003; Ciardhuan 2004).

This conference re-iterated the need for harmonised training materials and for the global exchange of training materials and the development of a "free" web training site. Although there was a shortage of trainers universities and private industry could support the development and delivery of training and educational modules. The delegates recommended *inter alia* that[22]:

- Interpol facilitate[23] a global training cybercrime investigations course for managers, first responders, basic, intermediate and advanced levels, and ensure appropriate assessment and certification;
- Interpol continues to support the International Cybercrime Training Action Group (ICTAG);
- Interpol takes responsibility for the collection, retention and dissemination of training materials created by regional working parties and other training organizations;

---

19 Representatives from America Online, Microsoft and the International Federation of the Phonographic Industry were noted in attendance.
20 The conference was attended by 70 representatives from more than 30 countries.
21 This is a similar developed to the response to forgery and counterfeiting for Interpol's secure website for a Universal Classification System for Counterfeit Payment Cards that provided up-to-date information on trends and techniques of forgery of payment cards and fraud. Apart from illustrating how Interpol's unique clearing house function can be adapted to meet new problems, the site served as an example of how international agencies can assist with essential tasks, such as secure shared intelligence, and the potential role of private non-state actors in the prevention of crime. According to recent information the website has fallen into disuse.
22 Adopted from the report of the conference at (visited December 12, 2006) http://www.interpol.org/Public/TechnologyCrime/Conferences/1stCybConf/Conference.asp.
23 Interpol could provide, it was argued, training using its Mobile Classroom and the available training facilities of its Sub-Regional Bureaus.

- Interpol Regional Working Parties on IT Crime, working in co-ordination, shall develop training modules for all levels and provide training packages to other regions;
- Interpol supports the establishment of an international training network with appropriate membership requirements, recognising the existing European training network (AGIS);
- Universities should be encouraged to continue activities in the development of accredited training modules;
- private industry should be encouraged to participate in the development, delivery and sponsorship of appropriate training initiatives, in particular, the provision of international 'train the trainer' programmes;
- Interpol facilitates a communications mechanism to enable students and trainers of Interpol courses to maintain contact and share information and experiences.

Expectations that Interpol lead these initiatives was unresolved by the issue of resources. Further action was expected by close of 2006 including a 2nd Conference for cybercrime training.[24] Elements of these recommendations resonate with the proposals made at the Eleventh United Nations Congress but focus on the role of a single central agency. An alternative is to develop networks of training. In the proposal adopted at the Congress the combination of research and training was assumed to achieve greater synergy by the convergence of several training networks associated with nodes in established agencies, universities and industry. To succeed this mechanism of coordination would require a *virtual hub* located in an international agency (*e.g.,* United Nations Office on Drugs and Crime (UNODC), or regional United Nations institutes such as KICJP, UNAFEI, AIC) or one of the university centres focusing on the social and technical problems of ICT. For a 'virtual hub' or forum to function as a training platform a dual function as an *on-line research forum* was ideal. Such a virtual hub could act as a clearing house about developments in cyber-crime, legislative innovations, the scope of relevant laws, capacities of law enforcement agencies, as well as disseminate research findings and act as an 'honest broker' of what constitutes best practice (Broadhurst 2005).

A training and research network would entail closer cooperation between the private IT security sector, academia[25] and law

---

24 At the time of writing the author is not aware of a second conference taking place.
25 The non-profit Computer Crime Research Center (CCRC) located in Zaporizhzhya, Ukraine is an example of cross-border initiative supported by public and private sponsors that seeks to improve co-operation on computer-related crime research, child pornography and cyber terrorism between CIS countries, Europe and the USA (see http://www.crime-research.org/, visited March 3, 2005).

enforcement than is usual and a degree of uncertainty about who pays and how cooperation could take place arises (Grabosky, Smith & Dempsey 2001). In addition a degree of potential rivalry and poor co-ordination among international agencies may risk the dilution of resources through the fragmentation or proliferation of similar efforts at addressing the problems.

Action: A Model Syllabus

Many police agencies in ICT advanced nations have recognised the increased interdependence of global markets and have responded to the general risks of cybercrime especially to commerce and financial services. For example, the response of the Hong Kong Police high-tech crime unit is typical of many police services and its mission broadly reflects the scope of public policing now required to address cybercrime:

- maintaining a professional investigation capability and broadening the investigation; *i.e.,* specialising and mainstreaming expertise;
- developing accredited computer forensics;
- proposing changes in laws and policies;
- prevention and education;
- intelligence management, and liaison with industry; and
- liaison with overseas law enforcement agencies and international MLA cooperation.

Each of these goals needs to be informed by adequately trained personnel capable of undertaking the operational demands of the comprehensive role envisaged by public policing agencies (see also Anon 2001; Johnston 2002). A highly useful function is formal risk assessment.[26] However, there are differences in the length and type of training that are provided by police agencies and very few courses have academic recognition[27] or are accredited outside the jurisdiction. In the following section I describe a proposed 'model' curriculum for on-line delivery in the UNODC/KICJP Virtual Forum in terms of aims, objectives, course outlines and delivery modes.

Aims and rationale of model syllabus

The online courses in cybercrime proposed by the UNODC/KICJP *Virtual Forum* seek to prepare introductory and advanced level

---

26 The UK, National Hi-Tech Crime Unit for example produced an annual hi-tech criminal and technological threat assessment as a component of the National Criminal Intelligence Service's national assessment.
27 The Hong Kong University of Science and Technology was an early partner with the HKP in developing a forensic diploma course.

256

courses for Law Enforcement Agency (LEA) investigators and prosecutors. These courses are based on evolving models of the investigative process drawn from variations of the standard crime scene protocol. A number of useful investigative models for digital environments have been proposed (see Casey 2000) and these recognise that awareness of the forms of malware is crucial to the subsequent nature of the (forensic) investigation. Because of the increased offender targeting of networks dynamic means of applying the investigative stages have also evolved – shifting from laboratory to site based practices. Recently Ciardhuan (2004) suggested a comprehensive model stressing awareness and effective chain of custody processes adding to the fundamental stages proposed by Reith, Carr and Gunsch (2002).[28]

The *Virtual Forum* programme shares some similarities with the comprehensive programme proposed by the AGIS group, and also emphasises "awareness training" for senior managers. However, the three progressive (accredited) levels or stages of training recommended for European cybercrime investigators (for details see Ciardhuan, Patel and Gillen 2003) are modified. Awareness training will be essential in the context of Asia as well as the advanced levels courses that focus on the management of hard and software infrastructure, systems planning and criminology. The training programme is developed with three audiences in mind:

1. Basic introductory levels courses designed to sensitize all levels in LEA and judicial officers to computer-related crime in the context of information communication technologies and convergence;
2. All LEA officers: guidelines and procedures for first responders;
3. Introductory and advanced level courses for investigators, prosecutors, case managers and forensic specialists.

The training gives students a basic understanding of cybercrime in the context of a globalisation and all of its diversity (from Information & Critical Infrastructure Protection through to individual Internet banking and cyber terrorism). Methods for counteracting cybercrime and developments in policing and intelligence that utilise high-tech solutions to crime are the core skill/competencies to be developed. The aim of the training programme is to provide up to date expertise in identifying and combating cybercrime including the new roles to be adopted by high tech crime units in law enforcement and national security. It also recognises the growing need for computer related forensic and investigative skills because many traditional crimes also involve the investigation of computers and networks.

A website platform with interactive features will be the means to carry the structured self-paced learning programme for students of

---

28 Namely: identification, preparation, approach strategy, preservation, collection, examination. analysis, presentation of evidence and archive.

varying LEA backgrounds and skill levels. The on-line learning will also enjoy features for teachers and students that are similar to that provided by university online course software such as *Blackboard* or other e-learning platforms. The preferred on-line delivery mode may not be practical in some jurisdictions so face-to-face and other delivery modes are to be developed in tandem.

Training Objectives - Virtual Forum

Core competencies and skills are crucial for the conduct of any criminal investigation and this is also the case in the investigation of cybercrimes. Training at advanced and introductory levels is required and the various skills necessary to respond to cybercrime are described below.

By the conclusion of the introductory courses students should be able to:

1. Demonstrate a basic knowledge and understanding of cybercrime and ICT;
2. Recognise the risks associated with ICT and global networks;
3. Be aware of current and emerging trends in cybercrime;
4. Describe the types of cybercrime and the tools or methods utilised to commit cybercrime;
5. Understand the practical and evidentiary requirements for the seizure and protection of computer-related evidence (*e.g.,* per the first responders role).

By the conclusion of the advanced (investigators) courses students should be able to:

1. Identify and trace computer-related crimes;
2. Apply investigative tools and strategies;
3. Apply data recognition, seizure and preservation procedures;
4. Understand the major forms of forensic interrogation of computers and related devices;
5. Describe the evidentiary aspects of cybercrime and the role of existing conventions and bi-lateral MLA arrangements;
6. Understand topical and emerging issues in the investigation and control of cybercrime;
7. Provide oversight and manage cases involving cybercrime.

By the conclusion of the forensic specialist courses student should be able to:

1. Acquire forensic images according to acknowledged protocols and methods;
2. Apply national and international legal and ethical protocols as required;
3. Recognise and resolve technical issues related to the examination of forensic images;

4. Critically use the products of analytical procedures;
5. Perform the role of the expert in investigations and in court.

Cybercrime training programme outline

An outline of the courses to be offered in the training programme provides for introductory, advanced, forensic and general courses covering the main subject areas.

A. Introductory level courses

Introductory courses are essential pre-requisites for advanced courses but may be offered as stand alone or terminal courses designed to increase *awareness* for a wider range of LEA personnel.

A.1 Pre-requisite course (or stand alone module)

A.1 Guidelines and procedures for first-responders at computer-related crime scenes.

1. Understanding Information Communication (ICT Technology)

1.1 Challenges of cybercrime in the information age;
1.2 Understanding computers and related devices;
1.3 Structure of the Internet, networks & the digital divide;
1.4 Emerging trends in ICT – ,*e,g.,* broadband, internet services (*e,g.,* VoIP) & wireless;
1.5 Vulnerabilities of ICT: including forms of intrusion & hacking, *etc*.
1.6 E-commerce (forms of electronic payment) & its threats: ID & account theft;
1.7 Forms of IT & Network security.

2. Understanding the Law of 'Cyberspace'

2.1 Criminality – definitions of cybercrime & computer-related crime;
2.2 History of cybercrime and its legal suppression;
2.3 Types of cybercrimes I – against the person (*e.g.,.* cyber stalking, content crime – offensive materials, identity theft & misrepresentation);
2.4 Types of cybercrimes II – against property (*e.g.,* telecommunications theft/ interception, piracy, electronic money laundering and tax evasion, vandalism, denial of service, extortion, sales & investment fraud, forgery, electronic funds transfer fraud and 'carding');
2.5 Forms of digital evidence, preservation & presentation of evidence (for non-forensic specialists);

2.6 Jurisdiction: the roles of national and cross national law enforcement (*e.g.,*. Cyber Emergency Response Teams);

2.7 International developments in the control of computer-related crimes

- The Council of Europe Convention on Cybercrime;
- European Commission on Computer-related Crime;
- ASEAN and APEC responses to cybercrime and threats to e-commerce;
- Compatibility of international conventions with domestic laws

2.8 Mutual legal assistance: methods, procedures and practices for online cooperation.

B. Advanced and introductory courses for specialists

In relation to the courses and topics outlined below both introductory and advanced versions could be offered depending on the target group and level of technical proficiency. Thus the course outlines below are generic and will require further specification. The course entitled 'Special Online-Seminars' is provided as a catch-it-all course designed to address current and emerging topics: its content should be dynamic and responsive to emerging problems.

3. Computer Investigations: Overview

3.1 Investigation procedures and management;

3.2 Computer investigation techniques: networks and PCs;

3.3 Cybercrime monitoring & the role of automated systems;

3.4 Digital and computer forensics for investigators;

3.5 Modus Operandi of computer-related crimes

- Computer viruses, worms, hacking/intrusion,
- botnets, *etc.*;
- Cyberstalking & bullying, electronic vandalism;
- Computer fraud, forgery and phishing: ID theft & money laundering;
- Computer espionage and terrorism ;
- Content crime : violation of juvenile protection ordinance/regulation;
- Illegal production/destruction of electro-magnetic data.

3.6 Applying counter measures: variable measure;

3.7 Investigative Best Practices: case studies, e.g., Bloomberg/ Honey Net Project;

3.8 Practicum: project exercise.

4. Computer Related Forensic Investigation

4.1 Computer security risks and remedies;

4.2 Incident response teams: priorities and team building;

4.3 Understanding and applying of the rules of evidence: the expert witness;

4.4 Principles of Computer Based Evidence (networks & PC));

4.5 Acquiring forensic images & preservation of computer evidence;

4.6 Evaluating & applying computer forensics software tools, (*e.g.*, Encase, X-Ways Forensic Addition, Forensic ToolKit (FTK), Linux dd, iLook- DOS, Windows, Windows NT/2000/XP forensics, *etc.*);

4.7 Analytical procedures and investigation techniques: overview;

4.8 E-mail investigation;

4.9 Keyword analysis;

4.10 Internet activity analysis;

4.11 Encryption and stenography;

4.12 Practicum.

5. Special Online-Seminars: Issues and Topics

5.1 Privacy and data protection;

5.2 Obscenity and offensive/racist materials;

5.3 Online Gambling: issues for prohibition and non-prohibition jurisdictions;

5.4 Assessment of potential threat from wireless technology;

5.5 Biomatrix/Bioinformation applications in cyberspace;

5.6 Intellectual Property
- Trademark infringement;
- Copyright infringement;
- Unauthorised access/download;
- Unauthorised reproduction of protected programmes;

5.7 Special interest topics raised by participants – open forum on special cases;

5.8 Cyber-terrorism: forms, functions and modus operandi;

5.9 New e-commerce payment systems: implications.

The provision of on-line support via a dedicated chat room and discussion/bulletin board will be part of any *Virtual Forum* along with on-line course supplementary materials and resources. These resources should include a 'hot' reports section, articles, case studies, links to other sites and a reference section. Depending on the level of computer connectivity (broadband or modem) alternate delivery methods must also be offered in addition to on-line learning. The courses should enjoy standing and be articulated to formal qualification awarded by the relevant national higher education institutions.

Implementation and counter-measures

The widespread provision of training particularly in the developing world will allow the leading e-countries to manage if not prevent many of the cross-border problems (*e.g.,* rendition of fugitives) now so evident in the delivery of phishing, DoS and other cybercrimes.

The development of cybercrime training and the ultimate improvements in investigative capability will still require the traditional craft skills of policing. In the on-line 'situation' the theft of information and the manipulation of identity and trust are the key. Consequently the focus of training has been on the means identity has been breached. Leading crime prevention scholars Newman and Clarke (2003) argue that a crucial factor is how trust is acquired and maintained when on-line merchants must be more intrusive about their (unseen) customers' identity and credit risk and the apparent ease in which trust is manipulated by fraudsters and others. Clarke and Newman also note the high risks posed in the post-transaction phase (*i.e.,* the delivery of goods or services ordered) is often overlooked. Efforts to reduce cyber-crime need to recognise these ingredients and the numerous pathways for crime. Therefore in the online environment crime prevention must be more integrated than the conventional environment. Neglecting routine police training or failing to build on the essentials of policing would undermine the benefits of high tech crime training. In some jurisdictions training may also be altered or 'humoured' in order not to offend particular regimes or practices. The more mainstream the rules of evidence and suspect rights are embedded in training and recommended procedures the more easy it will be to foster genuine 'rule of law' practices.

The nature and efficiency of private sector investments in security as an aspect of 'true' external costs must also be considered (Schneier 2003). Careful monitoring of the deployment of public police to counteract problems on the Internet or cyberspace needs to be tested against clear public interest criteria (Huey and Rosenberg 2004). The evaluation of police performance will have to be embedded in follow-up studies of the effectiveness of operations (and feedback into the needs assessment process of trainers).

The role of legal education

A key training and research focus are the regulations governing ICT environments such as the Internet and mobile phone networks. Many jurisdictions sought to use their existing criminal statutes to cope with unauthorized access, ID theft, malicious computer software and other offences while others introduced purpose built criminal laws or sought technologically neutral definitions to reduce ambiguities about devices and media that were rapidly evolving[29] (Schjolberg 2004).

The CoE's *Cybercrime Convention*, which came into force in 2004 offered the prospect of a potential global treaty for the prosecution of cyber-crime. The convention provides a sound model of the definitions of cyber-crime and is a force for comity and harmonisation of law. It has been drawn on by many non-CoE nations in the framing of their own laws (*e.g.,* Thailand). The many jurisdictions involved in the CoE convention realized that mutual legal assistance arrangements (MLA) were inadequate to deal with the speed and diversity of crimes generated by greater connectivity and efforts in improving MLA are as vital as harmonised definitions of the offences. The monitoring or mapping of legal changes (Kaspersen 2004) and jurisdiction (*e.g.,* Brenner and Frederiksen 2002) across the globe are crucial priorities because there are many challenges in achieving uniformity of terminology and practice such that cyber-crimes might be prosecuted as with piracy at sea by any competent tribunal anywhere. Building in awareness of the development of the emerging legal responses will be a significant challenge in updating training. The introduction of common training standards can help to foster harmonisation but allowance for country variation will also be necessary.

Although there is consensus about the risks of computer-related crime, apart from criminalising the conduct at a global level, there is much less consensus about what might be done to prevent it. There is concern that the technological solution is a mirage despite improved software resistance to intrusion. Faith in deterrence-based approaches may also be misguided since deterrence is likely to succeed only in some circumstances, and experience with conventional crime suggests that over-reliance on law as a deterrent or moral educator alone is unlikely to be enough despite community support[30]. Above all is the belief that training or education for investigators can be an 'all purpose solvent' but much depends on the quality and timing of training.

Countries differ in terms of their training priorities for law enforcement and the resources that are available. It would be useful to develop an overview of where cybercrime investigation and training fits among the many law enforcement training priorities. Part of the moderation of any 'global' training effort would be to understand (and address) the actual problems faced by individual countries. What kinds of cyber-crime are at the forefront:

---

29 Useful sites include 'FindLaw' see http://cyber.lp.findlaw.com/criminal/; and McConnell International see http://www.mcconnellinternational.com/services/Updatedlaws.htm.
30 Most incidents of cyber-crime do not proceed to conviction and we know little about the eventual sentences imposed or the levels of disparity within and across nations (Smith, Grabosky & Urbas 2004).

hacking, fraud, or theft of intellectual property? Are governments more concerned about infrastructure protection or child pornography? Given a basic training needs assessment the courses on offer may be tailored to incorporate material and cases that focus on the nature of the crimes most worrisome in the jurisdiction.

Recent developments in the general context of more data, places, customers and complexity suggest *likely priorities* for research and training updates as follows (see Grabosky and Broadhurst 2005):

- Accounting for changes in the form (*i.e.*, greater sophistication) and profit focus of criminal activity, especially fraud and deception-like offences (see Morris 2004). Updates in deception methods and malware deployment will be a crucial means of keeping investigators abreast of developments;
- The scope, prevalence, severity, and duration of cyber-crimes among different populations and how best to identify high-risk populations. Training that focuses on victims and their behaviour will be necessary in investigation but also crucial in crime prevention efforts. Crime prevention strategies will need to be based on mass campaigns;
- Understanding the role of organised crime and the overlap between traditional organized crime and new modes of crime facilitated by computers and Internet connectivity (see Council of Europe 2004, Brenner 2002). Training that focused on all stages of a network attack would help identify the role of serious criminal networks;
- Increased sophistication of malicious code now required better mechanism for the co-ordination of rapid and secure information sharing about such threats among CERTs. Common training regimes provide excellent support for a trusted intelligence environment;
- Despite increased cross-national cooperation, systematic evaluation of the progress made in developing comprehensive forms of MLA has yet to occur. The monitoring of compliance is a priority (Kaspersen 2004) and common training and standards among investigators will create the necessary climate for change.

Much of what we think will help in preventing cyber-crime is based on too little knowledge about offender and victim behaviour as it applies in the online environment. The poor training and capability some law enforcement agencies and the consequent risk of cyber-crime safe havens remains the most serious problem and fully justifies the priority given to training. Nevertheless, the separation of specialist knowledge (computer hardware and software content) from the disciplines of criminology and law must be bridged both in the academy and among LEA practitioners.

264

Conclusion

A number of issues related to the delivery and priorities of training in the Asian context are yet to be settled but some of these are summarised below. Questions about the sustainability of the *Virtual Forum* and audience priorities (*i.e.,* 'training the trainer' versus selected personnel and so on) are crucial to the success of this global pilot project. However, many specific details about delivery (including on-line versus intensive or combinations) can only be determined by a training needs assessment process for the pilot countries chosen to develop the on-line forum.

The *Virtual Forum* provides a plan for the implementation of a programme of courses appropriate for either an on-line or conventional learning environments. However, questions about the best means of involving tertiary educational institutions and the development of appropriate recognition of prior learning and specialist courses appear to depend on attracting Universities and industry to become part of the solution.

The issues below reflect the many matters that must still be addressed in implementation:

- What are the best forms of learning strategies (on & off-line) for different target audiences: from first responders to forensic specialists and prosecutors?
- Who are the priority targets for training: introductory, advanced, or awareness levels?
- Who will have final control over the access and oversight processes on the Virtual Forum?
- How will the online, practicum, project and other forms of examination or assessment be undertaken?
- How applicable are existing on-line courses for police in developing countries?
- Sustainability and technical assistance – who will pay in the long term?
- What are the best training delivery strategies for low-technology environments?
- How best to provide useful feedback for students and teachers/instructors?

Research on cyber-crime is in its infancy and providing an international evidence base for future policy development is a challenging task. Without this research and the requisite documentation the development of effective training regimes will be hampered.

The development of instructional handbooks and the reporting of case studies of individual investigations, successful or otherwise, are part of the learning process Practical means of engaging police managers and others occur if the computer can be de-mystified. One successful technique used has been to require trainees to re-assemble from its constituted parts a computer. The relative ease that this can be done re-assures the trainees and builds confidence[31]. Success stories can also help build confidence for new investigators. 'Recipes' for success may also be useful for training purposes. Studies of unsuccessful investigations are no less important and cyber-crime specialists need reflect systematically on cases that 'go wrong' (Broadhurst and Grabosky 2005).

Government has driven much of the response to cyber-crime but the private sector plays a crucial role in the prevention of digital crime and can also contribute to training and research. Microsoft's role in supporting with Interpol the training of police officers and prosecutors across the world in combating child pornography is but one example of what can be done. The NSLEC and similar agencies in other jurisdictions draw upon the expertise found in both industry and academia, however, many educational institutions lack the funding support to respond promptly and effectively to new problems. Until government and industry create strategic partnerships with Universities (especially those with technological capacities) the struggle to train and certify capable cybercrime investigators who are life long learners will continue. Shortages in the essential personnel with the appropriate (universal) standards of competence (as in other professions) will remain a significant constraint. Apart from the continuous demand for research and training two developments are essential: the creation of a viable international law enforcement mechanism supported by a cadre of capable investigators and prosecutors and, private and public partnerships that are genuinely collaborative and incorporate the role of universities in the education of those that are tasked to fight cybercrime.

---

31 Personal communication Nigel Jones for trainer for Centrax UK.

References

Anonymous (2001). Top 10 police needs for combating electronic crime. The Police Chief, Vol.68, 8,119.

Anonymous (2002). Rethinking cyber crime fighting: getting the digital collar: today's investigators need more than archaic forensic methods when collecting electronic evidence. New guides are teaching old detectives new tricks. Law enforcement technology Vol 29 (4), 34 -338

Bocij, P. (2004). Cyberstalking: Harassment in the Internet Age and How to Protect Your Family. Westport: Praeger.

Brenner, S.W. (2002). Organized Cybercrime? How Cyberspace May Affect the Structure of Criminal Relationships. 4 North Carolina Law Review and Technology, 1.

Brenner, S.W. and B.A. Frederiksen (2002). Computer Searches and Seizures: Some Unresolved Issues, 8. Michigan Telecommunications & Technology Law Review 39.

Council of Europe (2004). Summary of the Organised Crime Situation Report: Focus on Cybercrime. Octopus Interface conference: Challenge of Cybercrime, September 15-17, Strasbourg.

Broadhurst, R.G. (2005). International Cooperation in Cyber-crime Research, Proceedings of the 11th UN Congress on Crime Prevention and Criminal Justice: Workshop 6 Measures to combat computer related crime, Bangkok, April, 23-24, 2005: UN Office on Drugs and Crime/Korean Institute of Criminology.

Broadhurst, R. G. and Chantler, A. (2006). Cybercrime Update: Trends and Developments. In Expert Group Meeting on The Development of a Virtual Forum against Cybercrime Report, June 28-30, 2006, Seoul Korea, KICJP & UNODC 2006, 21-56.

Casey, E. (2000). Digital Evidence and Computer Crime. San Diego: Academic Press.

Ciardhuan, S.O. (2004). An Extended Model of Cybercrime Investigations. International Journal of Digital Evidence 3 (1), www.ijde.org.

Ciardhuan, S.O. Patel A. and P. Gillen (2003). Training Cyber Crime Investigation, EU Falcone Project: Project No. JAI/2001/Falcone/127 http://www.ifip.org/TESTIFIP/WebPages/openbiblio/opac/viewDocument.php?id=92&PHPSESSID=f11c46e158952626dca6ddad9b509c60

Demetriou, C. & A. Silke, (2003). A Criminological Internet 'Sting: Experimental Evidence of Illegal and Deviant Visits to a Website Trap'. British Journal of Criminology 43,213-222.

Kaspersen, H., (2004). 'Convention on Cybercrime – current state of implementation'. Council of Europe Octopus Interface Conference: Challenge of Cybercrime, September 15-17, Strasbourg.

Grabosky P., R.G. Broadhurst (2005). The Future of Cyber-crime in Asia. In Broadhurst, R.G and P. Grabosky (eds.), Cybercrime: The Challenge in Asia. The University of Hong Kong Press, pp. 347-360.

Grabosky, P. and Smith, R.G., G. Dempsey (2001). Electronic Theft: Unlawful Theft in Cyberspace. Melbourne: Cambridge University Press.

Huey L. and Rosenberg R.S (2004). Watching the Web: thoughts on expanding police surveillance opportunities under the cyber crime convention. Canadian Journal of Criminology and Criminal Justice 46 (5), 597-606.

Jones, N. (2005). Royal Canadian Mounted Police Gazette, Vol. 67 (3).

Johnston, R.L. (2002). 'The National Cybercrime Training Partnership: Helping your agency keep pace with electronic crime'. The Police Chief Vol.69, 1, 52.

Loeb, G. and W. Lucyshyn (2003). Sharing Information on Computer Systems Security: An Economic Analysis. Journal of Accounting and Public Policy 22 (6).

Morris, S. (2004). The future of netcrime now: Part 1 – threats and challenges. Home Office (UK) Online Report 62/04

Newman, G. and R. Clarke (2003). Superhighway Robbery: Preventing E-commerce Crime. Devon: Willan Publishing.

Noble, R. (2003). Interpol's New Approach: A Return to Basics, in R. Broadhurst (ed.): Bridging the GAP: A Global alliance on Transnational Organised Crime. Hong Kong Police: Printing Department HKSAR

Reith, M., Carr, C. and G. Gunsch (2002). An examination of Digital Forensic Models. International Journal of Digital Evidence, Vol 1 (3): online http//www.ijde.org/docs/02_fall_art2.html (visited December 14, 2006).

Schneier, B. (2003). Beyond Fear: Thinking Sensibly About Security in an Uncertain World. NY: Copernicus Book.

Schjolberg, S. (2004). Computer-related offences. Council of Europe Octopus Interface conference: Challenge of Cybercrime, September 15-17, Strasbourg.

Smith, R.G., Grabosky, P. and G. Urbas (2004). Cyber Criminals on Trial. Melbourne: Cambridge University Press.

Why Crime Prevention is an Essential Component of International Training and Technical Assistance: the Experience of the International Centre for the Prevention of Crime

Margaret Shaw[1]

Introduction

The need to train personnel working in the criminal justice field is probably universally acknowledged around the world. Regardless of wealth and resources, countries recognize the need to improve the effectiveness and efficiency of justice systems, to effect changes in legislation or responsibilities, or implement new strategies. For countries which wish to develop new approaches such as community policing, introduce youth or family courts, or implement more recent approaches such as restorative justice, the offer of training from countries with experience of setting up such systems, or from specialized training institutes and organizations can be of considerable value. This paper is concerned with the impact of recent global changes on training and technical assistance in the field of criminal justice, but more specifically on the area of *crime prevention*, based on the experience of the International Centre for the Prevention of Crime (ICPC).

At the international level there is a long history of bilateral training and technical assistance, but it has often been characterized as disconnected and uncoordinated, and at times counter-productive, with countries or institutions offering competing models and paying little attention to the interests of needs of the recipient countries (Hebenton and Spencer 2001; Herman 2001). A number of important changes have taken place in recent years, which open up the opportunities for far more effective and appropriate training and technical assistance:

---

1 Margaret Shaw, Ph.d. is Director of Analysis and Exchange in the International Centre for the Prevention of Crime (ICPC). Based in Montreal, Canada ICPC, is an international non-governmental organization, and member of the United Nations Crime Prevention and Criminal Justice Programme network. It was founded in 1994, initially by the governments of France, Canada and Quebec, to promote crime prevention and community safety. It is now supported by a number of member governments, and international, regional and national organizations, associations and cities actively involved in crime prevention. www.crime-prevention-intl.org.

- There is now recognition of the need for more coordination of training and technical assistance within countries and regions;
- There is more awareness of the need to be sensitive to context - that models developed in one country may not be appropriate nor easily transplanted to another;
- There is recognition that good experience and practice does not flow only from the North to the South, or from developed countries to those in development or transition;
- The impacts of globalization, and the exponential growth in technological change, have not only increased the demand for training among countries, but also the ease with which it can now be accessed and adapted;[2]
- Concern with transnational organized crime and corruption, and terrorism have helped to focus attention on the importance of training and technical assistance in the justice and security sectors and their role in development (Dandurand, Griffiths and Chin 2004).

The long history of international training and technical assistance in criminal justice has primarily been concerned with the justice system itself, with the training of police, prosecutors and defence lawyers, magistrates and judges, for example, or correctional service personnel. While these remain important, very rarely has such training been concerned with crime prevention. There are some important reasons why this needs to change.

Contemporary crime prevention has evolved very markedly from how it was conceptualized twenty years ago, and this evolution has resulted in a much wider range of institutions and people being involved in prevention activities and working in unfamiliar ways. New 'professions' have emerged, and all of this requires a new range of skills and capacities to be learnt. There are now international standards and norms for crime prevention, and more and more countries are beginning to develop national crime prevention strategies and policies. As with all aspects of criminal justice, there is a continuing demand for training in new skills, as attitudes and approaches evolve, but in the area of crime prevention this is more marked.

---

2 See Zimring & Johnson (2005) for a discussion of how these factors have affected the field of international work on corruption.

> Crime Prevention, as defined by the **2002 United Nations Guidelines for the Prevention of Crime,** *'comprises strategies and measures that seek to reduce the risk of crimes occurring, and their potential harmful effects on individuals and society, including fear of crime, by intervening to influence their multiple causes.'*

The field of crime prevention has evolved and advanced considerably over the past 25 years. The experience of ICPC, an international non-government organization established in 1994, mirrors these changes in crime prevention. Its creation was inspired in particular by the Bonnemaison model of nationally-supported city-based crime prevention developed in France (Bonnemaison 1982). Bonnemaison had established the *European Forum on Urban Safety* in 1987, an organization which now brings together some 300 local authorities on issues of urban safety.

ICPC's mission is to promote the use of crime prevention among governments at all levels, shifting the balance of attention and spending away from an exclusive reliance on policing, courts and correctional systems. It recognizes the limitations on the ability of the state to ensure the safety and security of its citizens without the support and participation of a wide range of institutions and organizations and of citizens themselves. This mission is accomplished through a combination of knowledge-gathering and dissemination, through facilitating exchange of expertise and experience between those involved in crime prevention, and through training and technical assistance. Even in the short history of ICPC, the field of crime prevention has advanced considerably.[3]

- It is no longer seen as the exclusive preserve of the police, or a minor activity limited to advice on household security, but one widely accepted as the responsibility of a wide range of government institutions at all levels, working together and in partnerships with community services, organizations and civil society;
- This evolution has been built on and supported by the accumulating body of evidence across countries demonstrating the effectiveness of a wide range of interventions and strategies which aim to prevent crime (*e.g.,* NCP 1999). By the mid-1990s it was possible to demonstrate the enormous gains to be made through investing in good, effective and sustainable crime prevention strategies and programmes (ICPC 1999);

---

3 In 2005, in recognition of this evolution and the impact of global changes, ICPC adopted its *Strategic Development Plan* 2005-2010.

- Many developed countries now have well-entrenched national crime prevention strategies which began to take shape from the mid 1980s, including Denmark and Sweden, France, Britain, Canada, Australia and South Africa, for example. Evidence-based crime prevention interventions have become a major component of many country policies;
- The *Safer Cities Programme* of UN-HABITAT originally established in 1997 at the request of African mayors, has now expanded to assist countries and cities in Africa, Latin America and Asia develop strategic crime prevention, especially at the local-government level.
- The growth of international interest in crime prevention was in evidence at the workshop on community crime prevention organized by ICPC at the Tenth United Nations Congress on Crime Prevention and Criminal Justice in Vienna in 2000. This was also manifest at the Eleventh Congress in Thailand in 2005 (see below).

Conceptually, therefore, crime prevention has evolved from a primarily police-based advisory activity in the 1960s, through a series of conceptions as an alternative to incarceration in the 1970s, the recognition of the role of cities and municipalities in promoting urban security in the 1980s, as an integral component of the transformation of the police away from hierarchical models towards more community-based and problem-solving approaches in the 1990s, and in the new millennium, as a form of integrated governance (Sansfacon 2005). It encompasses a range of social, educational, situational and environmental interventions targeting individuals, communities or places at risk of crime and victimization, to strengthen, support and protect them. And it includes interventions and support for the reintegration of those released from custody. More significantly, perhaps, it requires working across sectors and disciplines, and in partnerships, using joined-up or 'whole-of-government' approaches unfamiliar to many governments and actors.

Developing International Standards for Crime Prevention

Until 1995 there were no internationally accepted guidelines on how crime prevention should be undertaken. In that year the Economic and Social Council (ECPSOC) adopted the *Guidelines for Cooperation and Technical Assistance in the Field of Crime Prevention* (UN 1995). Subsequently, in 2002, the United Nations *Guidelines for Crime Prevention* were adopted by ECOSOC (UN 2002). These guidelines have helped to establish norms and standards which an increasing number of countries are now beginning to apply.

At the Eleventh Congress on Crime Prevention and Criminal Justice in Bangkok, Thailand in 2005, the workshop on *Strategies and Best Practices in Crime Prevention, in Particular in Relation to Urban Areas and Youth at Risk* demonstrated the growth of crime prevention strategies and practice worldwide (UNODC 2005a). Again organized by ICPC in collaboration with UNODC and UN-HABITAT, this workshop provided ample evidence of the application of the principles and approach recommended in the *Guidelines*, as well as the spread of crime prevention internationally (ICPC 2006). Presentations from Australia, Japan and the Philippines, Nigeria, Tanzania and South Africa, Belgium, the Czech Republic and the United Kingdom, Brazil, Chile and Peru, showed the breadth of current strategic plans and good practice models. To accompany the workshop, a Compendium of 64 promising practices from around the world, targeting urban crime and at risk youth, was also published (ICPC 2005).

Yet how useful are broad guidelines in this relatively new field of crime prevention? Establishing a national or local policy and strategic plan does not guarantee that implementation will be assured or straightforward, nor that well-developed programmes will be effective. Much depends on how well programmes are implemented, on setting appropriate targets, on having sufficient resources, on the capacity of the partners involved to respond to the serious demands of working cooperatively, or their knowledge and skills to undertake the appropriate monitoring and evaluation, for example. 'What works' in crime prevention does not rest solely with well-designed programmes, much depends on the capacity of actors in the field to establish the conditions and manage the 'process', as well as on policy makers to understand the need for longer-term investment and planning, and not focus only on short-term results. Ensuring that strategies are maintained, well monitored and sustained beyond the life of a government is a further challenge.

One of the major lessons learned about *policy transfer* from one country to another, in the past ten years, has been that local conditions, local needs and local constraints must be taken into account (Sparks and Newburn 2002). Programmes which have been carefully developed and replicated in one setting, and found to be effective in reducing crime or insecurity, may not work in another country or city. This has been well demonstrated in South Africa, for example, where some crime prevention approaches developed in the North have proved to be inappropriate for a South African context (Pelser 2002). Even among developed countries it is clear that programmes are rarely precisely replicable (Jones and Newburn 2002).

Another major lesson has been that the *process* of developing and implementing good programmes is as important as setting goals or funding programmes. Implementing crime prevention programmes requires a particular set of skills, experience and capacities on the part of communities and key individuals. England and Wales, for example, which has extensive experience in the development and evaluation of crime prevention, and which invested considerable funds in the 1998 Crime Reduction Programme, has witnessed substantial problems in the implementation of evidence-based programmes on a wide scale (Hommel, Nutley, Webb and Tilley 2004). Among other factors, there were just not enough people with the necessary skills to allocate and undertake the many projects funded across the country. More significant, perhaps, have been the limitations of scaling-up pilot and experimental programmes, and the over-reliance on evidence-based knowledge of 'what works', over-ambitious targets and time-scales, and slow-moving bureaucratic procedures (Maguire 2004).

On the basis of Canadian experience in the provision of technical assistance in the criminal justice field to developing countries, Herman (2001) argues that while many donor countries are good at providing support for 'commitment and knowledge development', *e.g.,* through seminars and study visits, or specific targeted technical training, they often fail to consider *process* and the strengths and weaknesses of the *institutions* within which such training and knowledge needs to be applied. This requires capacity building, but also a broad and longer-term vision. Technical assistance will fail unless there is a broad vision of the context of criminal justice systems, careful and prior analysis of the broad range of factors influencing the system (including social and economic factors) and an agreed-upon strategy based on this integrated model (Herman 2001).[4]

These international lessons are beginning to lead to a more nuanced understanding of the role of crime and crime prevention, especially in developing regions. A recent report on crime and development in Africa (UNODC 2005b), for example, outlines the links between crime prevention and development. There is a clear need, therefore, for more detailed and practical support and exchange on the ground to aid the development and implementation of crime prevention strategies and practice, taking account of local contexts and capacities, and without imposing models and formulas from elsewhere.

---

4 See also the Background Paper for the Programme Network Institute's workshop on maximizing the effectiveness of technical assistance, at the 15th Session of the UN Commission on Crime Prevention and Criminal Justice, April 2006. (Shaw and Dandurand 2006).

In relation to technical assistance and capacity building, the 2002 *Guidelines* (para.18) recommend that member states support the development of professional skills in crime prevention by:

- Providing professional development;
- Encouraging educational agencies to offer basic and advanced courses;
- Work to develop certification and professional qualifications;
- Promote the capacity of communities to develop and respond to their needs.

They also urge the greater use of exchanges between countries and regions.

To a large extent, most training offered in the field of criminal justice and crime prevention has been, and remains, police-related.[5] This reflects the strong links between the traditional and more contemporary role of the police in crime prevention. Community policing and problem-oriented policing approaches entail considerable crime prevention components. Training and tools specifically geared to the needs of other crime prevention practitioners, such as community safety officers at the local authority level, or social mediators began to emerge in the 1990s. The University of Western England in the United Kingdom, for example, was among the first to develop an Internet-based distance learning course on crime prevention. Since the implementation of the 1998 Crime and Disorder Act, which mandates local authorities to establish crime and disorder partnerships and implement planned strategies on a three-year cycle, there has been a huge increase in academic courses and qualifications which touch on crime prevention at university level.

Training needs for the 'new' crime prevention professions have also been recognized in Australia, one of the first countries to establish a strategy of locally-based crime prevention. Such new professions have few existing guidelines and there is a need not only for what has been termed 'know-how' knowledge, but also 'know-who' knowledge (Cherney 2004). Capacity building is not simply a question of gaining knowledge and skills, but also about how to work.

More recent initiatives are beginning to expand the range of crime prevention training. Presentations at the Eleventh United Nations Congress crime prevention workshop by UNODC, UN-HABITAT and CSIR, and UNAFEI (Redo; Petrella and Shabangu; Someda 2005) were all concerned with aspects of capacity building

---

5 See paper by Jay Albanese in this volume.

and technical assistance. Based on its ten year experience in supporting the development of Safer Cities programmes in Africa as well as the Latin American and Asia-Pacific regions, UN-HABITAT have been developing a tool-kit to aid local governments in the development of such programmes, and more recently worked in collaboration with CSIR (Centre for Scientific and Industrial Research) South Africa. CSIR launched its own Local Crime Prevention Tool-Kit in 2003, in collaboration with the South African Police Service and a non-government organization UMAC, which had since been considerably expanded.[6]

Other recent initiatives include UNODC's *South-South Crime Prevention Project* established in 2004 in partnership with the University of Cape Town and the University of the West Indies. This is in recognition of the importance of bringing together countries and regions facing similar social and economic constraints and crime problems. The programme links the Southern African region with the Caribbean, and includes the development of an Internet site for accessing relevant publications, research reports and evaluations of good practice (www.southsouthcrime.org).

UNAFEI launched its first *Senior Seminar* on crime prevention in January 2005. This was an intensive five-week course which brought together practitioners and policy-makers from the Asia Pacific region, animated by a range of academics and practitioners from the region, and from Europe and North America (UNAFEI 2005). It used a practice-oriented and integrated approach to expand and share experience and knowledge among participants.

In recognition of the importance of community safety as a component of urban development, the World Bank has developed a series of tools to support local government crime prevention in the Latin American region which are being used to build the capacity of cities in countries.[7] ICPC's web-site now contains links to over 100 web-sites, tools, guides and manuals on aspects of prevention relating to topics such as cities, policing, schools, the business sector, women's safety, and evaluation.

These examples remain fragmented, however, and a range of needs can be clearly identified including:

- Academic training and certification on concepts, theories, ethical issues, crime prevention approaches, good practice, effective crime prevention models, evaluation and monitoring, *etc.* for policy makers, practitioners, researchers;

---

6 CSIR www.crimeprevention.csir.co.za.
7 This series has been developed by the International Bank for Reconstruction and Development/The World Bank and included guides for urban safety audits, urban design, women's safety and city case studies (eg. Llorente and Rivas 2005).

- Learning exchanges – learning by doing eg. city-to-city exchanges;
- Tools and techniques – observatories or monitoring centres on crime and social problems; crime mapping and other technological aides;
- Process and implementation issues – the capacity of policy makers, practitioners and researchers to work across sectors and in partnerships *etc.*;
- Targeted training at different levels for practitioners, researchers, policy makers – high level, middle management, front-line.

Redo (2005) argues for technical assistance in crime prevention which is better targeted to capacity building, and which would allow governments to coordinate programmes. He also argues for better and more standardized data on crime and victimization, the importance of evaluating crime prevention projects (something also requiring capacity-building) and for the application of the *sustainable livelihood* approach, developed in the field of drug prevention, to crime prevention. Such an approach would include civic and citizenship education, the promotion of a culture of lawfulness, as well as job creation.

ICPC – Building Capacity in Crime Prevention

Over the past ten years ICPC has itself worked to further knowledge and commitment-building through exchanges and seminars, and the compilation of good and promising practices. It has long stressed the importance of taking a broad and comprehensive view of the problems of crime and victimization, of careful analysis of problems on the ground, the development of strategic plans, and the importance of focusing on implementation issues, tools and capacity-building. It has begun to utilize the burgeoning communications technologies with web-based information, virtual networks on specific issues, and e-learning.[8]

The gaps in training and technical assistance in this relatively new area are evident. As suggested above, the expansion of crime prevention has led to the creation of new roles and responsibilities. The new community safety professions have to learn to work laterally and co-operatively with other institutions and partnerships. This includes how to analyse problems comprehensively, develop plans which are shared and have clear indicators and realistic goals, to set up projects and implement them successfully, to

---

8 ICPC maintains a virtual network on Indigenous issues, for example,

monitor and evaluate their outcomes, and work to ensure their sustainability over the long-term.

It is also evident that there is a demand for senior-level training in crime prevention internationally. ICPC launched a pilot International Training Institute in October 2004 which confirmed that people working in senior positions within local, provincial or national governments felt a need for greater networking and exchange on crime prevention. Building on this pilot project, ICPC's first *International Training Institute* takes place in June 2006, bringing together practitioners, policy makers and researchers in senior positions from both the north and south, and using a problem-solving and contextualized approach, and to begin to strengthen international networks on the ground.

Building on its experience, ICPC has developed a series of projects which recognize the importance of local context and buy-in among local officials and practitioners if projects are to be sustained and embedded, and capacity built up. The *City Exchange Programme,* for example, was launched in 2004, and brings together the cities of Montreal in Canada, Bordeaux in France, and Liege in Belgium to work together on tackling problems of incivilities associated with drugs and prostitution. The cities have been meeting on a regular basis to work systematically on developing a detailed analysis of their respective problems, a strategic plan, and its implementation and evaluation. ICPC's role has been to facilitate the meetings and the process. The emphasis of this approach is on learning-by-doing and on the exchange of experiences with others confronted with the realities of balancing prevention, health and respect for rights, with maintaining safety and security and the quality of life in cities.

ICPC has collaborated in the production of a variety of tools for capacity development, including *observatories* on crime and insecurity, and crime prevention *tool kits* for municipal governments and the police. Observatories, or monitoring centres, have been established by a number of regions, national and local governments on issues such as drugs, crime or school violence, *e.g.,* in France, other countries of the European Union, and Latin America. They have an important role in informing public policy and programme development, but few have focused on crime prevention and community safety. For the most part, information on crime tends to be limited to police statistics and victimization surveys. ICPC has been involved in the development of a pilot observatory on community safety, victimization and crime prevention for the Canadian Province of Quebec.[9] Its overall purpose is to collate information from a wide range of sources to establish a good basis for the analysis of problems and

---

9 For more information on this project see ICPC's web-site www.crime-prevention-intl.org under Technical Assistance.

measurement of trends, and support the development of well-planned intervention strategies. One of the major benefits of such tools is that they bring together a variety of government and institutional sectors (such as housing, health, social services and environment as well as police and justice) to pool their data and work together, enabling them, often for the first time, to understand the interconnectedness of their respective roles and responsibilities in preventing crime and insecurity.

ICPC has also collaborated in the development of a local government toolkit *The Key for Safer Municipalities* (FPP/ICPC, 2005) which sets out the case for municipal leadership in crime prevention, how it can be developed in partnership with local institutions, community organizations and the business sector, and provides concrete examples of strategic interventions.[10] Similarly, a *Police Tool Kit: The Role of the Police Crime Prevention* was developed following a series of international police exchanges organized by ICPC (ICPC 2002).[11]

In the near future, a major opportunity for increasing the availability and appropriateness of technical assistance and training in the field, may be through the use of the Internet and the increasingly sophisticated communications technologies now available. The recent establishment of a virtual forum on cybercrime provides an excellent example (UNODC 2006). The virtual forum was initiated in June 2006 by UNODC and the Korean Institute of Criminal Justice Policy, with the aim of providing practical and educational information for law enforcement personnel engaged in the prevention and control of cybercrime. Its objectives include the provision of a medium for communication, delivery of training, education and technical assistance, and acting as a clearing house.

Conclusion

For the future, it is clear that training and technical assistance in crime prevention must become a priority for governments, as part of a more balanced approach to safety and security. Training in the criminal justice sector must also recognize the importance of developing good prevention strategies, which are likely not only to be cost-effective, but cost-beneficial, bringing benefits in terms of improved economic climates in cities, reduced health costs, and

---

10 The toolkit is available in English and French in paper and CD-Rom versions. It was produced by the *Fondation Docteur Philippe Pinel* in Montreal, with technical assistance from ICPC, and developed initially for a Canadian context. Adaptation and translation into Spanish is currently being developed.
11 The police tool kit was produced in collaboration with the National Crime Prevention Council of the USA.

more productive and engaged young people, families and citizens. This can help to relieve pressures on the justice system, and the heavy costs associated with policing, overcrowded court systems and prison facilities.[12] The importance of the links between good crime prevention and development have begun to be recognized, while local crime prevention programmes have a crucial role to play in fighting transnational organized crime, corruption and trafficking. Overall, it is important for the future for such training and technical assistance to include the following characteristics:

- To have a strong focus on processes and implementation, not just good practice and knowledge;
- To have a strong awareness of context – historical, cultural, political, economic and social realities and recognition of complexity of all social institutions;
- To be participatory – with the involvement of country or city or particular target groups;
- To focus on human rights and inclusiveness.

Training and technical assistance in crime prevention should also capitalize on the new communication technologies. Finally, it would benefit from a more coordinated regional approach, which recognizes the experiences of both developing and developed countries, is adapted to the needs of particular regions, and which includes the full range of types of training and capacity-building targeting different levels of involvement.

References

Bonnemaison, G. (1982). Rapport de la Commission des Maires sur la Sécurité. Paris, France.

Cherney, A. (2004). Contingency and politics: The local government community safety officer role. Criminal Justice 4 (2), 115-128.

Dandurand, Y. Griffiths, C. T. and Chin, V. (2004). Justice and Security Sector Reform and Development. Discussion Note - Americas Branch. Canadian International Development Agency (CIDA). Gatineau, Canada.

FPP/ICPC (2005). The Key to Safer Municipalities. Montreal: Published by the Fondation Docteur Philippe Pinel. Technical assistance ICPC.

Hebenton, B. and Spencer, J. (2001). Assessing International Assistance in Law Enforcement. Themes, Findings and Recommendations from a Case-Study in the Republic of Estonia. Helsinki: European Institute for Crime Prevention and Control, affiliated with the United Nations. Publications series No. 37

Herman, T. (2001). Aspects in International Technical Cooperation – Lessons Learned. International Cooperation Group, Department of Justice Canada. Paper given at HEUNI International Seminar on

---

12 See ICPC (2000).

Central Issues in Crime Prevention and Criminal Justice, Helsinki, December 14-15[th.]

Hommel, P., Nutley, S., Webb, B. and Tilley, N. (2004). Investing to deliver: Reviewing the implementation of the UK Crime Reduction Programme. London: Home Office.

ICPC (1999). Crime Prevention Digest II: Comparative Analysis of Successful Community Safety. Montreal: International Centre for the Prevention of Crime. www.crime-prevention-intl.org.

ICPC (2000). Investing Wisely in Crime Prevention: International Experiences. Montreal: International Centre for the Prevention of Crime.

ICPC (2005). Urban Crime Prevention and Youth at Risk: Compendium of Promising Strategies and Programmes from around the World. Prepared for the 11th UN Congress on Crime Prevention and Criminal Justice. Montreal: ICPC.

ICPC (2006). Strategies and Best Practices in Crime Prevention, in Particular in Relation to Urban Areas and Youth at Risk. Proceedings of the workshop held at the 11th UN Congress on Crime Prevention and Criminal Justice. Montreal: ICPC.

Llorente, M.V. and Rivas, A. (2005). Case Study Reduction of Crime in Bogota: A Decade of Citizen's Security Policies. Washington DC: International Bank for Reconstruction and Development/The World Bank. www.worldbank.org.

Maguire, M. (2004). The Crime Reduction Programme in England and Wales. Criminal Justice 2 (3), 213-237.

Jones, T. and Newburn, T. (2002). 'Policy convergence and crime control in the USA and the UK.' Criminal Justice 2 (2) May, 173-203.

NCP (1999). Pathways to Prevention. Canberra: National Crime Prevention, Commonwealth Attorney General's Department

Pelser, E. (Ed.) (2002). Crime Prevention Partnerships. Lessons from Practice. Pretoria: Institute of Security Studies.

Redo, S. (2005). The shape of the future technical assistance. Presentation given at Workshop No. 3, 11th UN Congress on Crime Prevention and Criminal Justice. Bangkok, Thailand April 18-25th.

Sansfacon, D. (2005). De la prévention et de la sécurité: réflexions sur la gouvernance durable de la sécurité des collectivités. Canadian Journal of Criminology, 47 (2), 463-479.

Shabangu, T. and Petrella, L. (2005). The Local crime Prevention Toolkit. Presentation given at Workshop No. 3, 11th UN Congress on Crime Prevention and Criminal Justice. Bangkok, Thailand April 18-25th.

Someda, K. (2005). Urban crime prevention and effective measures for youth at risk: training needs and technical assistance. Presentation given at Workshop No. 3, 11th UN Congress on Crime Prevention and Criminal Justice. Bangkok, Thailand April 18-25th.

Sparks, R. and Newburn, T. (2002). 'How does crime policy travel?' Criminal Justice 2 (2) 107-109.

UN (1995). Guidelines for Cooperation and Technical Assistance in the Field of Urban Crime Prevention. ECOSOC Resolution 1995/9.

UN (2002). Action to Promote Effective Crime Prevention. Annex Guidelines for the Prevention of Crime. ECOSOC Resolution 2002/13.

UNAFEI (2005). Crime Prevention in the 21st Century – Effective Prevention of Crime associated with Urbanization based on Community Involvement and Prevention of Youth Crime and Juvenile delinquency. 129th Senior Seminar. January-February. www.unafei.or.jp.

Shaw. M. and Dandurand, Y. (Eds.) (2006). Maximizing the effectiveness of the technical assistance provided by member states in crime prevention and criminal justice. Proceedings of the workshop held by the Programme Network Institute during the 15th Session of the UN Commission on Crime Prevention and Criminal Justice. Helsinki:European Institute fro Crime Prevention and control, affiliated with the United Nations.

UN-HABITAT (2004). Youth, Children and Urban Governance. Policy Dialogue Series No. 2. Nairobi, Kenya: UN-HABITAT Global Campaign on Urban Governance. www.unhabitat.org.

UNODC (2005a). Strategies and Best Practices in Crime Prevention, in Particular in Relation to Urban Areas and Youth at Risk. Background Paper. Workshop No. 3. 11th UN Congress on Crime Prevention and Criminal Justice. Bangkok, Thailand. April 18-25, 2005. A/CONF.203/11. www.unodc.org.

UNODC (2005b). Crime and Development in Africa. Research Section. June. Vienna: UNODC.

UNODC and Korean Institute of Criminal Justice Policy (2006). Report of the Expert Group Meeting on the Development of Virtual Forum against Cybercrime. Held in Seoul, Korea, June 28-30th.

Zimring, F. E. and Johnson, D.T. (2005). On the comparative study of corruption. British Journal of Criminology, 45 (6), 793-809.